THE CORNISH FISHING INDUSTRY

AN ILLUSTRATED HISTORY

JOHN McWILLIAMS

First published 2014

Amberley Publishing
The Hill, Stroud
Gloucestershire, GL5 4EP

www.amberley-books.com

British Library Cataloguing in Publication Data.
A catalogue record for this book is available from the British Library.

ISBN 978 1 4456 3805 8 (print)
ISBN 978 1 4456 3824 9 (ebook)

Typeset in 9.5pt on 12pt Sabon.
Typesetting and Origination by Amberley Publishing.
Printed in the UK.

Contents

Introduction   5

Chapter 1   The Great Cornish Pilchard Seines   7

Chapter 2   Pilchard Driving   19

Chapter 3   Cornish Mackerel Season   39

Chapter 4   Cornish Herring: The North Coast   61

Chapter 5   Plymouth Herring   72

Chapter 6   Irish Herring   79

Chapter 7   The North Sea Voyage   88

Chapter 8   Longlining   99

Chapter 9   Crabbing: Fishing for Lobsters, Crabs and Crawfish   119

Chapter 10   Trawling   134

Chapter 11   Mackerel Hand Lines and the Industrial Fishery of the 1970s   152

Chapter 12   Cornish Netters   166

Chapter 13   Scalloping   179

             Acknowledgements   183

             Notes   184

Introduction

Although the fishing industry plays a much smaller part in the life of Cornwall and its people than it did in the past, it is still very much with us.

Some of us can remember when St Ives, Newlyn, Porthleven, Mevagissey, Polperro and Looe each had their smartly painted fleets of longliners and pilchard boats, all following annual fishing seasons which seemed to have been going on for ever. Each cove had its little group of crabbers with their withy pots. Every winter, the tough Belgian trawlermen arrived to fish the Trevose and Wolf grounds, and the coming of spring was heralded by the colourful Camaret and Audierne crabbers and their cheerful Breton crews.

This way of life largely ended with the 1960s and the passing years have perhaps romanticised it. In those days, Cornish fishermen did not have the economic and bureaucratic pressures which they do now, but their way of life was hard, dangerous and, in many cases, very badly paid. Most of the methods of the present industry – beam trawling, gill netting for white fish and scallop dredging – had yet to appear.

Some histories suggest that fishing in the county ended with the sailing luggers 100 years ago. This book questions that idea and aims to tell the story of the work that has been going on in Cornish waters since that time.

Fishing in Cornwall has often been a story of boom and bust, of prosperity and failure – the great pilchard seines, the spring mackerel season and the East Coast steam drifters, the all too briefly thriving Plymouth herring season, the herring voyages to the North Sea, the Mackerel War and Crawfish boom of the 1970s and the revival of Newlyn as a beam trawler and netting port in the 1980s.

While some harbours like St Ives and Porthleven have seen fishing decline, others have reinvented themselves. Looe, whose pilchard drifter fleet spent years dying slowly, is a thriving trawl port whose fish market has a reputation for high quality. Mevagissey, another tourist hotspot, still hangs on to its fishing fleet and has recently invested in ring netting for pilchards (alias sardines) so that it is now Cornwall's second fishing port after Newlyn. Newquay, which lost its fishing industry with the end of the pilchard seines in the nineteenth century, became a fishing port again in the 1970s and still is, despite its surfing fame. Tiny Port Isaac, whose fishing industry had declined since the herring landings of the 1920s, reinvented itself as a shellfishing port.

Perhaps the most interesting question is, where next? The demise of the fuel-guzzling beam trawler has often been predicted but they are still a mainstay of the whitefish fleet. Some visiting foreign vessels have diversified into seining, twin rigging and the fuel-saving Sum Wing beam trawl. Fewer Cornish youngsters are prepared to follow their fathers into fishing and several boats rely on foreign crews. Recent years have seen increased investment in crabbing and scallop dredging. The ancient pilchard fishery, long written off as a lost cause, has been revived by a small but efficient fleet of high-tech ring netters, and Cornish pilchards have successfully been rebranded Cornish sardines.

The industry is dominated by quotas and regulations. No one can fish commercially without the appropriate certificates so it is no longer possible for fishermen's sons to take a trip and get the flavour of Dad's business. Much of the Cornish fleet is elderly and second-hand. The past century's newspaper reports do not lack gloomy outlooks but the Cornish fishing industry has shown its ability to revive old fisheries and generate new ones. Conservation of fish stocks is high on the agenda. Drastic reductions in the fleet have resulted in very healthy fisheries today, but the dinosaur quota system fails to recognise this. The European Common Fisheries Policy has failed, though the opening of European markets has been very positive. Perhaps Europe's recent promise to relax its monolithic grip and delegate decision-making is an optimistic sign.

CHAPTER 1

The Great Cornish Pilchard Seines

In 1602 Richard Carew published the first book all about Cornwall.[1] In it he describes fishing for pilchards with seine nets and begins his description, 'But the least fish in bigness, greatest for gain and most in number is the pilchard.' So the smallest fish gave the most profit for the fishermen.

This fishery was important long before Carew's *Survey of Cornwall*.

The pilchard season began about August or September, and in some years lasted until December. At the start of the season, the seiners were 'put into pay' as it was called. The essential staff were hired. Many more would be taken on when the pilchards arrived. These key workers were the 'huers', who watched for the fish from their clifftop lookout, the huer's hut; the 'seiners', who manned the seine boat with its monster net; and the 'blowsers' whose task it was to haul the net full of fish into shallow water using carefully sited capstans, positioned along the coast.

In 1893, when seining had started to decline, the St Ives seiners 'went into pay' on Monday 4 September. Twelve companies had 178 seines between them and jointly engaged

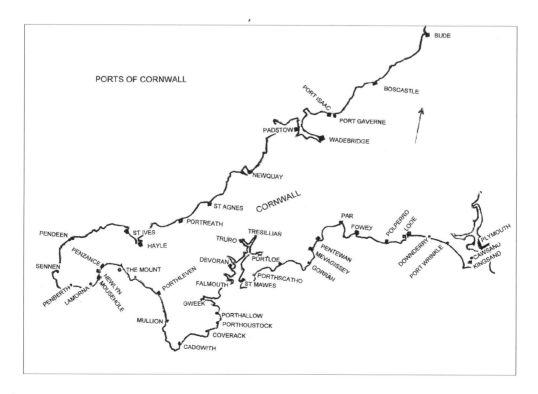

six huers, eighty-six seiners and sixty-two blowsers. The largest numbers were run by only three owners: Bolitho had eighty-two, E. Hain & Son thirty-three, and C. C. Ross twenty-four.[2] These three were prominent local capitalists and politicians, whose interests included banking, mines, property, land and shipping. (Charles Campbell Ross was to come unstuck with the fall of Penzance's Batten, Carne & Carne bank in 1896 but his name lives on at Penzance harbour's Ross Bridge.)

They had to wait a month for their first shot on the evening of Monday 9 October when the *Western Echo* described the outcome:

> Three seines were shot on Monday evening, and splendid shoals were enclosed. Unfortunately the seines were shot at high tide, and being the top of the spring, the strong current carried two of the seines round the Head, and these, with the fish, were lost. The third seine 'Went together' and the fish were also lost.[3]

They had more luck the following day when four seines enclosed 700 'hogsheads' (barrels). In an even better shot, a fortnight later, 3,000 hogsheads were hauled from two seines.

Because, in the balmy days of seining, huge profits could be made, there were many more seine nets than there was suitable coastal space to work them. This meant that there had to be very strict rules, enforced by Act of Parliament, giving everyone a turn. A free-for-all would have meant no one caught any fish.

In places with many seines, notably St Ives, the coast was divided into areas called 'stems'.[4] They were marked by pairs of tall white poles near the shore. For example, one stood on the outside of the St Ives churchyard wall near Chy an Eglos and another on the inside, on St Andrew's Street. When the fishermen at sea lined up these two poles they knew they were on the border between Carn Crowse and Pedn Olva stems. From the Hayle River to St Ives the stems were called Carrack Gladden, and this extended to the stream on Carbis Bay beach; The Leigh from Carbis Bay stream to the Carrack Rocks off Porthminster Point; Porthminster stem from the Carracks to the Porthminster beach stream; Pedn Olva from the stream to the corner of the parish churchyard; and Carn Crowse from here to the westward. It would seem unlikely that seines were shot west of St Ives Island but for the fact that the low flat rocks under the car park at Porthmeor beach are called Pilchard Pool. Perhaps, long ago, a tranquil, surfless summer day saw a shoal of pilchards surrounded by a seine on Porthmeor beach?

Each seine company was given its turn in its appropriate stem. The timing of changeovers was shown by coloured 'time balls' hung from a gibbet-like structure by the huer's hut.[5] Every detail of seining was carefully regulated: who had which turn in which stem; the length, depth and mesh size of the seine net, stop nets and tuck net; the length of the warp and tow rope used to haul them shorewards; the kind of anchor used to moor them; and the settling of disputes.

The seine net was 160 fathoms long and 8 fathoms deep at the centre and made of small mesh called 'Dungarvon'. It was fitted with large corks along the top, leads to weight it and wooden rollers at the bottom, to enable it to travel over the sand. The various nets had to be carefully looked after as described by the Union Seine Company's ledger of 1843,[6] which records that Jane Harry, Grace Uren, Nancey Goodwin, Hannah Hambly, Jane Noale, Betsey Honey and Martha Harry were paid 1 shilling 2 pence a day for 'repairing the Tuck Net and Making a Stop Net'.

The seiners' first task was to load the seine into the seine boat as described by H. D. Lowry in 1893.

> Down the gray granite quay, against the bluest of skies, march five-and-thirty tall and resolute fishermen in yellow oilers and great sea boots. Each walks some three or four

Mullion, 1860s. Farmers collect seaweed for fertiliser around half a dozen small crabbers, but at the top of the slope, five large seine boats wait for the big money to be made from a successful shot. On the left is the capstan to haul them up. (With permission of the Royal Institution of Cornwall – RIC.)

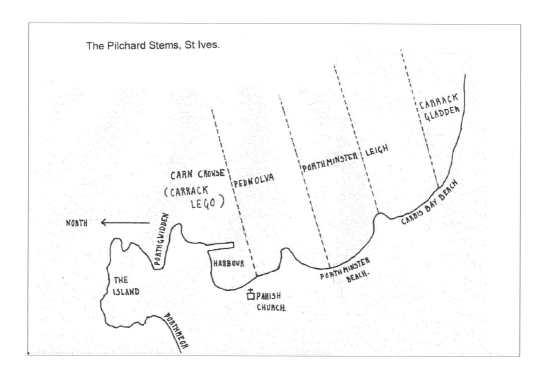

The Pilchard Stems, St Ives.

yards behind his leader; they bear upon their shoulders a great brown seine, which hangs in regular festoons between them. They are taking it from their cellar to the boat.

The heavily built seine boat was up to 40 feet long and 11 or 12 feet wide. It was sharp at both ends, i.e. had a pointed stern. The after part of the boat was the 'net room' with a 'bulkhead' (partition) at each end. The fore part had up to five 'thwarts' (seats) for the rowers. It was simply but very strongly built, with no frills. It was unusual, in Britain, for such heavy boats to be built for working from beaches but there was ample manpower to launch and recover them.[7] The seine season could be a very short one so the boats had to be rugged enough to stand the rest of the year dried out on the Porthminster boat plots, with perhaps the benefit of a coat of tar. Since there were dozens of St Ives seine boats, all black and more or less identical, they were identified by various devices painted on the bows: vertical white 'bars', painted discs called 'shots', or letters.[8]

The seine boat stayed anchored on its stem from dawn to dusk, waiting for the huer's call, its crew sheltering under a makeshift tent called a 'tilt'. Here they yarned and smoked away their days with brew-ups from a portable stove and, sometimes, tasks like mat making or fancy ropework. Their 11 shillings weekly pay was not a living wage so many of them went to sea all night in the drifters after their long days at anchor in the seine boat.

Coiling the warp on top of the seine, St Ives. The end of the warp had to be landed on the shore before the net was shot. (Tony Pawlyn Collection)

Waiting for the pilchards. Seine boats parked on the boat plots at Porthminster Beach, St Ives.

The huer, too, watched as long as there was daylight. He looked for changes in the colour of the water, and for gannets diving. His cry when it came was, 'Hevva!', which meant, 'A shoal!' He had a long speaking trumpet which he could use to call the fishermen, but more reliable communication was by a series of well-understood signs made with a pair of round white cloth signals with handles. These were called 'bushes'. In former days, the huer had torn real gorse bushes from the cliff side and used them.

On hearing the hevva, the seiners speedily dismantled their tilt and hauled in their anchor. On the huer's signal, they landed the end of the warp, the 600-to-700-fathom-long rope attached to the end of the net.

Carefully following the huer's directions, they began to shoot the seine around the shoal of pilchards in a U shape out from the shore, around the shoal and back again. Meantime the 'tow boat' had arrived on the scene. She carried one or two stop nets. Their function was to fill in the space between the ends of the seine and make the enclosure complete. So as the seine boat set off on its U-shaped course, the tow boat, directed by its separate huer, set off in a straight line across the ends of the U. The aim was to completely enclose the shoal of fish or a good part of it.

If the seine boat and tow boat crews were successful, the fish were surrounded by a solid wall of net. The seine was secured to the shore by the warp at one end and the tow

Seine boat anchored off Porthminster waiting for the huer's call. The crew shelter under their tilt.

The huer directs the seine boat with his bushes. (St Ives Museum, Comley Collection)

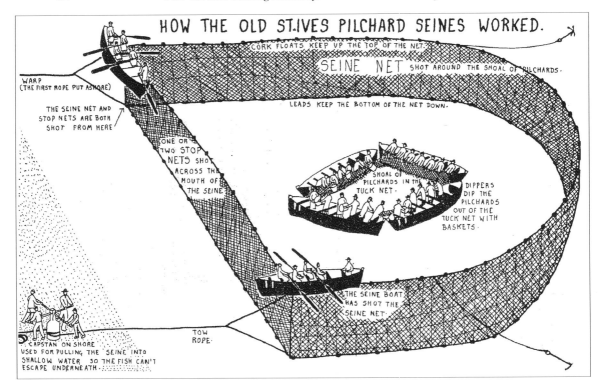

HOW THE OLD ST.IVES PILCHARD SEINES WORKED.

CORK FLOATS KEEP UP THE TOP OF THE NET.

SEINE NET SHOT AROUND THE SHOAL OF PILCHARDS.

WARP (THE FIRST ROPE PUT ASHORE)

THE SEINE NET AND STOP NETS ARE BOTH SHOT FROM HERE

LEADS KEEP THE BOTTOM OF THE NET DOWN.

ONE OR TWO STOP NETS SHOT ACROSS THE MOUTH OF THE SEINE

SHOAL OF PILCHARDS IN THE TUCK NET.

DIPPERS DIP THE PILCHARDS OUT OF THE TUCK NET WITH BASKETS.

THE SEINE BOAT HAS SHOT THE SEINE NET.

TOW ROPE.

CAPSTAN ON SHORE USED FOR PULLING THE SEINE INTO SHALLOW WATER SO THE FISH CAN'T ESCAPE UNDERNEATH.

rope at the other. The fish might still escape under the net so the next task belonged to the 'blowsers', who tramped around their shoreside capstans and wound the whole outfit into shallower water. This had to be carefully judged. The net had to be shallow enough to prevent the fish escaping underneath but not to squash the fish together so they would die. The success of the shot depended on the fish remaining alive and swimming inside the seine. If they died, they sank and could not be landed. This was known as a 'dead tuck'.

Once the net full of fish was in the right place, it was moored with special anchors, each with only one fluke. Ordinary anchors protruding out of the sand could have ripped neighbouring nets.

Enclosing the fish was essential but they still had to be got out of the seine. This was done with the tuck net, shorter but deeper than the seine, shot by a smaller boat called a 'follower' or 'follier', as described by William Cogar in 1911:

The tuck net is a strong miniature seine shot in the enclosure, and into which the fish are driven. Ropes are attached to its bottom so that it can be pulled up like a huge bag. Up comes a heavy mass, nearer and nearer the surface by slow degrees. Then the short expanse of sea water is broken with a moving surging dazzling glittering sheen. The fish are raised to the surface amazingly alive, and the boats are bought around a solid bank of fish, upon which seemingly, one could walk. The tuckers clad in oilskins and sea boots commence to fill up the boats by means of baskets. Boat after boat is loaded and sent ashore; the tuck net is gradually drawn up more and more, higher and higher, and emptied. Other tucks are made until the seine is relieved of its wealth … If the catch is a great one, it may take two or three days to save it all, when watch is kept at night by boats with lanterns.[9]

The blowsers haul the seine in to shallower water with their capstan. This was to prevent the fish from escaping under the net. Porthminster Beach, St Ives. (Paul Martin Collection)

The boats that surrounded the tuck net were called 'dippers'. The fishermen worked in pairs, two to each tucking basket. They leaned over the side and scooped the thrashing fish out of the net. The boats and the men dressed in their oilskins were soon covered in pilchard scales. The dippers were loaded down until they had just a few inches of freeboard, and towed into the harbour.

At St Ives there was ample parking space for the dippers on the 'boat plots' at Porthminster Beach. At many of the coves on the south coast, the seine companies had enough boats and equipment to enclose a shoal but not to carry the catch away. In this case, the call went out to the nearest drift net port – Mousehole, Newlyn or Porthleven – to send luggers to surround the seine, and these craft dipped out and carried away the catch. On Friday 1 December 1893, Skipper William Cattran's Mousehole lugger *Unity PZ 286* was lost off Lamorna with a cargo of seine herring from Mullion. Her four crew got ashore in their punt.[10]

Traditionally, the pilchards were unloaded at St Ives and other ports into 'gurries'. The gurry was a large box with two long handles nailed to its sides, carried by two men. It contained 1,000–1,200 fish,[11] about 28 stone in weight, the equivalent of the 'cran' measure for herring, or four 7-stone baskets.

Later in the nineteenth century, pilchards were taken to the cellars in carts with folding lids. This was to deal with the major problem of fish being 'cabed' (stolen). Cabing was described in February 1893:

> One man, manifestly of a temper not too well controlled, was followed at each journey by a score of urchins. Whenever his back was turned for a moment, one of the youngsters would dart forward and with one sweep of the hand send a score of pilchards flying out of the cart.[12]

The cellars themselves were large purpose-built structures, often called 'pilchard palaces' in East Cornwall. There was usually a central cobblestoned courtyard surrounded by covered pent houses where the fish were packed. Upstairs were the lofts where the enormous nets were stored, repaired and turned over at intervals to stop them getting damp and rotting. The geography of several Cornish towns and villages is still often dominated by

Tucking a seine. On the right the tuck net is hauled up. Left and centre, pairs of men dip out the fish with baskets. (St Ives Museum, Comley Collection)

Tucking a seine. Loading the lugger *FY 37*. Three pairs of fishermen dip out the fish with their baskets. Each pair has a helper with a long pole to shove the basket down. In the centre of the picture is *FY 37*'s flywheel capstan.

A carefully posed photo of Maid Betsey's pilchard cellar (Barnaloft), St Ives, 1871. In the centre the women have built a wall of pilchards and salt. In the foreground the fish are carefully packed into barrels in a rose pattern. On the left a gurry full of fish arrives. Left centre, the top hatted huer with his bushes has come to be in the photograph.

these pilchard palaces. For example, the large blocks of flats, gallery and studios along Porthmeor Beach, St Ives, follow the ground plans of former pilchard cellars. Port Isaac, Porth Gaverne, Porth Quin, Portloe and Sennen Cove still have traces of these large and prominent buildings.

The fish were preserved in salt. Traditionally this was done by groups of women who built a wall of layers of salt and pilchards, often as long as the courtyard and up to waist height. This highly labour-intensive business was called 'bulking'. However, in those days, labour was cheap. In the 1850s the women and girls were paid three pence an hour for bulking, sustained by nips of brandy, as the water was unfit to drink. The salt took all the moisture out of the fish and this preserved them. The fish remained several weeks in bulk.[13]

Next the fish were pressed using 'pressing poles' and 'pressing stones'. The walls of the cellars jutted out about 6 inches at the height of a barrel. A false lid called a 'buckler' was put over the barrel full of pilchards. The barrels were carefully packed with the fish in a neat rose pattern with all the tails facing the centre. One end of the pressing pole went under the ledge in the wall. The pole went over the buckler and a pressing stone was hung from a rope strop on the end. It gradually pressed the oil out of the fish. This took two or three hours. Then the barrel was topped up and pressed again. The pressing stone was a large, round granite boulder drilled to receive an iron ring. Many are still to be found all around the Cornish coast, often built into stone walls. Sometimes, instead of the ledge, rectangular slots, often built of red brick, were spaced along the cellar walls to take the ends of the pressing poles.

The pilchard oil, called 'train oil', drained out of gaps between the barrel staves down special wooden gutters to a barrel in the 'train pit'. It was a valuable commodity with many uses: curing leather, lighting smelly lamps (called 'chills'), waterproofing decks, even getting the rust off iron. It was boiled up with other ingredients to make an effective but slow-drying paint.[14]

During the 1870s, bulking, or 'dry salting' as it was sometimes called, was replaced by 'tanking'. The tanks were built from concrete about 8 feet long and 4 feet wide. Pilchards and salt were mixed in the tanks. The salt took the moisture out of the pilchards so that after a while the fish were floating in their own brine as described by William Cogar:

> The brine formed rises over the fish in the vats, and in three weeks the process of curing is complete. The fish are washed in wooden troughs by men and filled into wooden casks by women. When the casks are full they are put under screw presses in order to get out the excessive oil – which is used for leather curing and other processes – and subsequently refilled again, pressed, coopered up, marked and dispatched.[15]

Each tank held about twenty barrels of fish. The barrels were called hogsheads, often pronounced 'hosgits'. Tanking was much cheaper and less labour-intensive than bulking; it also gave a better product. Screw presses began to replace pressing stones at the same time as tanks replaced bulking. The barrel was placed under the press; the buckler was placed on top and screwed down.

When the hogsheads of fish had been pressed, they were ready for market. The main destination for Cornish pilchards was Italy. They were shipped off in sailing vessels to Naples, Genoa, Venice and Livorno (Leghorn). Many skippers bought lively and accurate paintings of their ships from local Italian artists. These 'pierhead paintings', usually painted in quick-drying gouache, often depict the ship under full sail with the volcano Vesuvius smoking dramatically in the background. Sometimes there was a second picture

A tank of pilchards and salt at Nick Howell's Newlyn pilchard works. (Brian Stevens Collection)

Packing pilchards. In the centre are the screw presses used to press the train oil from the fish.

showing the ship under storm sails battling with huge waves. They are excellent detailed records of nineteenth-century Cornish sailing ships. Often the sailors called their voyage 'Going to the Burning Mountain'.[16]

The pilchard trade 'to the burning mountain' was the beginning of another voyage for many Cornish ships. From Italy they sailed to the Black Sea and the ports of southern Russia, where they loaded cargoes of grain to bring home. This Black Sea grain trade played an important role in the growth of the two deep-sea Cornish shipping lines, Hain of St Ives and Chellew of Truro.[17]

The pilchard voyages were a barometer of the prosperity or poverty of the Cornish fishing ports. At St Ives, they were carefully recorded each year by Captain Short:

1824 November 22 – Sailed the schooner *Rebecca*, for the Mediterranean with 449 hogsheads of pilchards.
November 25 – Sailed the *Ambroke* with 340 hogsheads.
November 27 – Sailed the brig *Ann* of Liverpool with 750 hogsheads.

The diary continues with the *Emma, Jane Stewart, William and Mary, Grace, Furley, William, Laurel, Pomona, Meridian, Lambe, Nymph, Calpe, New Thomas, Flora, Industry* and *John and Joseph*, a total of nineteen vessels loading 10,778 hogsheads, a big season.

In December 1830, he wrote, 'Total pilchards exported to the Mediterranean this year from St Ives, 6,412 hogsheads; twelve ships loaded here.'[18]

Until the mid-nineteenth century, the seines which dominated the Cornish fishing industry provided a living to countless fishermen and women. In his will of 1797, St Ives' eccentric Customs Officer and Mayor, John Knill, made provision for £5, a considerable sum in those days, to any St Ives woman who

shall be the best knitter of fishing nets, £5 to the woman deemed to be the best curer and packer of pilchards for exportation and £5 to be given between two such follower-boys as shall ... be judged to have conducted themselves of all the follower-boys in the several concerns, in the preceding fishing season.[19]

In 1818 the *West Briton* enthused,

The refulgent appearance of the scaly tribe, struggling, springing and gleaming to the moon in every direction; the busy and contented hum of the fishermen, together with the plashing of the frequent-plying oar, altogether form a picture to which language is incapable of doing justice.[20]

By 1880, tanks and screw presses entirely replaced the old methods, and steamships had taken over from the picturesque schooners, brigs and brigantines. In 1883–84 a catch of 3,100 hogsheads from St Ives did not affect the overall gloomy picture for the local seiners, who claimed to have made losses of £40,000 during the previous twelve years. During the late 1880s, some poor-quality exports depressed the Italian market, and the 2-hundredweight half hogshead was introduced to improve quality and sales. The market for salt fish in Italy could also be affected by other imports, e.g. sardines from Spain or salt cod from the Newfoundland Grand Banks.[21] In the 1890s the Bolitho family, who were involved in many Cornish enterprises, pulled out of pilchard curing.

At the end of the century, the seines gave lively subject matter to St Ives and Newlyn's growing artists' colony and a sense of drama and excitement to those who witnessed them, as described by a 1904 postcard: 'Today we have been looking out at the first Seine or catch of pilchards. Many boats out but the tide being low they will probably not land much fish today.'

By January 1891, the *West Briton* reported,

Not a single pilchard has been caught by a seine off the Cornish coast during 1890. For several years this industry, once so lucrative, especially at St Ives, Newquay, Mullion and Cadgwith, has been gradually dwindling, but this is probably the first year in which not a single seine has been put into the water.[22]

By 1883 there were no seines left at Newlyn but the local luggers continued to bring home seine fish from the coves, when they were needed.

On Friday 1 October 1897, two heavily laden luggers unloaded pilchards from the Mullion seines at Mousehole. The following Monday, five luggers – the *Annie Harvey PZ 102* of Newlyn, *Billy Bray PZ 67* of Porthleven and the *Bonnie Lad PZ 251, Onward PZ 510* and *Valourous PZ 96* of Mousehole – came in with seine catches from Mullion and Cadgwith. Such was the urgency to get the fish to the cellars that the fish were brought ashore in punts until there was enough water for the luggers to enter Mousehole harbour.[23]

The last year of serious seine landings at St Ives was 1905 when, on 2 September, five seines enclosed a massive 4,500 hogsheads and the local paper enthused about the exciting scene of the seines being tucked:

> A large number of visitors witnessed the busy scene with the keenest interest – a sight they will not soon forget. One great reservoir of fish, the water literally boiling with pilchards – a teeming, convulsed mass of shining, glancing, silvery scales – one compact mass of thousands upon thousands of fish.

This apparently good news quickly had a downside, as the huge catch flooded the market and depressed prices from 11 shillings to 7 shillings and 6 pence per thousand. Until these big seine shots, the drift net fishery in the Cornish ports had been jogging along comfortably with reasonable prices.[24]

In August and September 1910, the Porthgwarra seiners made two excellent and much photographed shots which grossed £2,000. The catch was carried to Newlyn by local luggers, including the *Edgar PZ 131* of Mousehole and *Lamorna PZ 169* of Newlyn, both recently equipped with motors. Coverack's seiners caught 100 hogsheads at good prices.[25]

In October 1922, the *St Ives Western Echo* sadly recorded,

> On Friday last the well-known and long awaited cry of Hevva! was heard throughout St Ives and several of the seine boats were pulled out into the bay. The proceedings were watched by many interested spectators, but after about an hour's manoeuvring the boats returned to the harbour without having shot the seines.[26]

This was the last attempt at St Ives.

Newquay huers with their telescope and speaking trumpets, 1863: S. Clemens, Captain B. Barker and Jim Clemens. (Newquay Old Cornwall Society ON0502)

CHAPTER 2

Pilchard Driving

The seines were run by large companies. Their cost was beyond the pocket of the ordinary fisherman who fished at night with 'drift nets', long rectangular floating nets. Each boat shot its fleet of nets, all joined together in a row, at dusk. Their fine meshes hung down in the sea like a curtain. As they drifted along, attached to their boat, the 'drifter', by the 'swing rope', the fish swam into the meshes and were caught by their gills. As the nets were hauled in and carefully stowed in the boat's 'net room', the fish were shaken out. Drifting was certainly going on as early as 1602, when Richard Carew described it in his *Survey of Cornwall*:

> The drovers hang certain square nets athwart the tide, through which the shoal of pilchards passing, leave many behind entangled in the meshes. When the nets are so filled the drovers take them up, cleanse them, and let them fall again.
>
> The seiners complain with open mouth that these drovers work much prejudice to the commonwealth of fishermen, and reap thereby small gain to themselves; for (say they) the taking of some few breaketh and scattereth the whole shoal and frayeth them from approaching the shore.[1]

That pilchard drifting was important by the seventeenth century can be seen from correspondence which shows that the St Ives boats were already pilchard driving in Mount's Bay. In a letter about tithes from the St Aubyn Estate documents, Christopher Harris wrote on 4 November 1698 about the Mount's Bay boats fishing from St Ives:

> Its true they pay no tyth hear nor our [St Ives] boates payes none in the mounts bay about 26 or 28 yeares a gone … Mr Guavas [of Newlyn] did distraine our boates for the tyth of pilch'ds.
>
> Mr Guavas and Mr Norworthy did verbally agree that wherever the craft did belong there ye Tyth should be paid.[2]

In other words, boats paid tythes in their home port, no matter where they were fishing.

In another letter from the St Aubyn documents, written from St Ives in 1698, probably on behalf of the rector, about a tithe dispute, Mr Hichens writes,

> That St Ives boates when they fish at the Mounts bay, they goe many times to and beyond the … woolfe to take pilchards and bring them home to Penzance and pay the full value of the tythes … Thomas Puresoy hath fished there with drift nets since forty yeares or upwards and John Hichens merchant proves the like.

So the pilchard drivers had already been fishing around the Wolf Rock for over forty years.

Although the seine owners pretended, for the next two centuries, that they were the real fishermen and the driftermen were johnnie-come-latelies, the 1698 correspondence continues,

> The said 3 gents (John Hichens gent, John Hichens merchant and Thomas Puresoy) sweare that the drift nets have exceeded the saynes for that in St Ives there were anciently 30 saynes but the drift netts breaking those shoals of pilchards did take them before they came near the saynes so far that as for the saynes were generally laid aside here, as well as in the Mounts bay and mostly use drift netts.

The Mount's Bay boats were also coming to St Ives pilchard driving: 'John Hichens merchant – Tyth in kind received by him at St Ives from Paul boates of Pilchards and Herrings and that he was agent for the proctors of Paul there.' Paul was the parish church of Newlyn.

The powerful capitalist seine owners alleged that the rows of nocturnal drift nets broke up the shoals of pilchards so that they destroyed the livelihood of the 'proper' fishermen, the seiners, who fished in daylight. They asserted that drift nets drove away the shoals. Until its end, pilchard drifting was known as 'Pilchard Driving' and the boats as 'Pilchard Drivers'. Laws were made and enforced, preventing the drifters from fishing near the land. In April 1819 the *West Briton* printed an apology:

> A prosecution having been commenced against us, the undersigned, Edward Scantlebery, of Polruan and Nicholas Thomas, of Mevagissey, fishermen, for having in the month of September last taken pilchards with drift nets within the distance of one league and a half [a league was about 3 miles] from the shore of this county, contrary to an Act of Parliament, passed in the reign of king Charles the II, for the protection of the pilchard fishery … we do hereby promise not to offend in like manner again.[3]

This was how the seine owners usually operated. They prosecuted the drift fishermen, but not too harshly. This was self-interest as they depended on the driftermen's womenfolk to cure and pack their fish in their pilchard palaces. The seiners who awaited the huer's cry at St Ives were paid 11 shillings a week, less than a living wage. When their seine boat was back on its moorings each evening, they started their night's work in the drifters. The seine owners steered the tricky path between enforcing their will and alienating the community, in the days when Cornish communities were close-knit.

The St Ives seine owners were still flexing their muscles as late as December 1877 when they prosecuted the crews of the drifters *TB*, *Magpie* and *LEH*. The magistrates fined Thomas Bryant and his crew of the *TB* a hefty £2 each, with the alternative of prison, resulting in uproar from the fishermen present in court. The seine owners were still representing their interest as the public interest.[4]

In 1818 there were forty-four pilchard seines at Mevagissey and only six drifters. Forty years later, the situation was reversed; there were only two seines left in 1867, and by 1881 there were more than sixty drifters.

In March 1828 the *West Briton* published figures which show the relative importance of the seine and drift fisheries:

> Number of seans employed 186 (not employed 130).
> Number of men employed at sea on seans 2672.
> Number of drift boats 368.

Number of men employed on drift boats 1599.

Number of persons on shore, to whom the fishery affords direct employment 6350.

At this time the government was considering withdrawing its bounty (subsidy) of six shillings per hogshead, so the industry was making its case. This was not an accurate picture of the real situation. Employment by the seine companies was seasonal and often very short-term. Besides the catching and curing, it also mentioned some of the ancillary trades depending on the pilchard fishery: 'The building and repairing of sean boats, ... the manufacture of netting, cordage and canvas, the making of casks.'[5]

Captain Short's St Ives diary shows that the drifters were playing an important part in the fishery early in the nineteenth century. In November 1821 he wrote, 'The largest quantity of pilchards ever known on the drift at one time: from 50,000 down per boat; in all over 500 hogsheads.' In 1824 the seiners went into pay as early as 26 July but although they shot several times on shoals of sprat, the main landings were by the drifters, 10,000–15,000 pilchards on 2 August; 20,000 on the 18th; 10,000–15,000 on 2 September; and 160,000 on 26 October. In November there were mixed landings of pilchards and herring.[6]

Mount's Bay pilchard boat *Omeo 487 PZ*, built 1886. (With permission of the Royal Institution of Cornwall – RIC.)

Mevagissey luggers going to sea pilchard driving, *c.* 1907. *FY 109 Millie*, 15 tons, built in Mevagissey in 1888 for W. J. Robins. (S. Dalby Smith, St Blazey)

Looe fishing fleet going to sea past the Banjo Pier. After a good pilchard season in 1911, the Looe luggers were fitted with engines.

The pilchard season varied from place to place. The shoals often appeared at harvest time, leading to the rhyme:

When the corn is in the shock
Then the fish are on the rock.

In St Ives the main season was often in September and October when it was followed by the herring season. In Mount's Bay, it was in the summer, from July to September. However, fishing sometimes continued on a reduced scale for the rest of the year. Mousehole and Porthleven boats sailed from their home ports in the days of sail. In the twentieth century, the St Ives fleet worked from Newlyn, which was packed with pilchard drivers. In later years, this was called 'Going to the Wolf', as much of the fishing was around the Wolf Rock lighthouse. In East Cornwall, the main fishing was in the autumn from Falmouth, Mevagissey, Polperro, Looe and Plymouth. During the First World War, the summer season failed in East Cornwall, and between the wars the Looe and Mevagissey fleets came to work from Newlyn.[7]

There could be record landings, as described by the *Cornishman* on 15 September 1910 under the headline 'A WEEK'S REMARKABLE CATCHES. PROSPECTS OF A RECORD SEASON':

The pilchard season in Mount's Bay during the past week underwent a remarkable change and from despondency and despair the local fishermen turned to jubilation … The catches during the week were nothing short of remarkable, and with prices unusually high the season promises to be a record … About 180 luggers are at present engaged in the pilchard fishery, and a reliable computation of the landings from Monday to Saturday places the catches at 2,480,000 pilchards. They were of splendid size and quality, the hawkers giving 25 shillings per 1000 and the curers 20 shillings per 1000. The value of the fish amounted to £2,500, of which … the Mousehole fishermen secured over £900.[8]

In 1911, the *St Ives Weekly Summary* described the Mount's Bay pilchard season:

It is a fine sight to see the little boats over three hundred in number go out from the ports of Newlyn, Penzance and Porthleven to the Mount's Bay, just as one is having

Ketch *Lewisman* discharging salt for the St Ives pilchard cellars. (Paul Martin Collection)

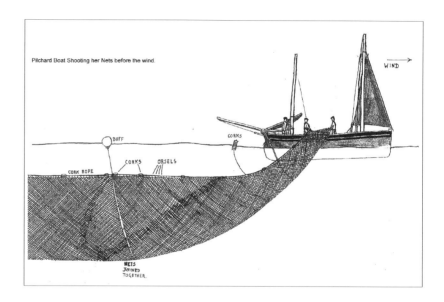

Pilchard boats sailing out of Newlyn. In the background are Breton crabbers anchored in Gwavas Lake.

five o'clock tea. They look exceedingly pretty with their tanned sails and there is a rush to get out to sea altogether, they are closer than in a regatta, almost with danger of collision. They are well handled however and accidents are rare amongst them. The bigger boats are manned some with four men and a youngster, some with three and a half, and the smaller ones with two and a half.

The same process takes place in a smaller scale at Mevagissey, Looe and other ports along the Cornish and Devonshire coasts. At nightfall they shoot out their nets to drift, and soon after midnight haul them in again with the enmeshed fish.[9]

It is puzzling that this lively description includes Penzance as a fishing port, which it wasn't, but leaves out Mousehole, which certainly was.

In 1921 S. G. Harmar recorded his memories of the sailing pilchard fleet for the *Western Morning News*:

During the evenings of August 1913, it was my custom to stand at the end of Newlyn pier and watch with interest and admiration the picturesque sight of the pilchard fleet slowly proceeding to sea for the night's fishing. It is no exaggeration to say that the fleet itself comprised over 100 vessels, including flotillas from the ports of St Ives, Porthleven and Mousehole. The excitement, bustle and agility with which the crews, arrayed in their snow-white jumpers, hoisted the dark brown lugsails and mizzens, as the little vessels rounded the lighthouse, attracted scores of visitors to the pier-head, and presented many a brilliant picture to numerous artists.

As in other methods of fishing, chance plays a great game. The nets which have a very small mesh, are shot at sunset. After about two hours drift, they are partly hauled, and if prospects are encouraging, are shot again; hauling finally about 4am. It has often been said by merchantmen approaching the Lizard that the congregation of such a large number of lights so close together is very confusing to navigation. That is easily understood because from Penzance Promenade the twinkling of so many lights stretched right across Mount's Bay closely resembles a huge pier lighted up profusely.[10]

During the First World War, the pilchard fishery was reduced by the lack of shipping for exports to Italy. Fishing continued for home consumption. After German submarines began to sink British fishing boats, pilchard drivers fishing the Wolf grounds were provided with a naval escort.

NETS

The pilchard drift net was a rectangular curtain of fine cotton meshes. Until the invention of the net loom in the nineteenth century, they were hand-made of hemp, several pieces being joined together to make one net.

The actual net, the 'twine' as it was called, was machine-made of thin cotton. It had to be fastened to ropes to 'set' it properly and to enable the fragile meshes to be robust enough to be handled. In Scotland and East Anglia, nets had ropes at the top and bottom. In Cornwall they were roped at the top only and known as 'fly nets'.

The nets and their ropes and corks were beautifully and skillfully put together. A 100-yard-long net fastened to a 100-yard-long rope would not fish. It needed to be slack. Before being set on its 'cork rope', a St Ives pilchard net was 100 yards long; at Mousehole and Porthleven 87 yards; and at Mevagissey 120 yards. A St Ives 100-yard-long net would be

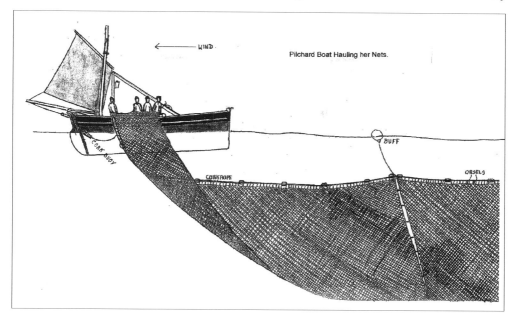

set on a rope about 63 yards long. A Mevagissey 120-yard-net was set on an 80-yard rope and a Looe 180-yard net on a 120-yard rope.

The nets arrived from their makers complete with 'norsels' or 'orsels', short double lengths of cord fastened to the top, about 5 inches apart. When setting the nets, the cork rope was stretched out tight in the loft. The first norsel was tied to the rope. The fisherman next picked up the fifth norsel along the net and tied it to the rope. He matched four spaces between norsels on the net (about 4 x 5 inches) to a distance about three spaces along the rope (about 3 x 5 inches). So about 20 inches of net was hung from about 15 inches of rope. The norsels were tied to the cork rope all the way along.

The cork rope was made of two, three, or four pieces of rope, lashed together. This was to prevent it twisting and rolling up the top of the net when it was hauled. The large oval corks were fitted between the ropes of the cork rope and tied in place, about 4 feet apart, depending on their size. The cork rope had a loop called a 'buckle' spliced at one end and a 'tail' at the other to join them together. The 'twine' had ten meshes deep of heavier net called the 'heading' at the top, five meshes called the 'guarding' at each end, and heavy twine called 'skilven', the 'end cords' at each side.[11]

Originally the cork rope floated on the surface of the water but, from the early nineteenth century, pilchard and herring nets were submerged about 4 fathoms below the surface, hanging on strops from cork buoys, and at the end of each net was a large inflated canvas ball called a 'buff' or 'mollac'. These cork buoys were about 11 yards apart. A St Ives net had four cork buoys and a buff.

In the twentieth century, the nets were produced by net looms at Edwards, Way and Hunkin of Mevagissey; Eddy, Kitto and Cowls at Porthleven; England at St Ives; Gundry and Gale at Bridport in Dorset; and Knocks of Kilburnie in Scotland.

Nets had to be looked after. Mending could go on all year round. They were 'barked' in a hot 'cutch' liquid at the local 'bark house' to preserve them and to kill the bacteria from the fish. When the boats were fishing, the nets were hauled up on deck every weekend; otherwise they would heat up and could spontaneously catch fire. Dipping in hot bark killed the bacteria, which would rot the nets, and preserved their fibres. The downside

Setting a net at Newlyn. The orsels are tied up to the headrope. (Margaret Perry)

Overhauling pilchard nets at Porthleven. The cork buoys are on the ground. Each pilchard net was suspended from four cork buoys and an inflated canvas buff.

Net mending at Mousehole. (Geraldine Underell)

was that 'barking' shrank the meshes and hardened the twine so that the nets fished less effectively with repeated barkings. This was solved by dipping them in creosote, known as 'pickle'. 'Pickling' lasted longer than barking and did not shrink the meshes, but pickled nets were vile to handle. The pickle coated hands and oilskins alike, and the fish buyers reasonably complained that creosoted nets tainted the fish.

WORKING PILCHARD NETS

The pilchard nets were all joined together to make one 'fleet'. Each tail on the cork rope was tied to its neighbouring buckle. The sides of the nets were tied together every foot to 13 inches by 'tachings'. When the nets were stowed in the net room, the cork rope was at the back and the foot of the nets at the front.

The boats went to sea at about four or five o'clock and aimed to shoot their nets at dusk, when the fish that had been feeding near the seabed all day rose closer to the surface. To

Skipper John F. Toman and his crew spreading the *Nazarene*'s nets to dry on St Ives Island. (St Ives Archive)

Taking aboard nets after barking, Mousehole, 1940s. (Geraldine Underell)

shoot the nets, two of the crew faced each other on the starboard side of the net room, one at the front and the other at the back. The skipper steered the boat before the wind, and at his signal one picked up the cork rope and the other the foot of the nets, the 'twine', and they threw them overboard. The man shooting the twine had to work much harder than the one shooting the cork rope. As explained above, the nets were roped only at the top, so the cork rope man would shoot about 60 yards for each net in a St Ives boat while his opposite number shot 100 yards of twine. Usually a third man shot the cork buoys and buffs. Each time the man shooting the cork rope got the rope strop to a cork buoy, he passed it over his head. The man shooting the buoys stood behind him. He pulled each buoy out of the net room and threw it overboard. In East Cornwall, the cork buoys were called 'corbles'.

The nets were shot slowly under reduced sail. Often a staysail would be hoisted on the foremast for shooting. When the nets were all out, the boat swung around, facing the wind, tied to its nets by the swing rope. The mizzen sail was reset and sheeted flat to keep the boat head to wind, the foremast was lowered down to an angle of about 45 degrees to reduce wind resistance, and the riding lights were lit.

When it was time to haul, the roller was put in place on the starboard rail alongside the net room. The length of the roller was the same as the width of the boat. It was fitted with an iron 'pawl', which prevented it from turning outwards. The front of the roller fitted in to a curved wooden chock, which prevented the nets being entangled with it.

One crew member hauled the cork rope and stowed it at the back of the net room, and another hauled the twine, which was stowed at the front. Two or three crew stood on the 'hauling boards', which went across the fishroom just below deck level. These fishermen unmeshed most of the fish. The nets were supported at convenient working height by one or two poles called 'prangers', which were lashed in place before work started. In bigger boats, the cork rope was hauled forward, near the bows, and passed aft where another crew member stowed it at the back of the net room. This helped to pull the boat along her nets and keep her in line with her gear.

When not in use, the roller, prangers and oars were stowed in the 'lumber irons', a pair of metal crutches on the port side. Until the Second World War, drift net fish were all counted and sold by the 'hundred', actually 120 fish.

MOTORS

The biggest change in drifting was the installation of engines, mainly during the First World War, with the help of the Motor Loans Committee of the Ministry of Agriculture and Fisheries. Mr Hamer, who had recorded his memories of the pilchard luggers in 1913, wrote of how things had changed in 1921:

> During the evenings of August 1921, it is again my custom to stand at the end of Newlyn pier and watch the departure of the pilchard fleet. I see the same number of boats, the same sturdy crews in their snow-white jumpers, but the bustle, animation and excitement as the vessels round the lighthouse is absent. They now proceed to sea in single file, like so many miniature destroyers. The fascinating and familiar dark brown lugsails that once delighted the hearts of famous artists have gone, and gone for ever. The mainmasts are lowered (as if in mourning), and the throb of the motor tells me that progress has robbed a world-picture of its greatest charm.[12]

Motors certainly eased the fishermen's task. Nets were now hauled under power. The boats were fitted with two engines, one on the centre line and the other on the port quarter. The centre engine was turned off and the port engine, known as the 'quarter engine', was used, at slow speed, when hauling. Its propeller on the port side was clear of the nets being hauled to starboard. The gear levers could be controlled from the deck and hauling was punctuated by the Skipper's calls of 'Go ahead!' and 'Knock her out!' ('Put the engine out of gear').

Skipper Robert Welch's St Ives pilchard boat *Mizpah 56 SS* going to sea from Newlyn. (Tony Pawlyn Collection)

The large fleet of motor pilchard boats at Newlyn in August 1925. Among them are the *Our Girls PZ 457, Ebenezer SS 340, Ripple SS 19, Seagull FY 408, Auld Lang Syne PZ 486, RJG PW 182, Irene SS 186* and *Leader FY 287.* In the foreground is a row of St Ives pilchard boats.

Porthleven pilchard boats moored in the outer harbour, *c.* 1930: *PZ 113 Ivy, PZ 62 Charity,* and *PZ 192 Marjorie,* whose stove is smoking well! (Tony Pawlyn Collection)

BETWEEN THE WARS

Initially the post-First World War outlook seemed promising. There were nearly 100 boats at Newlyn in September 1920, with prices of 30s per 1,000 for cured fish and 3s 6d – 4s per 120 for home consumption. Two years later, the fishery was bustling with large quantities being packed for the Italian market but prices had dropped to 22s 6d per 1,000 for curing, and 2s 9d to 3s 6d per 120 for the home market.[13]

In May 1949 the *Cornishman* took a nostalgic look back to these busy days of the 1920s:

> Those were hectic seasons when practically the entire fleets of Newlyn, Mousehole, St Ives, Fowey, Looe and Mevagissey landed millions of pilchards at Newlyn, and where at times, boats came into port laden to the rails. Unmeshing was in progress for more than 24 hours, and the harbour was a hive of industry, with curers' small boats being sculled to and fro, landing fish to the nearest vantage points to the stores, for horses and carts to complete the journey.
>
> In those days it was a common occurrence to see boats beached under Fore Street and Newlyn Slips, the Old Harbour, under the Fish Market, anchored in the harbour and lying against the Quay, all landing huge catches of fish, and with curing houses stretching from Street an Nowan to the Mousehole road. Practically all landings were for export, and the firms of Stevenson, Chiffers, Pawlyn, Edwards, White, Barnes, Hunkin and others cured hundreds of tons for Mediterranean ports.[14]

This seems a rosy picture but the motor boats were oversupplying the markets. In 1922–23, 13,000 casks of pilchards were stored until the following season. There was also foreign competition. By the mid-1920s, pilchard canning in British Columbia was expanding rapidly, supplied by efficient purse seiners.[15]

Another perspective on the industry comes from a report of April 1924. A Porthleven fisherman applied to Helston Board of Guardians for relief. His boat had earned £4 during the previous week and he shared 3s 6d. His earnings since the previous November were £34, from which nets and ropes had cost him £12. A board member said, 'It was a wonder how the family had lived at all.' The Board could not let the family starve.[16]

At the end of September 1926 the General Steam Navigation steamer *Guillemot* loaded over 3,000 barrels for export to Italy. She was the third steamer to load at Newlyn for the season.[17]

On Friday 6 June 1930, skipper Robert Care's St Ives gig *Cutty Sark SS 117* shot her nets deep off Newlyn. While hauling their nets, they got mopped up with one of the cork buoys in the propeller. Her four crew hauled their gear without the engine, a long and tedious job, and then set off for Newlyn under sail, against a strong breeze. When she was still missing on Saturday evening, skipper James Pender's Mousehole motor lugger *Boy Willie PZ 602* put out from Newlyn, found her off the Bucks rocks and towed her into port.[18]

There were seventy drifters, including many newly built St Ives motor gigs, at Newlyn for the 1932 season but prices for curing had fallen to 12s 6d – 15s per thousand fish. The pilchard drivers' lives were made harder by sharks wreaking havoc with their nets. Nights of toil were followed by daylight hours of mending.[19] The situation improved later in the season when ninety St Ives, Mount's Bay and Looe boats found good shoals around the Wolf.[20]

Sharks were an ever-present menace, whose damage resulted in hours of net mending in the loft. Each boat carried a shark line. Two large longline hooks were stuck into a whole pilchard. The line came in over the side and under the stringer where it was tied to the

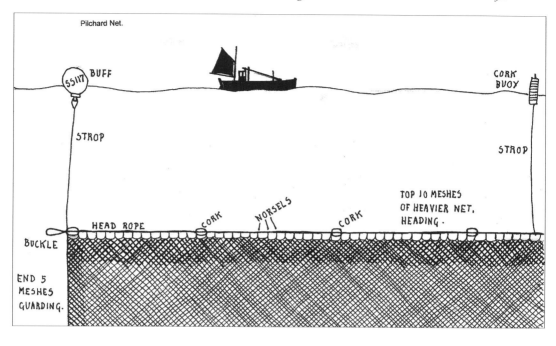

The pilchard fleet hard at work in Newlyn harbour: *PZ 302 Faithful* of Mousehole, *FY 70 Mayflower* and *FY 35 John Wesley*, both of Looe, and the St Ives gig *Glorious Peace SS 37*. (G. E. Low)

Clement Toman's St Ives gig *Bonnie Girls SS 54* and Mr Atkinson's Looe motor lugger *Seagull FY 408* landing at Newlyn Old Slip. (Richards Collection, Penzance Morrab Library)

handle of the bucket. Each time a shark was caught, the bucket rattled and it was hauled up and dispatched.

Since motor boats were more efficient, the drifter fleet reduced from its pre-1914 levels, and prices fell in times of oversupply. A fisherman remembered, 'The problem in the 1930s was the price of pilchards. They went down to 10 bob or 7s 6d a thousand. That was a very poor price. Men had to catch boatloads of fish to get anything out of it.'[21]

Record catches did not always bring prosperity, as in September 1933, when huge catches resulted in lost nets caused by the weight of the fish, which sank them:

Three million pilchards, the largest catch for half a century, were landed at Mounts Bay on Thursday. The *Sheerness SS 10* (St Ives) which netted from eight to nine lasts (about ninety thousand fish) was packed from mast to mast, although she is the largest boat in the local fleets.

Unfortunately this enormous haul, which should have done much to relieve the depression in the industry, was accompanied by the loss of over 100 nets, valued at between £500 and £600.

The losses listed were from the *John Wesley FY 35* of Looe, twelve nets valued at £108; *Israel Britain PZ 528* of Newlyn, fifteen nets at £75; from the Mousehole fleet *Boy Don PZ 459*, eighteen nets at £90; *Girl Joyce PZ 156*, twelve nets at £60; *Penzer PZ 324*, six nets at £30; and from the St Ives boats, *Our John SS 64*, seventeen nets at £102; *Maggie SS 113*, sixteen nets at £96; and eight nets from the *Ripple SS 19* at £48.[22]

The Abyssinian Crisis of 1937, when Britain objected to the Italian dictator Mussolini's invasion of the country and put an embargo on exports, destroyed the main export market for Cornish pilchards and devastated the fishery. Although pilchard canning had been introduced at Mevagissey as early as 1873 (its produce known as 'Cornish sardines'), the canners could not replace the Italian market. The pilchard fishery had been the backbone of fishing in the county and, although the bigger boats could go lining and the smaller ones crabbing, these could not replace the drift fishery. These pre-war years were desperate ones for Cornish fishermen, and many boats were sold.[23]

With the coming of war in 1939, the Royal Navy imposed controls on fishing, and most of the larger Cornish boats were requisitioned by the forces, though a modest pilchard fishery continued for home consumption.

Seen in a cottage window, St Ives Downlong:

Marinated Pilchards for Sale.
Prepare to Meet Thy God.

and

Figgie Duff, one penny.
More Figgier, one penny halfpenny.

POST-SECOND WORLD WAR

With the return of peace, the pilchard drift fishery revived, as recalled by Skipper Gordon Stevens of St Ives:

The crew of the Pender family's *Lyonesse PZ 81* of Mousehole unmeshing a big shot of pilchards. (Richards Collection, Penzance Morrab Library)

A deck full of pilchards, *Provider PW 89*. (Richards Collection, Penzance Morrab Library)

Bonnie Lass PZ 306 hauling pilchard nets in daylight. (Jan Pentreath)

After the War, the smaller boats would make a whole season of it from April or May month, catching smaller quantities. But the proper season, Going to the Wolf, started at the end of July or beginning of August. Then we would fish on 'til Paul Feast, which is in September I believe. We have fished after that. From there we went to Plymouth.

That fishing ranged from Plymouth to Mevagissey and eventually came back down to Falmouth. Lots of Mevagissey men came to Plymouth too. The Looe men worked from home. We used to be in Plymouth just after the War about Guy Fawkes Day and stayed there to the middle of March.

Of course, when the echo-sounder came along, that stretched the season. You knew the fish had sunk over the full moon. We would stop fishing over the moon, and when the fish would rise, go to sea again. The echo-sounder made fishing much easier.[24]

Fishing has always been a dangerous occupation and the post-war years saw several incidents. In January 1946 the *Nellie PZ 211* was disabled by damage to her rudder off the Lizard and brought in by the Trinity House steamer *Satellite*.[25] The fishing community was

Unmeshing a good catch at Plymouth Barbican, 1946. (Plymouth City Archive)

Cornish pilchard drivers going to sea from Plymouth, 1948. *SS 10*, Matthew Stevens' *Sheerness* of St Ives. (Plymouth City Archive)

struck by tragedy when on 25 June 1948 the Porthleven drifter *Energetic PZ 114* was sunk in collision with the American liberty ship *Chrysanthy Star* in thick fog 10 miles south-west of the Lizard, with the loss of the five Richards brothers and their friend who was out for a trip. The fog also claimed the life of fifteen-year-old François Vandorstraeten of the Ostend trawler *Simone Marcel*, which went ashore near Gurnard's Head.[26] In September 1957 the *Nazarene SS 114* of St Ives was wrecked at Pednevounder near Porthcurnow, fortunately without loss of life.[27] In the following days, over sixty St Ives and Mount's Bay fishermen helped skipper John F. Toman to haul his fishing gear to the clifftop.

There was encouragement in the opening of new marketing outlets. In October 1947 Cornish Products Ltd planned a new cannery at Looe.[28] Firms like Cornish Canners and Shippams now bought much of the catch but they were sometimes concerned about irregular supplies of fish. Traditional curing still took large supplies. By December there were fifty-five drifters fishing from Plymouth. In November 1950 the steamer *Albatross* loaded 150 tons of pilchards, destined for the Mediterranean, at Newlyn.[29]

In 1950 the summer fleet at Newlyn had increased and again included craft from Looe, Mevagissey, St Ives and Porthleven. After trials by a pair of Scots ring netters, the Mousehole boats *Renovelle PZ 107* and *Mark H Leach INS 207* tried ring netting with some success, particularly in the autumn when the shoals were more concentrated and they made some good landings of excellent quality at Plymouth.[30] The Scots ring net did not take off in Cornwall but its cousin, a miniature 'purse seine' (usually known as a ring net), was worked by several West Cornish boats – *Sweet Promise SS 95*, skipper E. Stevens; *Girl Renee SS 78*, skipper J. Stevens; *JBS SS 17*, skipper J. M. Veal; *Coeur de Lion PZ 74*, skipper Dick Sampson; and the second *Renovelle PZ 177*, skipper E. Madron – in the late 1950s. The *Sweet Promise* and *Renovelle* made a success of this technique at the autumn Cornish pilchard fishery and herring fishing from Dunmore East in Ireland. Another development was sponsored by Shippams cannery, who built the 40-foot-long *Chichester Lass PZ 63* in Fraserburgh in 1956. In January 1960 she pioneered midwater trawling for pilchards under skipper Bobby Jewell of Porthleven. In one shot of her trawl, she caught over 9 tons of pilchards just off Falmouth.[31] They were unable to get the fish aboard and had to tow the catch into port. At the same time, Skipper Ernest Stevens' *Sweet Promise* made some record shots with her ring net, her best night's landing being over 1,000 stone.[32] Her fish were of exellent quality, not having been meshed in drift nets. John Stevens said, 'Our fish were perfect with not a scale off them. We were in, landed and

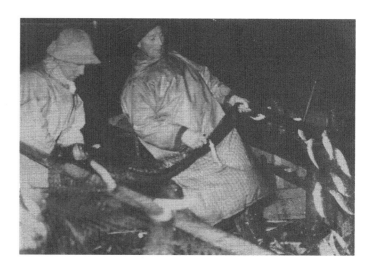

Hauling pilchards aboard the *Janie PZ 30*, 1950s. On the right, behind the net, is the line hauler, known as the jinny. (Harry Penhaul, Penlee House Museum, Penzance)

moored up while the rest of them were still hauling.' Such perfect fish were a problem for the cannery, whose machinery was clogged up by quantities of pilchard scales.

By the 1950s many of the drifters were ancient, having been built in the days of sail. Several new boats were built for Cornwall, most with help from the White Fish Authority grant and loan scheme. New builds included the *Provider PZ 19* and *Chichester Lass PZ 63* for Porthleven, *Hesperian* for Mousehole, *Ocean's Gift PZ 18* and *Coeur de Lion PZ 74* for Newlyn,[33] *Little Pearl FY 23* for Mevagissey, and *Sweet Promise SS 95*, *JBS SS 17*[34] and *Lamorna SS 45* for St Ives.

In January 1954 the drifters were doing well off the Eddystone. Each day, after the shipping forecast, there were radio broadcasts requesting vessels 'to keep to luuard of pilchard drift net vessels fishing between the Eddystone and the Wolf'. These messages started after complaints about large merchant ships, including the French liner *Île de France*, steaming through nets.[35]

When a ship got too close, it was customary to set off a 'flambow', a primitive paraffin flare. The flambow was a traditional but effective device. It consisted of a metal jug with a close-fitting lid. Inside the lid was a metal rod, ending in a ring that enclosed a piece of rag. The flambow was about half full of paraffin. When it was needed, the lid was taken off, and a match applied to the paraffin-soaked rag.

There appeared to be many optimistic signs for the pilchard industry, but the problem, as always, was in marketing. In 1947, 3,000 tons were landed; the number had increased to 5,700 tons in 1956. In 1954 there were nine canneries at work. However, in 1955 a national trade agreement with South Africa allowed cheap imports of tinned pilchards from Walvis Bay. These imports soon undercut the Cornish canneries, which closed within a few years. This and the failure of the autumn fishery doomed the industry. In September 1957 the St Ives gig *Cape Cornwall SS 23* landed a massive 1,300 stones.[36] However, after only three days of good fishing, the cannery was unable to cope and the boats were kept in harbour. By August 1958 the fleet at Newlyn was made up of fewer than thirty boats, and by 1964 landings were down to 1,500 tons. A description of hauling pilchard nets dates from this time, but it could equally well have applied to the previous 400 years:

Chichester Lass PZ 63 pioneered trawling for pilchards.

The iron pawl on the net roller clink clinks as it turns. The men's wet oilskins reflect the deck lights hanging over them. The fine black meshes of the net ripple over the roller and the net room coamings and jerk as the silver fish are shaken out. Smoke drifts sleepily from the cabin stove pipe across the dark shape of the mizzen sail. The deck pounds fill up as fish scales fly and coat everything they touch. The heap of nets in the net room rises. Over all is the shriek and flapping of herring gulls getting bolder and greedier by the minute until a wild yell from one of the crew sends them off. Mount's Bay appears like a floating village as the deck lights are lit and more boats start hauling. One of the crew says, 'There's Uncle Us gone to work,' and we see the *Cape Cornwall*'s lights appear, over to starboard. It is eleven o'clock on a beautiful summer's night. The last of the Cornish drifters are hauling their nets.

The drift net fishery faded away in the 1960s. Expensive trials were made to assess pilchard stocks. It was agreed that the shoals were still there off the Cornish coast, but without marketing opportunities there was no incentive to catch them.

In the early 1970s, midwater trawling for pilchards took off, and very large shots were landed. In January 1972 the Brixham midwater pair trawlers *Angel Emiel* and *Angele Erika* landed 7,800 stones of pilchards worth nearly £1,600 at Plymouth Barbican. The Cornish pair trawlers *Galilean*, *Rose of Sharon*, *Spaven Mor* and *Kilravock* landed 6,000 stones at Falmouth but took thirty-six hours to land because of lack of facilities. Skipper Bobby Jewell of the *Galilean* commented, 'Pair trawling is allowing us to catch fish in quantities which local markets and storage resources cannot handle.'[37]

That appeared to be the end of the story until the 1990s, when Skipper Martin Ellis of Cadgwith took up the challenge of ring netting and began making landings to Nick Howell's pilchard works at Newlyn,[38] which, as a living museum, was still exporting cured pilchards to Italy until 2005. Cornish pilchards were rebranded as 'Cornish sardines' and began to go upmarket. British holidaymakers who enjoy grilled sardines in Europe have been persuaded that the same delights are available from Cornwall. The supermarket chains now sell Cornish sardines as a quality food, and the health benefits of eating oily fish are becoming better known.[39] Interestingly, this rebranding as 'sardines' had been suggested over fifty years earlier by Commander Luard of Cornwall Sea Fisheries Committee, and ignored.

9,000 stones of pilchards aboard the St Ives trawler *Rose of Sharon FR23*, January 1972. Left to right: Maurice Goulden, James Matthews Perkin, David Perkin, Raymond Stevens, Paul Stevens, Skipper David Stevens, Skipper Michael Hosking of the *Kilravock BS 18* of Porthleven and crew. (Shamrock Lodge Collection)

In the twenty-first century, several high-tech ring netters have been built or adapted. In 2009, the *Little Pearl FY 23*, *Pride of Cornwall SS 87*, *Resolute FY 119* (the same number as the Lakeman family's famous lugger *Ibis*) and the catamaran *Lyonesse PZ 81* fished very successfully from Newlyn during the pilchard (alias sardine) season. In 2010 several new ringers were being fitted out. All the new boats are built of fibreglass. Their catches are dictated by the market and they fish almost to order. They have modern electronic navigating and fish-finding equipment. Their nets are hauled by hydraulic 'power-blocks' and winches. Side thrusters enable them to avoid the traditional danger of getting mopped up in their own nets. The older boats, without thrusters, work with partner 'tow boats' to keep them out of the net. The 1950s generation of Cornish ringers shot their nets to finish up downwind.

A crew of three can now catch the equivalent of half a dozen drifters, and their landings are measured by the ton instead of the stone, 1,000 or 120. Modern ringers are very expensive and prices are still low: 'It takes over a ton of fish just to pay for the lorry.' The emphasis is on quality. The fish come aboard from the purse seine alive (as they did from the seines a century ago) and are immediately stored in large plastic containers containing seawater and ice. They are landed in perfect condition. Many of these developments have been learned from our Celtic neighbour Brittany, whose sardine industry has also experienced a decline and revival on a larger scale. In September 2011 the Newlyn ringer *White Heather LK 3390* landed shots of 30 tons, equivalent to a night's landings for a whole fleet of drifters in the late 1950s. In November, Ocean Fish's new ringer *Asthore PZ 182* was fishing in Bigbury Bay and landing in Plymouth as the drifter fleets had done, half a century before. Sadly, the sea takes its toll. On the night of 20 December 2011, the heavily laden Mevagissey ringer *Heather Anne FY 126* sank very suddenly in calm weather, in Gerrans Bay, having already landed a good shot. Although both crew were rescued from the water, tragically experienced fisherman Ian Thomas died. The *Heather Anne* was one of several Mevagissey ringers to regenerate sardine fishing at the port.[40]

Skipper Stephan Glinski's very successful ring netter *White Heather*. (Francis McWilliams)

CHAPTER 3

Cornish Mackerel Season

According to the Cornish historian Cyril Noall, mackerel drifting was introduced to St Ives by Breton fishermen. After the Edict of Nantes in 1685, Huguenot refugees settled in St Ives. There were conflicts between these Protestant Huguenots and the Catholic Bretons who stored their nets in a barn-like building on St Ives Island called the Bretons' hut. After one of these conflicts, nets were found at Porthgwidden beach with mackerel enmeshed in them.[1]

R. Morton Nance's research, published in the *Mariner's Mirror*, shows that seventeenth-century Cornish drifters, known as 'coks', were little two-masted open boats setting square sails. One mast was amidships and the other in the bows, as in the eighteenth-century Breton sardiners.[2]

By the eighteenth century, the drifters were three-masted luggers, still very small open boats. Much more is known about these. For example the *Caeser*, registered in St Ives on 1 March 1792 and owned by six locals, including 'Ann Harry, widow', was built at St Michael's Mount in 1777. Her skipper was John Pearce. She is described in the register as a 'round sterned lugsail boat' of 18 tons, with a length of 35 feet 9 inches and a beam of 11 feet.[3] By 1795 there were fifty mackerel drivers in the Mount's Bay ports.

On 26 March 1791 the Mount's Bay mackerel fleet was caught out in a terrible gale. One boat was lost, as were many nets, and there was heavy damage to boats and nets. Several boats were driven as far as Plymouth.

In the early nineteenth century, the Cornish luggers were three-masters. They were open boats except for the foredeck. The St Ives and Mount's Bay fishermen sailed to Ireland and the North Sea in these little craft. (With permission of the Royal Institution of Cornwall – RIC.)

Herbert Richards wrote of these early days at Newlyn,

> The first drifters were so small that the crews were forced to sleep in the net room when the nets were shot, and cover themselves with a thick cape, and the harbour was so small that many of the craft were hauled up in the winter on the beach between Lariggan and Newlyn. From 1825 the boats were larger and more seaworthy. The produce of the industry was mostly consumed near home and it was only when large quantities were taken that they went as far as Plymouth ... as more and larger boats were built, fast sailing smacks came to Newlyn to take consignments of mackerel to Bristol markets.[4]

Mackerel have to be eaten fresh and the age-old problem was getting them to market quickly. Captain Short's St Ives diary evokes the maritime scene. The mackerel men hoped to start their spring season by March but, as always, the weather had the last say: 'April 26 1822 – Twenty five mackerel boats attempted to go to sea, but were obliged to run for the harbour again.' The incentive to sail in poor weather was the previous year's season, when some boats had made £100 in a week, a fortune in 1821. In April 1836, 'One boat landed 1,200 very fine mackerel, sold at 2½*d* (pence) each.' Captain Short records some excellent landings in the 1820s. On 22 April 1829, 'Skiffs Dolphin and Globe took on board mackerel for Bristol.' These 'skiffs' were pilot cutters. 'May 1 – Mackerel boats, from 3000; sold at 25*s* and 27*s* per hundred. Mount's Bay boats fishing here.'[5]

In 1827 the *West Briton* reported,

> Owing to arrangements made for conveying fish from Bristol to London by vans or light carts, the price of mackerel has been kept up to 20 shillings to 25 shillings per hundred. The fish caught on our coasts are taken to Bristol, where they are purchased by regular dealers and sent to London; fish caught on the Cornish coast have been offered for sale at Billing's gate on the third day from their being taken – the price of mackerel in the London market is stated at 70*s* to 90*s* per hundred.[6]

Perhaps modern tastes might not regard three-day-old mackerel, without benefit of ice or refrigeration, as a high-value luxury.

Washing and packing mackerel with straw in pads, baskets with lids. Until the building of the Norway Ice Stores at Newlyn, where ice imported from Norway in sailing ships was stored, mackerel were washed and packed in straw for dispatch, without the benefit of ice.

Running mackerel to Bristol was a profitable business but brought misfortune to the six crew and a boy of the Penzance lugger *Blucher*, which was wrecked with the loss of all hands at St Minver, near Padstow, on 29 March 1827.

The local market also played a role, as reported by the *West Briton* in 1836, a report which dents St Ives' traditional claim to keep the Sabbath holy, and shows how the merchants' desire for a quick buck came to grief:

FOUR HUNDRED FISHCARTS ON ST IVES BEACH. So great was the bustle of catching fish and selling mackerel on Sunday, that the day had no appearance of the Sabbath, and on Monday as early as two o'clock, carts from the neighbouring parishes began to arrive, and continued throughout the day. At one time more than 400 carts were on the beach. Messrs Tremearne, Bamfield and Co. commenced the sale of their mackerel, but they raised the price from 24s per gurry, holding about two hundreds and a half, to 44s and more than half the carts in consequence returned to Redruth, Camborne, Crowan, Gwinear, Phillack, Ludgvan, Marazion, Perran, Towednack, Zennor, St Just and other parishes, without a supply.[7]

The next boost to the market was the Hayle–Bristol steam packet steamer service, started in 1842, following the completion of Brunel's Great Western Railway from London to Bristol. Captain Short spotted how this improved prices: 'May 13 1851, Boats from 500 to 1,500 mackerel; sold at 12s 6d per hundred for the steamer and 5s 6d for home consumption.'[8]

In this Great Exhibition year there were three paddle steamers on the Hayle–Bristol run: the *Cornwall*, *Express* and *Brilliant*.

The completion in 1859 of Brunel's Royal Albert Bridge over the Tamar, Cornwall's natural frontier, had a tremendous effect. Cornwall ceased to be almost an island and, with through rail travel, England came to be regarded less as a foreign country. The following year, £80,000 worth of fish, much of it mackerel, left Cornwall by train for London and the large provincial cities. This figure carried on rising until the First World War. There was a boom in building mackerel boats, the largest class of Cornish lugger, and their lines and sails were refined and improved to produce sturdy decked vessels, capable of going anywhere. These magnificent craft were soon to dominate fishing in the Channel and Irish Sea, where they were flattered by being widely copied in the Isle of Man, the west of Scotland, Ireland and the Channel ports. The number of luggers at Newlyn rose from sixty in 1838 to 116 in 1883.

This sudden and welcome expansion of the market for mackerel also brought problems in the shape of the Lowestoft luggers, whose traditions were very different from Cornwall's:

April 29, 1860; An East-country fishing boat came into the Roadstead with about 1000 mackerel, caught on Saturday night, which was purchased by two strange buyers. A gig's crew of St Ives fishermen refused to allow the fish to be landed, and after some altercation threw the fish into the sea.[9]

Why the uproar? Because the fish had been hauled on a Sunday. Since the Wesley brothers' crusade a century before, many Cornish fishermen were deeply religious, and the commandment 'Keep holy the Sabbath day' meant not fishing on Sunday.

The *West Briton* reported on 14 May 1871,

The Cornish fishermen suspend work on Sundays, but the east country fishermen who come to St Ives for the season, have no such scruples. Last year there was a disturbance and this year the St Ives men have again prevented the others from landing … fish caught on Saturday night or Sundays. The result is the eastcountrymen have gone to Hayle.[10]

The East Anglian boats, always known as 'Yorkies' in Cornwall, despite their Norfolk and Suffolk origins, were allowed to land at Newlyn, though with declining enthusiasm, as large landings on Mondays often ruined the market for the rest of the week. In 1875 there were between 300 and 400 boats at the fishery, landing about 50 tons a day. In 1896 they were joined by the Yarmouth fleet.

In May 1882 the mackerel fleet was caught out in a severe storm. About 100 St Ives boats were at sea and several only survived by riding to 'rafts' (makeshift sea anchors). There were crippling losses of nets valued at a massive £2,500 at St Ives.[11]

In May 1883 the *Cornishman* reported, 'MOUNT'S BAY SPRING MACKEREL FISHERY. The first general success for the season was on Wednesday morning, when the boats shot off Scilly and landed at St Mary's 1,500 pads of mackerel, which were got away in good time by the *Lady of the Isles*.'[12]

From the 1870s the Isles of Scilly were used as a base for the mackerel drifters. The steam tugs *Gamecock* and *Stormcock* were chartered by the London & South Western Railway to ship mackerel to Plymouth and Southampton. Since the Great Western Railway was running main-line fish trains, this seems a strange venture, but the GWR was accused of a lackadaisical interest in the fish trade. On 17 May 1886 the *West Briton* reported that the *Stormcock* brought over 250,000 mackerel from Scilly, and the island steamers *Lady of the Isles* and the

St Ives mackerel fleet landing fish. The boats moor in the harbour mouth and land their catches by punt. As soon as the fish are landed, they are away to sea again. The lugger on the right is off.

Lowestoft drifter *LT 48* at Penzance. Centre, one of the steamers which brought mackerel from Scilly during the 1880s. To the right of her funnels are another Lowestoft drifter and three local luggers with their mizzens set. On the left a Plymouth smack is getting her punt aboard.

paddler *Queen of the Bay* also brought big cargoes.[13] Other steamers, the *St Kilda*, *Curzon* and *Scott Harley*, came to run mackerel from Scilly to Penzance during the 1880s.

Despite its very inadequate tidal harbour, St Ives appears to have been the top Cornish fishing port in 1893, with ninety mackerel drivers and eighty pilchard boats crewed by 800 fishermen. Newlyn had seventy-nine mackerel boats and thirty-eight pilchard boats crewed by 540; it was closely followed by Mousehole, whose tiny harbour packed in forty-five mackerel boats, sixty-three pilchard boats and 472 fishermen.[14]

On Saturday 19 May 1894, about 400 St Ives, Newlyn and Mousehole fishermen came home from Scilly for the weekend at a reduced steamer fare of 1s. During the following week, the steamers brought 6,330 pads (baskets) of mackerel from the islands.[1]

The tragic loss of the lugger *Jane* and her seven crew, while running for Penzance harbour on 7 October 1880, highlighted the need for a proper harbour at Newlyn. The *Jane* had just returned from the North Sea herring voyage.[16] The old medieval harbour could only take a fraction of Newlyn's fishing fleet, most of which moored in Gwavas Lake, the anchorage outside the village. When poor weather threatened, they headed for the safety of Penzance harbour.

The building of Newlyn's new harbour, completed by the North Pier in 1894, changed the situation, and it quickly came to dominate the Cornish fisheries with its local and

The Cornish mackerel fleet at St Mary's, Scilly.

Newlyn mackerel boat *Jenny Lind PZ 58* leaving Penzance, 1890. Until the completion of Newlyn North Pier in 1894, the Newlyn boats often moored at Penzance. The *Jenny Lind* has her foresail aback on the wrong side of the mast. When she tacks, it will be on the correct side. Her punt is on the starboard side, beside the net room, right in the way for shooting her nets. When it's time to shoot, the skipper will call, 'Aft punt!' and it will be shifted back on the port side of the mizzen mast.

Lowestoft sailing drifters at Penzance. (Margaret Perry)

visiting fleets, especially the Lowestoft and Yarmouth drifters, which entirely took over the port during each spring mackerel season. While the local men stayed in port to 'keep holy the Sabbath day', the Yorkies fished over the weekend, and their Monday landings glutted the market for much of the rest of the week.

The new harbour was a great improvement, but not perfect. The luggers were moored in rows and subject to big surges in heavy weather. On 7 April 1899, in a north-westerly gale, thirteen luggers parted their moorings and were washed out of the harbour. Ten were totally wrecked. The harbour became secure in 1915, when the South Pier was lengthened. The boats could now safely berth alongside the North Pier.

MACKEREL NETS

Unlike pilchard and herring nets, mackerel nets floated right on the surface. They had a bigger mesh but were both shallower and shorter than pilchard and herring nets, so the boats worked many more of them, perhaps sixty-four in total. A St Ives mackerel net was 80 yards long before being set, and only 50 yards roped. They were always worked with a footline, a strong rope which hung down below the nets, fastened by strops to the cork rope. If the nets were cut by ships ploughing through them, the footline enabled the surviving nets to be hauled.

Each mackerel driver was fitted with a capstan. The footline came in through a cage roller on the bow and was wound several times around the capstan. As the capstan slowly turned, it pulled the boat along her fleet of nets, which were cast off from the footline and hauled in over the net roller on the starboard side. The footline went down through a hole in the deck to the footline locker where the cabin boy coiled it down. As he pulled the rope down from above, the water ran up his sleeves. If he didn't pull hard enough, the men stamped on the deck and shouted, 'Pull down! Pull down!' In 1884, William Garrood invented the steam capstan, and by the 1890s all the large West Cornish mackerel boats from Mount's Bay and St Ives were fitted with steam capstans. Several boats chose the Cornish-made Penryn steam capstan. The steam came from a vertical boiler aft in the cabin. There was also a coal-fired cooking stove beside it in the cabin, which must have been an inferno on a hot summer day. The smaller boats and the Looe and Mevagissey fleets were fitted with hand-wound flywheel capstans, which could be unbolted and taken ashore when not in use.

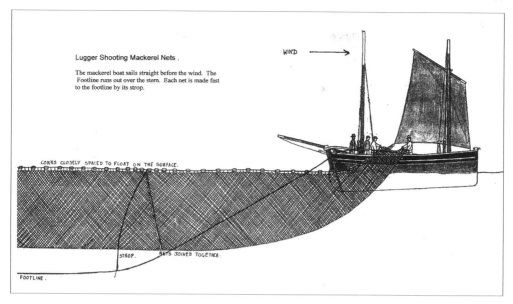

Lugger Shooting Mackerel Nets.

The mackerel boat sails straight before the wind. The
Footline runs out over the stern. Each net is made fast
to the footline by its strop.

WIND

CORKS CLOSELY SPACED TO FLOAT ON THE SURFACE.

STROP.

NETS JOINED TOGETHER.

FOOTLINE.

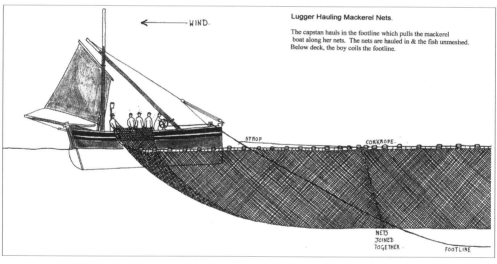

WIND.

Lugger Hauling Mackerel Nets.

The capstan hauls in the footline which pulls the mackerel
boat along her nets. The nets are hauled in & the fish unmeshed.
Below deck, the boy coils the footline.

STROP

CORKROPE.

NETS
JOINED
TOGETHER.

FOOTLINE

The *Barnabas SS 634*
hauling her nets. Built at
Porthgwidden, St Ives, by
Henry Trevorrow in 1881, the
Barnabas fished until 1955.
After rebuilding, she is still
sailed by the Cornish Maritime
Trust.

MACKEREL VOYAGE

By the end of the nineteenth century, life was getting tough for the Cornish mackerel drivers. Matthew Stevens of the St Ives lugger *Jane SS 563* kept a record of landings and earnings. The *Jane*'s 1894 mackerel season began on 23 March:

23. 7 hundred, 15/6d per hundred.
27. ¾ hundred, 16/- per hundred.
28. 2¼ hundred, 23/- per hundred.
29. Score Mackrell.
April 24. 6¼ hundred, 16/- per hundred.
25. Not out last night strong Gale. Half of the Fleet out Riding. More damage done with nets than it has been for many years. We had 15 damages. Lost 5.
26. Not out repairing damages.
27. Still repairing Damages.
28. Not out Barking.

The *Jane*'s 1895 mackerel season began on 20 March and ended on 21 June. They shot their nets thirty-eight times and grossed £91 3s 0d. For the whole season, each man shared £3 14s 0d plus £2 4s 6d allowance, a total of £5 18s 6d per man, not a living wage.[17]

The West Cornish fishermen certainly felt that the East Anglian landings from their weekend fishing were destroying their livelihood. Those East Coast drifters that did not fish on Sundays carried a star on their mizzen sails and were known as 'Bethel Boats'. In modern times, this device has become part of the livery of Newlyn's Stevenson's trawler fleet. In 1889 the Bethel Boats *Nil Desperandum LT 111*, *Young John LT 526*, *Never Can Tell LT 283*, *Queen Bee LT*, *Despatch LT 313*, *Energy LT 60*, *Iris YH*, *Martha LT 493*, *Celt YH 892* and *Ferry Boat YH 884* landed their catches at St Ives.[18]

An anecdote from this time is about a Lowestoft drifter trying to find her way into St Ives in thick fog. The crew heard a noise and sang out, 'Who's that?' Came the reply, 'What's it got to do with you who I am? You mind your own business. I'm tealing potatoes.' 'Where are you tealing potatoes?' 'Just under Providence Mine [Carbis Bay].' The Yorkies shouted, 'Thank you!' and found their way safely into harbour.

Skipper Ben Downing's mackerel boat *Sweet Home PZ 514* at Scilly. The *Sweet Home* was built at Porthleven in 1893 for Edward and Benjamin Downing of Mousehole.

Until Newlyn North Pier was widened in 1907, mackerel were ferried ashore by bummers' gigs. On the left is a Plymouth lugger, *PH 73.*

In May 1896 the Sunday fishing question boiled over into the Newlyn Riots. On Monday 18 May 1896, over 1,000 of the people of Newlyn marched down the quay, boarded the Lowestoft boats and threw over 100,000 mackerel into the sea.[19] The St Ives fleet was at Scilly and, according to local folklore, they promptly set sail for Newlyn with flags flying to come to the aid of their fellow Cornish fishermen. The strife was only ended by 350 soldiers of the Berkshire Regiment who were rushed to Penzance by train and marched into Newlyn with fixed bayonets to restore order. The gunboats HMS *Curlew* and *Traveller* and the destroyer HMS *Ferret* headed for Mount's Bay at full speed. The East Coast mackerel fleet moved to Penzance, where the warm welcome they received did nothing to improve relations between the two towns.

The ringleaders were punished, but leniently. A compromise was agreed by which the Yorkies were not to fish on Saturday nights, but the agreement was not kept. The spring mackerel fishery continued to grow, but the Cornish share in it declined.

While Sunday-caught fish were landed at Newlyn, St Ives stuck to its guns, as related by the *Western Echo* in April 1901:

> During a strong southwesterly gale, several Lowestoft fishing boats put into St Ives Bay and harbour. Most of the crews who observed the Sabbath the same as the Westcountry men, came into harbour and landed their fish. The boat *Buttercup* however which was a Sunday fisher, remained in the Bay until the next day when the captain brought his craft into harbour and wanted to sell his fish. This the salesmen and fish buyers would not countenance.[20]

THE STEAM DRIFTERS

The first English steam drifter, the *Consolation LT 718*, was built in 1897.[21] From 1900 there was a boom in building these highly successful craft in East Anglia. There was no way the local Cornish luggers could compete. The Cornish fishermen often watched, becalmed or weatherbound, while the jaunty new steamers with their puffing 'Woodbine' funnels sailed for the mackerel grounds, almost regardless of the weather.

Newlyn North Pier under construction, *c.* 1890. No wonder some of the locals thought they were building a harbour for strangers. The local mackerel luggers, left, are outnumbered by the Brixham and Plymouth smacks off the South Pier, right.

Lowestoft steam drifters in Mount's Bay: *LT 177 Gratitude*, built at Galmpton, 1902; *LT 212 Boy Ben*, built by Chambers & Co., 1906; and *LT 1062 GMV*, built by John Chambers in 1907. (Jan Pentreath Collection)

On 5 June 1899 the *West Briton* gave an enthusiastic description of the fishery:

> During the past week, it is computed that more than a million mackerel were landed at and dispatched from Newlyn ... This means that several hundred fishermen secure the fish anywhere between 60 and 70 miles from land. Two or three hundred craft are engaged ... Perhaps 300 miles of nets were shot for that purpose ... it calls for the aid of a little army of workers on shore ... horses, wagons, lorries, a flotilla of row boats, or bum boats, many scores of packers, ice-preparers ... tons of ice used for keeping the fish cool ... tons of straw and paper used for package, perhaps 20,000 boxes laden and sent up the line.[22]

Sam Hendy Stevens enterprisingly converted the St Ives 'dandy' *William Warren SS 31* into the steamboat *Rebecca SS 118* but, despite landing a top shot of 14,000 mackerel in May 1901,[23] she was a failure, and was sold to Norway in 1908.

In 1902, two Newlyn mackerel drivers, fishing the Bristol Channel, landed in Milford Haven. The steam drifters followed suit. The Smith's Dock Trust of Yarmouth sent eleven of its drifters to the 'Westward Voyage' in 1902. In 1905, seventeen of these 'Iron Boats' were based at Milford Haven for the mackerel fishery.[24] It was thought that Milford, with its improved facilities and direct rail link, might make Newlyn's new harbour redundant. Its recently completed mackerel market helped to make Newlyn more competitive. Until its construction, mackerel were landed straight on to the beach. It was dominated by East Coast fish merchants like Hobsons and Peacock & Co. of Lowestoft and Yarmouth's Smith's Dock Trust. The visiting steam drifters were supplied with coal by Lowestoft merchants like Bessey and Palmer & Craske Ltd.

Contemporary press reports give a lively idea of this vigorous fishery at Newlyn. In April 1903, the *Cornishman* reported, 'The large fleet, comprising Dutch, East Coast and Westcountry boats, covers a great portion of the sea from the Eddystone to Padstow, and the fish appear plentiful throughout the area.' Nevertheless, prices were low, down to 9s 6d a hundred, and the fish merchants bickered about the poor service provided by the railway:[25]

The *Cornishman*, May 1903:
Newlyn. The very fine steamers from Rotterdam which made Newlyn their rendezvous this season carry 17 hands. These vessels far exceed anything which has hitherto come amongst us for the mackerel season, and they are only specimens of a large fleet at the Dutch port.

30 May 1903, The *Western Mackerel Fishing*:
But today an immense fleet from Lowestoft and Yarmouth numbering two hundred craft, largely made up of steamers, is strengthened by foreign craft as we have FRENCH AND DUTCH BOATS competing with the English in the endeavour to bring mackerel to market.[26]

Western Echo, Saturday 16 April 1904:
A Variety of Fishing Craft. On Wednesday during a strong south westerly gale, a large number of fishing craft ... sought shelter in St Ives bay ... Amongst the various fishing craft might be seen four steam trawlers from Hull, Milford etc, one large French sailing mackerel drifter and a Dutch steam drifter, several Lowestoft steam and sailing boats besides the St Ives luggers and one Mount's Bay boat.[28]

The Boulogne steam drifter *Antoinette B 27* loading her boxes at Newlyn after landing her catch, 1935. Boulogne and Fécamp owners sent their drifters to the mackerel fishery to keep them working between the more profitable herring seasons. The *Antoinette* was built at Rotterdam in 1907.[27]

There were over 500 drifters at the 1905 spring mackerel season, twenty from Porthleven, eighty from Newlyn, fifty from Mousehole, eighty from St Ives, sixty from Mevagissey and Looe and 270 from Lowestoft and Yarmouth, over 200 of them steamers. There was not room for this huge fleet at Newlyn, where the steamboats crowded in, their bows to the quay.

There were some big shots. In February 1905 the drifter *Emulator* hauled a huge catch while working 60 miles north-east of the Longships. Several of her nets sank with the weight of fish. The *Lily Maud*, which was fishing nearby, came to her aid. They put in to Newlyn with about six lasts, 60,000 mackerel.[29] In May 1907, there was such a glut of mackerel at Newlyn that the price fell to 1s 6d per 120, and local boats and Yorkies alike had to throw their catches overboard.[30]

From 1907, when Newlyn North Pier was widened to allow two-way cart traffic, the drifters could land their catches straight on to the pier, and the 'bummer's gigs' (fish ferry boats) were redundant. At the same time, the steamboats began to be fitted with 'cranning poles' (derricks) to discharge their fish.

In April 1903, the steam drifter *Berry Castle* ran down and cut in half Skipper Richard Jacka's Newlyn mackerel boat *Vanguard* off the Bucks rocks, fortunately without loss of life. In May 1903, the *Eighteen YH 611* of the unimaginatively named Smith's Dock Numerical Fleet was run into by the Liverpool coaster *Foylemore*, and put into Penzance for repairs at Holman's drydock. In March 1912, the Lowestoft steam drifter *Energetic* sank 18 miles north-east of the Longships. Her crew were rescued by the steam drifter *Record*. The 83-foot *Energetic* was one of twenty-nine wooden steam drifters built at Porthleven, mainly during the pre-1914 steam drifter boom. Built by Kitto, she was fitted with her engine at Lowestoft.[31] On Thursday 18 April 1912, the Lowestoft drifter *Tuberose* was steaming across Newlyn harbour when she collided with the coaster *Test*, which was loading roadstone at the South Pier, badly damaging her.[32] The *Pearl LT 461* grounded in Mount's Bay in 1915, and the *Golden Light LT 706*, *Golden Gift* and *Victor Mary* in 1920. The *Golden Gift* and *Victor Mary* grounded within yards of each other off Penzance Prom in thick fog.[33]

The *Lord Haldane LT 1141* went ashore at St Mary's in 1929. Until the building of Tater Dhu lighthouse, the Bucks rocks, west of Lamorna, took a steady toll of shipping, including the Lowestoft steam drifters *Excellent* in May 1899 and *Young Charlie* in June 1926.

By 1912 the competition of the steam drifters had made the Cornish mackerel luggers obsolete, and there was acute distress in the Mount's Bay ports and St Ives. A government commission, chaired by Cecil Harmsworth, was set up to enquire into the Cornish fisheries and grants for fitting engines. It reported in 1913. One of the Commission's members, Stephen Reynolds, wrote,

> On a grey Sunday, near about sundown, we walked to Lelant where the St Ives boats are laid up. There on one side of the broad sand and mud flats of Hayle harbour, we saw a fleet of seventy or eighty boats, mostly luggers, moored up with old chains or rotting ropes to the rusty railings of the old broad gauge, along a grass grown quay. In local phrase, they are the St Ives boats that have died. The unpainted hulls of many were rotten. On their still standing masts, the running gear, left as it returned from sea for another season that never came, flapped in the wind until it parted.

The real problem was that the beautiful but outdated West Cornish sailing mackerel boats were competing in the 'first division' with the East Anglian steam drifters, a competition they were bound to lose. The Looe and Mevagissey boats were not involved in this unequal struggle. They had an excellent pilchard season in 1911, and many of them fitted engines then.

The St Ives mackerel fleet running into Newquay for shelter. They include the *Mary Bennetts SS 584*, *Young John SS 18*, *Mary Jane SS 517*, *Pet SS 348* and *Lord Beaconsfield SS 2*. (Newquay Old Cornwall Society ON0468)

St Ives Weekly Summary, 9 March 1907: 'Mackerel.– The Lowestoft steam drifter Result put into St Ives on Wednesday and landed 3,500 mackerel which sold from 15s to 16s per 120.' The *Result LT 259* was built of wood at Oulton Broad in 1903. She must have been a Bethel Boat or Sunday Keeper, or she would not have been allowed to land at St Ives. (With permission of the Royal institution of Cornwall – RIC.)

Newlyn mackerel market, *c.* 1905. The merchants' offices are Hobsons of Lowestoft and Smith's Dock Trust of Great Yarmouth.

In 1929, the Lowestoft steam drifter *Lord Haldane LT1141* went ashore near the Steval, St Mary's. She was towed off by the St Mary's lifeboat. (Gibsons of Scilly)

St Ives mackerel boats laid up at Lelant 'to die'. (Tim and Rita Lait Collection)

The Harmsworth Report provides a fascinating record of the numbers of boats in the Cornish ports in 1913, and how many were already fitted with engines. It clearly shows the difference between East Cornwall, where nearly all the big boats in Looe and a third of those in Mevagissey already had engines, and West Cornwall, where Mousehole, Newlyn, Porthleven and St Ives had only thirty-one motor boats between them. It can be seen that the numbers of first- and second-class boats at St Ives had halved since 1904, a huge loss:[34]

Port	No. of 1st class boats	No. of 2nd class boats	No. of 3rd class boats
Looe	36	35	17
With motors	31	7	0
Mevagissey	75	23	
With motors	26	0	
Polperro	0	37	3
With motors	4	1	
Falmouth	3 steam, 7 sail	18	?

With motors	5		
Porthleven	1 steam, 1 sail	95	4
With motors	1	3	2
Newlyn	36 + 2 steam	59	16
With motors	6	2	2
Mousehole	28	76	7
With motors	2		
St Ives	40 [81 in 1904]	60 [125 in 1904]	44 [50 in 1904]
With motors	6	3	

Motors were seen as the answer, but few West Cornwall fishermen could afford them. In 1912, over 100 St Ives fishermen were unable to pay their rates. St Ives Customs Officer Michael McWilliams, my grandfather, reported which boats had engines: 'Motor engines were fitted in the *Gleaner SS 123* and *Family SS 61* in 1910 and in the *Golden Lily SS 14* and *Snowdrop SS 311* in 1911. Another boat *Mayflower SS 498* is getting ready for one.'[35]

Many Cornish fishermen gave up the struggle and emigrated. Fourteen St Ives mackerel boats were sold to Ireland at rock-bottom prices of £100–£150. The legendary *Water Lily* and the *Uncle Tom* continued to work from Kilkeel for half a century.

However, what the Harmsworth Report failed to achieve, the Kaiser did. During the First World War, the steam trawler and drifter fleets were called up into the Royal Navy, where they and their fishermen crews served with distinction. The pressure was off the fishing grounds, which restocked. With the country in danger of starvation as a result of the German submarine campaign, the Cornish fishing fleet was rapidly motorised with the help of the Motor Loans Committee of the Ministry of Agriculture and Fisheries. This regeneration boosted the Cornish Fishing Vessels Insurance Society, which, because of the war emergency situation, insured vessels from South Wales right around to the South Coast. Motor Loans were refused unless the boat and its engine were insured.[36] Manned largely by old men and boys, the mackerel fishery revived, though not without incident.

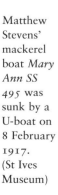

Matthew Stevens' mackerel boat *Mary Ann SS 495* was sunk by a U-boat on 8 February 1917. (St Ives Museum)

The auxiliary mackerel boat *Mary Ann SS 495* was sunk by a German submarine on 8 February 1917. When Skipper Stevens protested, 'Surely you're not going to sink a little boat like ours?' the U-boat commander replied in perfect English, 'My orders are to sink everything.' The Germans placed a bomb in the *Mary Ann*, which blew her to pieces. Fortunately her crew were rescued from their punt by the steamer *Sheerness*. Skipper Matthew Stevens went to Porthleven and ordered a new motor boat, which was named *Sheerness SS 10* in honour of their rescuer. As a result of this sinking, the local motor drifters *White Heather SS 84*, *Gratitude SS 626*, *Perseverance SS 40*, *Helena Maud SS 537*, *Mayflower SS 498* and *Snowdrop SS 9* were each fitted with a gun manned by two naval ratings. All except the new *White Heather* were motorised luggers. The Mount's Bay boats were escorted to the mackerel grounds by an armed steam drifter.

After the First World War, the West Cornish boats again joined the mackerel fishery with renewed optimism. Now that they were fitted with engines, they could go and play with the big lads, the Yorkie steam drifters. In 1919, thirty St Ives boats and many from Mount's Bay fitted out and made a great success of the fine April weather. The venerable motor lugger *Ebenezer SS 340*, built back in 1867, landed a record shot of 45,000 mackerel.[37] There was life in the old girl yet.

The following year, eleven St Ives motor boats, some of them very small, put in mackerel nets. The celebrated Small Boats' Gale of 11 March 1920 shook them up. The fleet was caught with their nets out and had a heavy buffeting.[38]

Three of them had to run for shelter in Newquay. John Trevorrow related the experience of the *Ripple SS 19*: 'That little man, Mr Noall was with him in the Little Boats' Gale. The other boats were throwing mackerel overboard to lighten them. Barber said, "I haven't come out here to catch mackerel and throw them away." They ran up to shelter.' It was realised that the little pilchard boats were not adequate for this deep-water fishery, even if they did have engines. William Barber had the little *Ripple* sawn in half and lengthened by an 11-foot section in the middle.

The local boats did well the following year when, in June, the St Ives, Mousehole and Newlyn mackerel drivers were working on the grounds together, most of them landing in Newlyn with earnings of £120–£250. Barney Thomas remembered selling the *Young John SS 18*'s catch: 'We used to land our mackerel in Newlyn. You'd go up with a basket,

Ebenezer SS 340 landed 45,000 mackerel.

Local fishermen help to land a huge catch of mackerel from the steam drifter *Sarah Marian* at Newlyn. (Ken Brown)

a sample of the boat's catch, they'd ring the bell and then your fish would be auctioned.' However, it soon became uneconomic for the Cornish motor boats to go mackerel drifting. The cost of fuel was too high, and the shoals on the westward grounds, Jones Bank, Labadie Bank and the Great Sole, too far from land for these little paraffin-engined boats.

The numbers of local boats declined sharply, and between the world wars the fishery was dominated by the Yorkie steam drifters. A Newlyn local remembers, 'The drifters would be moored up half way across Newlyn harbour. You couldn't see the sky for their smoke.' In June 1924, Cornwall Sea Fisheries Officer Mr Barron reported the declining Cornish share in the mackerel fishery with the number of Cornish boats taking part in 1900 and 1924:

	1900	1924
St Ives	95	25
Mount's Bay	100	20
Falmouth	4	–
Mevagissey	42	–
Polperro	3	–
Looe	23	6
Total	267	70

Meanwhile the steam drifters, working from Newlyn, had done very well, with earnings of up to £3,000 per boat for a twenty-week season.[39]

The steam drifters brought their own infrastructure to Newlyn with them. Lowestoft and Yarmouth buyers arrived for the Westward Voyage. Spare nets were stored in local lofts. Coal bunkering facilities were provided. Sacks of coal were sculled to the drifters in rugged little coal barges, which were moored in the Old Harbour out of season.

Over 100 steamers arrived for the 1925 season, and by April they were landing record shots, which caused prices to plummet from 5s 3d to only 1s 6d per 120 mackerel but there were only half a dozen Mount's Bay boats left in the fishery.[40] The Newlyn Riots were soon forgotten, and the Yorkies continued to come on their Westward Voyage and were made welcome. Several Lowestoft fishermen settled in Newlyn and some skippered local boats including Billy Capps of the *Forget Me Not PZ 47*, William Pope Balls of the *Penlee PZ 85*, Jack Williams of the *Betty INS 198*, Stanley Beckett of the *Madeline PZ 88*, and William Love and Joseph Carr of the *Efficient FR 242*, now *Excellent PZ 513*.

For the local boats left mackerel driving, there could be surprises, as reported in May 1925:

> The crew of the Mousehole mackerel drifter *Hopeful* (PZ 634) were hauling their train of nets 18 miles off the Bishop Rock on Friday night, when they discovered a huge fish enmeshed in the gear by the head. After a great struggle the men deemed it advisable to cut away one or more brand new nets and be entirely free of the monster.
>
> From their point of observation the length of the fish easily exceeded forty feet, and it was probably as long as the boat itself. Boulogne steam drifters, fishing a distance of 120 miles from the Bishop, have sustained damage to gear by the enmeshing of the dolphin species.[41]

On 30 March 1927, the drifter fleet fishing off Scilly was hammered by a terrific gale, and there was great anxiety for their safety. Many were badly damaged. The Yarmouth drifter *WPG* came in with her flag at half mast, having had a man swept overboard. Many had their bank boards and punts washed away, their mizzen sails blown out and wheelhouse windows smashed. The *Faithful Friend* had her wheelhouse so badly damaged she had to be steered in by tiller. There was concern for the *Eileen and Emma*, *Playmates*, *Lord Hood* and *Forethought*, as they did not return to Newlyn for three days, but fortunately they were all safe. There was also anxiety for the little sailing French crabbers from Camaret, but they all returned safely.[42]

In March 1929 more than twenty steamers had arrived, with others yet to come, but 'the present season is the slackest in Newlyn for the last two decades.'[43] In July 1937 there were only twenty-two steam drifters, the lowest number since the First World War, but

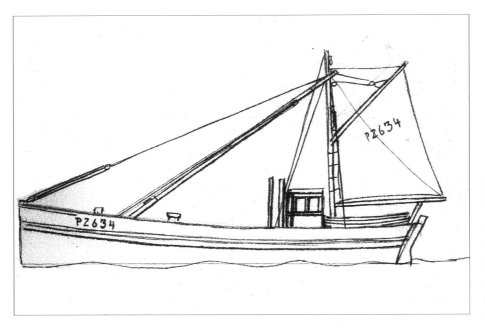

In May 1925, the Mousehole drifter *Hopeful PZ 634* caught a huge fish in her mackerel nets.

they had a very successful season. A few local boats continued to join the mackerel fishery later in the season. In May 1938 the *Francis SS 49* and *Freeman SS 65* of St Ives, and the immaculately maintained *Seagull FY 408* of Looe, put in mackerel nets and worked from Newlyn.[44] The little *Freeman* and *Seagull* fitted flywheel capstans to haul their mackerel footlines. Mr Atkinson's *Seagull* was crewed by 'yachties', fishermen who spent much of the year away crewing rich men's yachts. He also owned the Newlyn longliner *Swift FY 405*, skipper Sidney Thomas.

Twenty-four steam drifters came for the 1939 spring mackerel season. Roaming German aircraft put a stop to mackerel drifting during the Second World War, after the loss with all hands of the Yarmouth drifter *Helpmate YH 129* in March 1941.[45]

However, with the return of peace, the Cornish boats again put in mackerel nets, including the new gig *Sweet Promise SS 95*, the elderly *Francis Stevens SS 49*, and the new *Girl Renee SS 78*, *Lamorna SS 45*, *JBS SS 17*, *Renovelle PZ 177* and *Coeur de Lion PZ 94*. Skipper Dick Sampson of the *Coeur de Lion* said, 'It didn't take a lot to make a good catch. If you only had 100 mackerel in each net, that would do it.'

The longliner *Swift FY 405* and mackerel drifters: John Stevens' *Francis SS 49*, Matthew Freeman's *Freeman SS 65* of St Ives and Mr Atkinson's *Seagull FY 408* of Looe. The *Francis* has her mackerel nets piled on deck. (Morrab Library)

Skipper Ernest Stevens' *Sweet Promise SS 95* leaving Newlyn on a mackerel driving trip, *c.* 1950.

Lowestoft steam drifter
Sunny Bird LT 305 hauling
mackerel off the Wolf, 1946.
(Ken Brown)

When Skipper John Madron Veal's new *JBS* first tried mackerel nets, it is recalled that 'she caught so many scads [horse mackerel] they were two days alongside in Newlyn, unmeshing them all'.

Skipper Edwin Stevens of the *Francis Stevens SS 49* recalled,

> We started off mackerel driving out here off St Ives in the Channel. Those mackerel were fine big fish too, lovely to eat, not like the ones you catch here whiffing. Then we went round to Newlyn. A footline was worked on the boat nets, the first 30 nets. The footline came in through a roller forward, a roller with four vertical guides. Its position could be altered. The footline was hauled on the barrel of the trawl winch aft. Then it led forward along the port side and down though a hole in the deck. It was coiled in the footline room by Scrans [Mr Peters, the lifeboat coxswain].[46]

The locals wondered if the Yorkies would return. They did, but in nothing like the pre-war numbers. On 2 March 1949, hopes were raised by good catches by the *Ocean Unity* and the *Strive*. Local Newlyn men were employed to help unmesh the mackerel. A dozen drifters arrived in February 1950, and the *Welcome Home* and *Shepherd Lad* began the season with good shots of 1,500 stones. They were often outfished by the French drifters from Douarnenez, one of which landed 3,400 stones the following day.[47] In June 1951 the Lowestoft drifter *Merbreeze LT 365* sailed for home with the customary blasts on her foghorn, having broken all mackerel drifting records with earnings of nearly £8,000 under Skipper Albert 'Brandy' Bailey.

In 1954, the *Wyedale YH 105*, *Merbreeze LT 365*, *Justifier LT 224*, *Calm Waters LT 407*, *Playmates LT 180* (sadly lost with all hands on the mackerel grounds in March 1955), *Fisher Queen LT 679* and *Lord Hood LT 20* came to the Westward. On 3 May they returned to Newlyn with heavy losses of 50–100 nets each. In March 1955, the steam drifters *Lord Hood*, *Friendly Star* and *Shepherd Lad* landed mackerel from 170 miles west of Newlyn. Three weeks later the *Justifier* had her mizzen sail blown out. When Skipper Ernie Thompson's new motor drifter *St Luke LT 156* landed an 800-stone shot in May 1958, the *Swiftwing LT 238* and *Quiet Waters LT 279* had already sailed for home.

The last Yorkies to come to the Westward were all steel motor boats, among them the *Harold Cartwright LT 231*, *Dauntless Star LT 367* and *Frederick Spashett LT 138*.

The Lowestoft drifters were often out-fished by the little wooden drifters from Douarnenez in Brittany, which were called Sashies or Chasse Marées after the old Breton coasting luggers. The *Bluette et Marie Pierre D3825*, built in 1951, was only 54 feet long with a Baudouin 120-hp engine. (Michael Pellowe)

Yarmouth motor drifter *Ocean Sunlight YH 167* leaving Newlyn on a mackerel voyage. (Harry Penhaul, Penlee House Museum, Penzance)

Four drifters came in 1964. When they sailed from Newlyn on 16 April 1964, with the customary farewell blasts on their sirens, after the shortest and worst season in living memory, a crewman said, 'I have been coming to Newlyn for a great many years, fishing for mackerel, and I cannot remember one as bad as this.' The total landings from the *Frederick Spashett, Dauntless Star, George Spashett* and *Harold Cartwright* were 11,251 stones. The following year, two drifters landed a similar total. The year 1967 was the last Yorkie season. The *Norfolk Yeoman LT 137* landed her first shot of 1,748 stones on 4 February.[48] By her last landing on 18 March, her total was a mere 2,744 stones. By this time, landings from local handline boats far exceeded the drifters'. Small & Company, the last Lowestoft drifter owners, decided that drifting was no longer economic and sold their fleet.

The Cornish too had come to the end of the mackerel drifting story, as Raymond Stevens described:

I was mackerel drifting in the *Girl Renee*. We had 70 nets, 55 yarders. That was the length on the headrope. We only had 70 as there were only four of us in the crew. There was a footline on the first nine nets. We were out here 50 miles off in the Channel. There was this great French trawler, a steel sidewinder cut off two of our nets. He came and gave us them back. When he threw them down on the deck, there wasn't a mackerel left in them, only scads. The trouble was: by the time we got in, the whiffers [hand liners] had already landed. That was the last mackerel drifting from St Ives.[49]

The very last drifters to fish the western mackerel were the French boats from Douarnenez, which were known as Sashies or Sashie Marees in Cornwall, a nickname derived from the old Breton coasting luggers, which were called *Chasse Marées*, literally 'Chase the Tides'. Fisherman Lili Colin of Douarnenez spent a season mackerel driving:

Each man carried six nets so we could have up to 120 nets. The newer nets were closer to the boat, the old ones at the end of the fleet. We had acetelene dan lights on the nets. The problem was, if they blew out, you could lose your nets. [The Douarnenez drifters did not ride to their nets like the Cornish and Lowestoft boats.] We shot them in one fleet. When we sold our catch at Newlyn we had to land our mackerel by the stone.[50]

These drifters had no net rooms and carried all their nets on deck. Among them were the famous *La Brise D 3398*, which spent the war years at Newlyn, the *Winston Churchill Dz 3673*, *Annick and Eugene Dz 3853*, *Face au Vent Dz 3728*, and the canoe-sterned *St Kourentin Dz 3674*.[51]

CHAPTER 4

Cornish Herring: The North Coast

The herring fishery on the North Cornish coast is an ancient one, as shown by a letter of 25 October 1688 from Christopher Harris about fish tithes at St Ives: 'The herrings continue plenty with us: this day makes up the full account of herrings to what I gave you last year. If continues with us one month longer I hope to double the last years account of herrings.' In another letter of 4 November, the St Ives herring season is still going well and eighteen Mount's Bay boats have come to St Ives to join in. 'The Herrings continues still with us … we are over comed with Mounts bay boates, that beinge now with us att least Eighteen takeinge of herrings, having took great quantities of herrings, I suppose the Tyth comes near 50£.'[1]

During the nineteenth century there were prosperous St Ives herring seasons in 1814, 1823, 1825 and 1837. In 1825 Captain Short wrote, 'November 13-24,- Drift boats: large catches of herrings, the Frenchmen giving 13s per hundred.' Sir Edward Hain noted, 'French smacks formerly came to St Ives in considerable numbers for the purchase of herrings for curing purposes.' These exports were probably for the kipper houses of Fécamp or Boulogne. In 1837 Captain Short recorded, 'October 11, Drift boats from 200 to 1200 fine herring, sold at 2s 6d per hundred.' But the herring were unreliable as his Diary also notes, 'The herrings have not appeared on this coast for 14 years.'[2]

From the 1890s until the 1930s the most important fishing season on the North Cornish coast was for herring. This season lasted from October until after Christmas. The boats worked from St Ives, Newquay, Padstow and Port Isaac. Newquay had few fishing boats of its own and the Porthleven fleet came for the autumn. In the early twentieth century, they were joined by the little steamboat *Pioneer PZ 277*, the single powered vessel among the fleet of sailing luggers. The bigger Mounts Bay boats from Newlyn and Mousehole fished from Padstow, which was a safer harbour once they had navigated the dreaded Doom Bar at the entrance to the port. In 1911 a group of Scots steam drifters came to work the herring from Padstow.

Miles of herring nets were got ready. They were mended and barked to preserve them, then spread out to dry. It was an exciting time for the children, who liked to play around the piles of fish boxes, barrels and gurries. They knew that if the herring failed to arrive, there would be few Christmas presents. In a good season, many tons of fish were caught. In the 1892 season, over 1,000 tons of herring were sent by rail from St Ives in just four days. In the three weeks up to 16 December 1893, over 3,000 tons of herring were sent away by rail; the largest daily total was 365 tons. Five big mackerel boats shipped away cargoes of salt herrings. Three returned with potatoes from Ireland, one with paraffin from Southampton and one with coal from Newport.[3] In February 1894 Paul Quick's mackerel boat *Quick* was lost on rocks at Wexford while running a cargo of salt herring to Ireland.[4]

When there were bumper shots of herring, the market was oversupplied and prices fell. An attempt to provide further outlets was kippering. W. Rouncefield opened his smoke

The Mount's Bay herring fleet at Newquay. On the right is the little steamboat *Pioneer PZ 277*. (Newquay Old Cornwall Society ON 0674)

PZ 192 Marjorie of Porthleven leaving Newquay. (Newquay Old Cornwall Society ON 0675)

John Woodger's kipper house at Porthgwidden, St Ives. On the roof are the louvres to let out the smoke. (William Thomas collection St Ives Archive)

house at the bottom of Court Cocking, St Ives, early in 1894.[5] He supplied bloaters, kippers and red herrings. This business was later taken over by Pawlyn's, who had another kipper house at the top of Fish Street. Next to this was Holmes's. Brown's had a large works at the bottom of the Rope Walk. Veal's was opposite the Island Meadow, now the site of Porthgwidden Shop. The largest was Woodger's above Porthgwidden, later the Box Factory and now the site of Porthgwidden Studios.[6] John Woodger from Newcastle invented the kipper. A smoke house can still be seen at Porth Gaverne's old cellars, built for Port Isaac's brief herring boom of the 1920s. Padstow had a large kipper house by its trawl dock, on the site of the modern Lobster Hatchery. This was a big investment in properties which worked for only a few months each year.

The Scots lassies came from the Scarborough season to work in these Cornish kipper houses. They worked at long wooden troughs called 'farlines', splitting and cleaning the fish. The herring were next washed and cured in brine. They were hung on poles to drain and then placed on racks in the smoke house over smouldering fires of oak chips and sawdust. Bloaters were smoked for a few hours, kippers for 24 hours and red herrings for up to three weeks.

Keith Ross remembered the Scots lassies at work on St Ives Prom opposite Pawlyn's kipper house.

In their hand a short bladed knife – razor sharp. They worked on the harbour side, no railings then … in the open in almost any weather. The speed and skill with which they split the herring, dispatched the soft roes into one container, the hard roes into another and the split herrings into yet another, was fascinating, mesmerizing …[7]

When the boats came in, the fish were landed in baskets and brought up the beach in carts. Here the crew tipped the fish into gurries, each holding about 28 stones. The crew's wives counted the herring in 'casts' of three. Two women counted at each gurry, a score of casts each to make 120 fish known as a 'long hundred'. The counted out loud and when they got to a score, called out 'Score Ma!' and the skipper's wife made a tally mark in her notebook.

Herring nets were very similar to pilchard nets, roped and set in the same way, but a bit deeper as their meshes were bigger. A St Ives herring net was 100 yards long before being set and 62 yards long when set on its ropes.

The North Cornish coast, with its shallow water, is a tricky place to work. St Ives and Newquay are both tidal harbours, afflicted by notorious groundswell. In December 1902 the *Western Echo* reported dramas among the St Ives fleet.

St Ives herring fleet left harbour in a strong WNW gale but the weather became more squally and the majority of them returned … The crew of the *Willie* reported that the *A1* had lost her rudder … Meanwhile the *A1* was making for the harbour and steered by an oar, she arrived safely just after the lifeboat's departure.

The *Three Brothers* and *Golden Lily* collided in the Bay and the *Golden Lily* was towed in. The *Nazarene* carried away her mizzen boom in collision with the *Margaret Gyles*.[8]

At St Ives, the big mackerel boats were laid up in Lelant when they came home from the North Sea. The smaller decked pilchard boats were used for the herring fishing in the Bay. The pilchard boats were very safe but had disadvantages. With their high freeboard, they lost herring from their nets. Their deep draught was a problem in St Ives' tidal harbour.

The 1880s saw great enthusiasm for building clinker-planked rowing and sailing gigs for the St Ives herring fishery. These were open boats of about 26 to 32 feet length. Many were

Kipper girls cleaning herring at Woodger's Porthgwidden smokehouse, 1930s. (William Thomas collection, St Ives Archive)

Workers at Holmes' kipper house. 'R HOLMES and SONS. SELECTED WEST COAST KIPPERS. ST IVES.'

Counting herring from gurries into baskets. Two women counted from each gurry. They each counted twenty casts of three herring to total 120 fish, a 'long hundred'.

Packing herring, St Ives, 1900s. (St Ives Museum, Comley Collection)

fitted with centre boards and were smart sailers. They were cheap to build and could go to sea from St Ives's tidal harbour when the bigger luggers were still aground. With their low freeboard, they lost fewer herring when hauling their nets. However, they were only big rowing boats and were very vulnerable. Sadly, several were lost through overloading with herring or stress of weather. On 6 October 1900 the *Fortitude* was caught on a lee shore and driven aground on the Western Spits near Hayle Bar with only one survivor from her crew of four. On 23 December 1908 the gig *Maggie* capsized and sank in the Bay while overloaded with herring. Fortunately, her crew were speedily rescued by the *Daisy* and other boats. Only six days later, the well-found and recently built 34-foot pilchard boat *Pendeen SS 193* failed to return from Bassett's Bay in a south-easterly gale with the loss of all her six crew.[9] The 26-foot clinker gig *Lily and John* was fishing in fine weather on 11 November 1910 when she caught a hefty 10,000 herring (approximately 300 stone) in her eight nets. Just after setting sail for home, she filled over the stern and quickly capsized. The gig *Little Johnnie* plucked Thomas Toman from her waterlogged gunwale but there was no sign of the other three crew. Like many of the clinker gigs, the *Lily and John* was fitted with a centre board, an unusual feature for a working boat.[10]

There was great pressure on fishermen to overload and get the most out of the herring, as the mackerel fishery was now dominated by the Lowestoft and Yarmouth steam drifters and the Cornish boats were also failing at the North Sea fishery. In 1912 over 100 St Ives fishermen were prosecuted for the non-payment of Rates and many emigrated to the USA, often to work in the growing car factories of Detroit and Flint. While the herring brought some prosperity to the Cornish fisheries in the first decades of the twentieth century, it was at a cost in human lives.

In 1896 the *Jane*'s crew grossed £51 13s 10½d for 53 nights' work and shared £3.00 each, plus 10s allowance, a total of £3 10s each, worth about £200 today.

In 1909 the St Ives lugger *Gleaner SS 123* was fitted with a Fairbanks petrol motor. She promptly set off for the herring grounds off Newquay on 11 November and came in with a £100 shot of 7,000 herring. The *Mayflower* was fitted with a Danish Alpha paraffin engine.[11]

In 1910 many of the Mount's Bay boats opted for Padstow for the first half of the herring season.

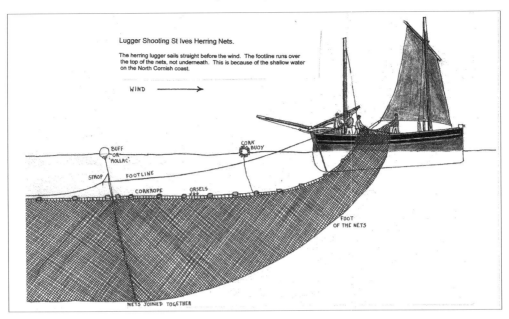

Lugger Shooting St Ives Herring Nets.

The herring lugger sails straight before the wind. The footline runs over the top of the nets, not underneath. This is because of the shallow water on the North Cornish coast.

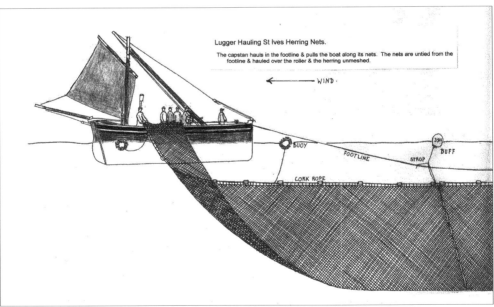

Lugger Hauling St Ives Herring Nets.

The capstan hauls in the footline & pulls the boat along its nets. The nets are untied from the footline & hauled over the roller & the herring unmeshed.

The herring season started at Padstow, and most of the Mount's Bay sailing and motor boats started at that port instead of Plymouth, as in previous years, where they have met with a deal of success, returning recently to overhaul for a couple of days, when off they went to Plymouth.[12]

During the First World War, when the large steam trawlers and drifters were called up as Naval auxiliaries, the German submarine campaign brought huge losses to Allied merchant ships, many being torpedoed in sight of the Cornish coast, including the *St Chamond*, which was sunk by *U 60* in sight of the population of St Ives on 29 April 1918.[13] The

A St Ives gig un-meshing herring, 1900s. The catch is shaken out over her oars. The nets are piled forward. Her cork buoys are on the sand, foreground left. They have lots of help.

country was desperate for food and the role of the Cornish fishing ports became more important. Led by charismatic West Country Fishery Officer Stephen Reynolds, the Cornish fishing fleet was motorised with the help of the Motor Loans Committee of the Ministry of Agriculture and Fisheries. This programme was an immense success, and this and the urgent need for food supplies brought great prosperity to the Cornish ports, where the boats were largely manned by old men and boys as most of the younger fishermen were Reservists, serving in the Navy.

Stephen Reynolds wrote of the St Ives 1914 herring season:

> ... the herrings came properly into the bay, the first time for years, and prices were high. They went as high, some days, as thirteen to fifteen shillings a long hundred. Boats returned laden from sea. Men staggered up the beach inside the harbour under the weight of the hand barrows or 'gurries', of fine full herrings. The women were out counting the fish, or standing by their menfolk's catches. Salesmen and merchants shouted prices; half the town, it seemed, was down along ... Ponies strained into their collars, and went at it with a run, to drag the packed barrels up over the steep hill to the station.

The fishery, like the rest of British life, was not immune from the Great War story. In October 1914 the clinker gig *Richard Williams SS 161* was renamed *Highflyer* after the recent victory over the German armed liner *Kaiser Wilhelm der Grosse* by the elderly British cruiser HMS *Highflyer*, which had many Cornish Reservists in her crew.

The Thomas family laid up the big *Young John SS 18* and used the smaller and handier *Barnabas SS 634* for the herring season. On Monday 7 December 1903, skipper Barnabas Thomas was swept overboard while hauling. Fortunately, he hung on to the footline and was speedily recovered.[14] Barney Thomas vividly remembered herring fishing in the Bay shortly after the *Barnabas* had an engine fitted in 1917.

> The nets got caught around the propeller while we were shooting. We had to haul them right away and it was a storm of wind. We had to sail her back to St Ives under the fifty yard foresail, towing that great bunch of net under our quarter. The tack of the foresail went to the eye in front of the mast. There was no question of dipping the

sail in that weather. When we came to tack, outside the Harbour, that great bundle of
net on the quarter helped to bring her around and we got in safely.

There were some freak herring seasons, as in the summer of 1919, when huge shoals of
large, excellent quality fish appeared from the Eddystone to the Longships and the Cornish
drifters enjoyed a month-long bonanza with shots of 20,000 a boat and earnings of up to
£400.[15]

On 19 November the St Ives motor drifter *White Heather SS 84* filled up with a record
100 cran shot. But the combination of poor weather and big catches also resulted in
expensive losses of nets among the St Ives boats.[16]

In *Sea Change*, art historian David Tovey quotes artist Frances Hodgkins at St Ives, '…
the herring season at its height and everyone doing well and making money.'

More records were broken the following year: 500 tons of herring were landed at St
Ives on 20 November. The *White Heather* was again in the news on 1 December when she
saved the pilchard boat *Golden Lily*, anchored with engine trouble, from certain loss on
the dreaded Stones Reef.[17]

From the end of the Great War, many of the St Ives clinker gigs were replaced by the
bigger and safer motor gigs. Bumper herring landings during the War, the coming of peace
and good seasons in the 1920s brought a spirit of optimism and almost forty motor gigs
were built for St Ives, beginning with Dan Roach's *Glorious Peace* in 1919. The last was
the *Sweet Promise*, completed by Tommy Thomas for Ernest Stevens in 1947. Many of
the little clinker gigs soldiered on, fitted with engines. They were still allowed to join the
annual August sailing Regatta, provided their propellers were removed for the event!

The harbour was alive with bustle and sound. Carts rattled over the cobbled streets full
belt for the Station and the smoke houses. The Scots girls sang at their work in the kipper
houses, whose pungent smoke brought a tang to the nostrils and a jingle to the pockets.
The harbour echoed to the tapping of caulking mallets and the screech of planes as Tommy
Thomas, Henry Trevorrow and Phillip Lander built nine new gigs for the herring fishery
in 1926 alone.

The boom season of 1923 inspired a whole series of evocative paintings from St Ives
artist Charles Simpson. In big seasons, oversupply could reduce the price to starvation
level. John Trevorrow recalls skipper William Barber of the *Ripple SS19*.

> He came in here with a boat load of herring one time. When he was offered a
> price for them, he wouldn't accept it. My Father was in her. That was after she was
> lengthened [1927]. He said to them, 'Go home and get a tin [of provisions].' They
> went up to Swansea and sold them there.

On Christmas night 1923 the St Ives pilchard boat *Peggy SS 62* was shooting her gear
when she got 'mopped up' with the nets around her propeller. The gigs *Our Girls SS 131*
and *Guide Me SS 106* and the St Ives lifeboat *James Stevens No. 10* went to her aid in
the nick of time, as she was nearly aground in the breakers off Gwithian and being driven
towards Godrevy. The *Peggy* and her crew were saved and her lost nets later recovered by
the *Our Francis SS 155* with eight gurries of herring in them.[18] (The *Our Francis* is still
afloat as the yacht *Deu Kerens*.)

December 1924 saw good herring landings for St Ives of 22,575 hundredweight and
Padstow 17,272 hundredweight, worth £14,413. Plymouth was top West Country herring
port with 24,018 hundredweight for the month.[19]

The 1925 season got under way on 21 October with shots of up to 12,000 fish per
boat for the twenty drifters which landed at St Ives. It was thought that the shoals of

Packing herring, St Ives Prom, 1920s.

Fishing fleet off Pentire: Mount's Bay boats at the Padstow herring season, 1920s.

herring were to be found around the dangerous Stones Reef, which lies between Godrevy lighthouse and the Buoy of the Stones on the edge of St Ives Bay. Top herring fisher Job Boase in the *Our Girls SS 131* often worked this ground. This led to the loss of the motor gig *Day Dawn* on the Shoaler Stone on 28 November 1927.[20] Three of her five crew managed to survive by clinging to the net buoys and were rescued at great personal risk by the crew of the *Godrevy*.

At the start of November 1928 the Mousehole fishing fleet left home for the herring fisheries, some for Padstow and the majority for Plymouth. On the 22nd, the Padstow steam tug lifeboat *Helen Peele* took off the crew of the Port Isaac drifter *Our Girlie* which, after hauling in a fine 20-cran shot, was anchored on a dangerous lee shore off Port Quin with a swamped engine. The *Helen Peele* was in the nick of time, as the anchor ropes parted and the *Our Girlie* drove ashore and was demolished.[21] A sturdy little boat, the *Our Girlie* was one of a class of five new motor boats built for Cornwall by the Ministry of Agriculture and Fisheries after the Great War, as a shot in the arm for the Cornish fisheries.

The local press was enthusiastic about the 1929 St Ives season.

Animated scenes have been witnessed at St Ives during the past four weeks, where the local fishing fleet are enjoying a splendid harvest. For the past few seasons the herring season at St Ives has been very disappointing and the town generally has suffered considerably. But the scenes now being witnessed daily are reminiscent of the days twenty or thirty years ago, and the whole town is at present a hive of industry.

The first catch was made about the latter part of October and since then, catches have averaged 20 lasts (200,000) a day, the lowest quantity landed being ten lasts and the highest 70 lasts.

About 80 boats are engaged in the fishery, employing about 400 men, but in addition to this a similar number are engaged in carting, kippering etc. In connection with the latter, about 50 fisher girls have arrived in St Ives from the North of England.

… On Monday night, in the face of a strong gale, practically the whole of the fleet put to sea.[22]

But when the Boulogne steam trawlers trawled up ship loads of herring on the Smalls spawning grounds,[23] this soon destroyed the North Cornish fishery. The 1930s seasons were very hit and miss.

In some years there was a mixed fishery, including herring, in Mount's Bay. In June 1926 the *Western Echo* reported on the excellent herring landings at Newlyn: 'The scene presented on Newlyn pier on Tuesday morning was typical of a large herring fishing centre. Boxes … filled with herrings lay along the quay while quantities of the fish were strewn over various boats. Approximately 1,400 boxes were landed.'[24] Pawlyns sent Newlyn herring to their St Ives smoke house, at Court Cocking, for kippering.

But the St Ives season continued to fade away as reported on 27 November 1937: 'One St Ives crew working in Mount's Bay on Tuesday landed 5,700 mixed fish, which it is reported was better than the combined catches of nearly fifty drifters engaged in the herring fishery in St Ives Bay.'[25]

Cyril Stevens of St Ives recalled a big shot in Charlie Andrews' 28 foot long pilchard boat *Primrose SS 20.*

The best shut we ever had was 31,000 herring in one night in 1939. I shared £22 – and I was the Boy. When we got into the Harbour, we had to beach her as she was taking in so much water. We were all that day unbuttoning at the foot of the Slipway, and fine great fat herring they were too. When I picked up the money, I had my hat cocked to one side.[26]

The last big St Ives seasons were in 1940 and 1943 when Arthur Brown remembered the family's kipper house in the Rope Walk, 'That was the year my uncle lost his pipe in a herring barrel. We were all day looking for it!'

Donald Perkin remembers the 1940 season in Ernest Stevens' gig *Boy Ernest SS 2.*

We caught so much herring, we had to let the last nets go. Ernie's brother John was with us and he told him, 'If you put any more herring in this boat, you're going to sink her. Better to lose the nets than lose the boat.' We put up a flambow [flare] for someone to come and take our nets but everyone else was the same .The *Vivid SS 209* [an old, clinker-built gig] caught so much, she was on the sand in the Harbour and her planks opened up.

In the early post War years the Plymouth pilchard season kept the St Ives fleet busy in the autumn, though a few boats continued to try in St Ives Bay with herring nets, mainly, it appeared, with the herring subsidy in mind. There was a brief flash in the pan in December 1955 when a few hundred stones of herring were landed. Several drifters optimistically returned from Newlyn but that appeared to be the end of the St Ives herring story.

In September 2011 two small inshore boats landed 500 stone of herring from monofilament nets set in the Bay and there were landings again in 2012. So never say never.

Boulogne steam trawler *Suzanne et Marie B 35*, built in 1907. Boulogne steam trawlers trawled up shiploads of herring on the Smalls Grounds. This may well have put an end to the St Ives herring fishery. (Jack Daussy, Fécamp)

St Ives herring fleet, *c.* 1936. The boats are going out to anchor over the low tide.

St Ives herring season, *c.* 1934. *Thrive SS 148, Unique SS 17, Guide Me SS 106, Our Boys SS 150, Caronia SS 70, Glorious Peace SS 37* still unmeshing her catch, and *Nazarene SS 114.*

CHAPTER 5

Plymouth Herring

While the North Cornish herring fishery brought some years of prosperity, it was worked on an exposed and dangerous coast, lacking safe harbours. In contrast, Plymouth's Sutton Harbour provided a safe, all-weather refuge for the Cornish and East Anglian drifters which fished in nearby Bigbury Bay until local trawlers started trawling over this spawning ground in 1934 and, in three years, destroyed yet another prosperous fishery.

For the Plymouth fishery, the nets were four fathoms (24 feet) below the surface. Plymouth was then a busy commercial port and cargo steamers could safely sail over the nets.

The 1906/7 season saw good landings of nearly 33,000 hundredweight but low prices, an average of 4s 11d a hundredweight. On 10 October 1907, *The Cornishman* reported good fishing from the Mount's Bay boats *Mary and Emily PZ 533* with over a 'last' and the *Annie Harvey PZ 102* with three lasts at prices of 3s 11d to 4s 8d per 126.[1] (A last was nominally ten thousand fish, actually 13,200.)[2] One of the Mount's Bay boats had an excellent shot with good prices in early January but the rest of the season was a poor one.[3]

On Thursday 17 December 1908 the luggers *Progress*, *Our Lizzie*, *Martha Jane* and *Annie Harvey* left Newlyn for Plymouth, where the Mousehole men had landed some good catches.[4] After three weeks of failure, they began to return home.[5] In 1908/09 only 4,260 hundredweight was put ashore but low supply increased the average price to 11s 10d.

In 1910 many of the Mount's Bay fleet began their herring season at Padstow but,

> ... returning recently to overhaul for a couple of days, when off they went to Plymouth, and it is good news to report that the *Alonzo FY 375*, fitted with a 10hp Gardner, secured a catch which realised £100. Other motor craft which left at the same time were the *Phyllis* and *Ailsa Craig*, both fitted with Ailsa Craig engines, *Treryn Castle PZ 190* fitted with an Alpha engine, the *Sea Queen PZ 574* and *Golden Lily SS 14*, both fitted with Gardner engines and the *Joseph SS 77* fitted with a Fairbanks engine.[6]

Sadly, in January 1913 Mousehole fisherman John Madron of the *Velox PZ 63* was drowned in Plymouth's Sutton Harbour. He was a former coxswain of the Penlee Lifeboat and left a widow and seven children.

Wartime shortage inflated prices to 15s 11d in 1914/15, 22s 7d in 1915/16 and 46s 5d in 1917/18. During the 1918 season Skipper Richard Richards' big new Mount's Bay drifter *Our Katie PZ 697* grossed £2,000 for one week's fishing.[7] Early in 1919 the skipper of the Newlyn boat *Auld Lang Syne PZ 486* was prosecuted for fishing in a Prohibited Area off Plymouth Breakwater after a mine became entangled in his nets. His protest that the whole fleet was working there did not save him from a £30 fine.

East Cornish luggers leaving Plymouth. (Steve Johnson)

In 1918, the new Mount's Bay motor drifter *Our Katie PZ 697* earned £2,000 for a week's herring fishing at Plymouth.

After she caught a mine in her nets, the skipper of the Newlyn motor lugger *Auld Lang Syne PZ 486* was prosecuted for fishing in a prohibited area.

In *Once Aboard a Cornish Lugger*, Paul Greenwood describes the record shot caught in a storm in Bigbury Bay by skipper Roger Dingle's Looe lugger *May Blossom FY 51* in 1920.

> After several grueling hours of work, they prevailed and the nets were once more stowed back into the net room, and a huge catch of herring was their reward. The *May Blossom* was now deeply laden, her fish room was full and she was loaded rail to rail on deck.

The *May Blossom* ran for Brixham, where her catch sold for £634 (worth £19,000 today).[8]

In January 1924 the elderly Porthleven motor lugger *Ocean Reaper PZ 71* (known for some reason as the *Pie Crust*), built back in 1885, sprang a leak and foundered while fishing out of Plymouth. Her crew were rescued from their punt.[9] Her owners, well known fish merchants Pawlyn's, were paid £495 by the Cornish Fishing Vessels Insurance Society but it is likely that this was the value of her 13 and 26 hp Kelvin engines.

Cornwall Sea Fisheries Committee reported on the 1924/25 Plymouth season:

> The boats from the various ports fishing out of Plymouth had worked under very trying conditions on account of the abnormal quantities of dogfish which were literally swarming. The havoc wrought, coupled with the loss of nets, had been a very serious matter. The majority of these boats had made a very fair season, while others had not grossed enough to cover out of pocket expenses. The East Coast steam drifters who were able to work in practically all weathers, made a very good season. The largest individual catch for one night's fishing was 200 cran, or 170,000 fish.
>
> During the herring season some very large catches of mackerel were secured, ranging from 7 lasts (700,000) per boat … The fish were caught in an area extending from the Dodman to Rame Head. On several occasions so great was the weight of fish that nets were taken to the bottom, and in some instances the boats lost as much as one half of their 'train'[of nets].[10]

Total herring landings for the season were almost 113,600 hundredweight. This was beaten in 1927/28 by 122,400.

Scientific research in the late 1920s suggested that there was a later spawning class of fish west of Plymouth around Gribben Head which was under fished.

There were many nights when the big East Coast steam drifters landed good shots while no Cornish motor boats managed to go to sea. For example, during the 1927/28 season, the steam boats fished twenty-two nights and landed a total of 29,708 hundredweight when there were no landings by the Cornish boats. The steam drifters had bigger crews and much higher expenses than the local motor boats but they consistently outfished them. In 1921/22 thirty-one steam drifters landed approximately 10,500 hundredweight of herrings while 155 motor boats landed approximately 6,500. In the 1925/26 season a record 153 'Yorkies' came to Plymouth, almost matched by 158 locals. The steamers landed approximately 82,800 hundredweight while the Cornish caught approximately 22,900.[11]

Bigbury Bay is just outside Plymouth and in *The Driftermen*, David Butcher quotes Herbert Doy of Lowestoft: 'Sometimes you could go out round there, shoot yuh nets, haul 'em back in an' be back in agin in time t' go t' the pictures. You'd shoot in the afternoon just afore tea (that got dark early, see) git a little shot o' herrin' an' be back in agin in time t' go t' the pictures.'[12]

In his report on the 1924–27 seasons, E. Ford of the Plymouth Laboratory points out that, as on the north coast, there were other players.

Plymouth Barbican filled with herring barrels and boxes, while steam drifters crowd in, bows to quay. (Mike Smylie)

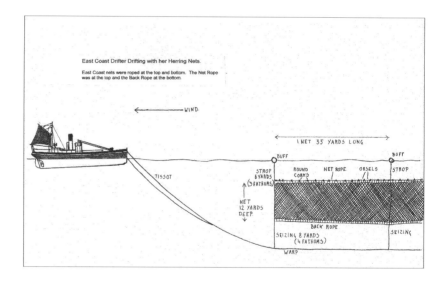

East Coast Drifter Drifting with her Herring Nets.

East Coast nets were roped at the top and bottom. The Net Rope was at the top and the Back Rope at the bottom.

East Coast steam drifters at Plymouth. *LT 526 Devon County.* (Steve Johnson)

Now in the first weeks of 1927, some thirty or forty French trawlers were intensively engaged by day on grounds where a few hours later the Plymouth drifters were shooting their nets for herring. It is neither illogical nor unreasonable to suspect that this trawling had a material effect on the prospects for the subsequent drifting.[13]

The grounds off Plymouth were regularly trawled by the Boulogne steam trawlers, whose crews called them *Les Metans*.[14]

On 12 February 1930 the St Ives boat *Edgar SS 66* was returning from the Plymouth season when young James Maddern Polmeor was lost overboard off Clodgy while repairing the mizzen boom.[15]

In *A Mousehole Man's Story*, Skipper Jack Pender evokes the highs and lows of the Plymouth season during the 1920s in the *Boy Fred PZ 528*.

One Friday night just before Christmas we were fishing in Plymouth and there were no herring ... then one little boat came in with a couple of cran ... I said to the crew, 'It's Christmas next week, how about carrying on through the weekend?' They were agreeable ... and on the Saturday night we went to sea and found our herring.

On the Sunday morning we were landing a good shot on the Barbican to the sound of the Salvation Army band.

Largely on the strength of their success at Plymouth, the Pender family had the 50-foot *Lyonesse PZ 81* built at Porthleven in 1930, equipped with 50hp Bolinder and 30hp Kelvin diesels. After herring fishing in Mount's Bay:

When we arrived off Plymouth the skipper of [the *Internos PZ 46*] closed over to us saying he was going in for the night, 'To hear the news.' I said to our chaps, 'What about going down the bay and making our own news?' This we did and we went into Plymouth next morning with over twenty cran of herring which was a good start ...

...At that time there was a large fleet of boats fishing out of Plymouth from Mount's Bay, Lowestoft, Looe, Mevagissey and St Ives. During the big fishing weeks German trawlers would anchor in the Cattewater and buy cargoes of herring ... one of them bought our fifty cran to make up his cargo and we went alongside to discharge ... as he was well down in the water it was easy work, we just filled up our quarter cran (7 stone) baskets and tipped them down the chute over his rail.[16]

Sutton Harbour was congested.

During the past two seasons, the total visiting fleet numbered about 300 vessels of which nearly one half were steamers. This considerable increase ... has sorely taxed the available accomodation within Sutton Harbour and the landing and packing operations have been conducted under the most congested conditions ... The fish market itself is small and comparatively little surrounding ground is available for the packing of fish landed and the storage of boxes and barrels...[17]

The 1930 St Ives autumn season was a failure and practically the entire local fleet headed for Plymouth. There were over thirty of them there in January getting moderate catches after heavy weather kept them in port for the first week of 1931. By mid-January the East Coast steam drifters were beginning to leave the port in twos and threes as catches declined.[18] German steamers known as 'klondikers' visited Plymouth to buy herring. The last klondiker left on 12 January.

The Pender family's *Lyonesse PZ 81* of Mousehole was a successful boat at the Plymouth herring season.

The 1930/31 Plymouth season was a success. Seventy-three East Coast steam drifters and 280 Cornish motor drifters caught 26,000 crans valued at £55,000. There were also landings of 3,000 crans at Newlyn. St Ives landings, of 5,000 crans, were half those of the previous season.[19] The fish fetched high prices, on average 42s 6d a cran at Plymouth and 52s 7d at St Ives.

On 7 January 1932 skipper Edward Bassett's *Blush Rose SS 152* landed a respectable 25 cran shot at Plymouth, not a huge catch in the herring fishing world, but at approximately 680 stone, good going for a little St Ives gig.[20] The ancient St Ives motor lugger *Ebenezer SS 340*, built by William Paynter back in 1867, also landed some good shots. But the 1931/32 season was the worst for a decade and many herring nets were damaged by static gear, mainly ray nets, set in Bigbury Bay.[21]

On 12 December 1933 the motor lugger *Ripple SS 19* was preparing to leave St Ives for the Plymouth herring season when a serious fire brought her fishing career to an end.[22]

In some years, e.g. 1934, the herring were found further up the coast off Beer and the Looe boats fished from Brixham. In 1935 the steam drifters were very successful, with high earnings. In very poor weather, the steam drifters could fish when the little Cornish motor drifters could not. Most of the Cornish boats worked 'fly nets', nets which were not roped at the bottom, which meant they could not fish with the steam drifters as their nets would drift at different speeds and might become entangled. Some of the larger Cornish boats which worked roped nets had a good season.[23]

The winter of 1937/38 was the first time for 80 years that no Mousehole or Porthleven boats sailed for the Plymouth herring season. No local fisherman could remember this happening. The Plymouth season had ended.[24]

And while the Cornish fishermen were convinced that trawling in Bigbury Bay was to blame, some scientific evidence suggests that natural conditions, particularly the water temperature, biological and chemical content, caused the pilchard to replace the herring. Certainly during the 1940s and early 1950s the Plymouth pilchard season was a big earner. In the nineteenth century the West Cornish luggers had gone to Plymouth in October to fish the mackerel. In the 1970s the Scots and Hull industrial fleet fished huge shoals of mackerel off Plymouth during the winter. So clearly no seasons were set in stone.

Skipper William Pope Balls' Newlyn drifter *Penlee PZ 85* at Plymouth. A Lowestoft fisherman, Skipper Balls had the *Penlee* built by Peakes at Newlyn in 1924. The Lowestoft drifters alongside the market include *LT 671 James and Walter*. The Belgian trawler is *O 314 Oscar Angele*, built in 1931. On the right is a Plymouth trawling smack. (Bill Ball)

CHAPTER 6

Irish Herring

The longest-lived season where the Cornishmen left home was in Ireland. In 1838 the Royal Cornwall Polytechnic Society reported:

> The Cornish fishermen carry on a considerable fishery for herrings on the coast of Ireland. This fishery was commenced in the year 1816 by a person of St Ives called Noall. The attempt which was a bold one succeeded. At first only two or three engaged in it; the next year the number had increased to twelve. In 1821 [May] two boats sailed from Newlyn, and the success of these and the St Ives boats was so great that the fishermen of Mousehole were induced to commence it in 1823. The number has increased every year. In 1836 and 1837 the boats were very successful, and brought home £10,000 each season after paying the whole of their expenses.

The first Newlyn voyage to Ireland 'was ... proposed by a Newlyn fisherman named Kelynack ... The boats fished out of Howth, Ardglass and the Isle of Man. Herrings were then sold by the mase-500 fish.'[1]

But the Irish voyages in these little, open three-masted luggers were not cost free. In August 1827 the 39-foot Newlyn lugger *Start* was lost. Fortunately her crew were picked up by another boat fishing nearby.[2] On 20 August 1828 the Newlyn luggers *Seven Brothers* and *Wellington* left Ireland for home. The *Seven Brothers* was lost in the night on the Swash Bank off Wexford with skipper Ephraim Noy and his four crew.[3]

A worse tragedy happened in May 1839 when the Mount's Bay luggers *Bounty* of Mousehole with skipper John Pender and his five crew, skipper John Blewett's *Neatly* of Newlyn and the Kelynack family's *Victory* of Newlyn were lost with all hands in the North Channel.[4]

The Cornishmen sailed from home at the end of May or early June and returned in late August or early September. Captain Short's St Ives diary records many of their departures and returns but not all seasons were bonanzas, e.g.: 'August 23, 1828. All the boats have arrived safely from Ireland, very bad success, many not having enough to pay for the outfit of the voyage.'[5]

In the 1830s the fishing out of Kingstown (Dun Laoghaire) was booming and so many Cornish used the new harbour that they founded their own Methodist chapel. The Isle of Man was central to the thriving Irish Sea herring grounds and the Manx fishermen were soon influenced by the visiting Cornishmen. They fitted their cutter-rigged fishing boats with mizzen sails after seeing how the Cornishmen lowered their foremasts and drifted to their nets with their mizzen sails set.

The Cornish fishermen had a high reputation in Ireland. In the 1840s the country was struck by the Great Famine. Hundreds of country people died of starvation and thousands emigrated to survive. But ironically, there was abundant food in Irish waters. In 1847 Wallop Brabazon wrote:

...the St Ives and Penzance fishermen – go up the Irish Sea until they meet the shoal of herrings that – come down by Ardglass to Dublin Bay. These men, in their well appointed luggers, follow the shoal in company with its many enemies, small whales, porpoises, herring hogs, and numberless sea birds who follow, with unerring precision, the course pursued by the herrings.

He noticed that the Cornishmen could adjust the depth their nets were fishing: '...the St Ives men are certain of a good take as soon as they find where the shoal is, as they can adapt their nets to the depth of water at which the fish are swimming.'[6]

This was still happening a century later, as Donald Perkin recalled: 'When we were drifting in Ireland, over the moon, the strops were lengthened to lower the nets.'

By the 1860s, instead of staying home for the summer pilchard season, most of the St Ives fleet was in Ireland.

June 29, 1864. A great many boats sailed for Ireland.
July 6, 1866. A great number of boats left for Ireland for the herring fishery.
June 24, 1869. Most of the boats sailed for the Irish herring fishery.[7]

In the mid-1860s the first Manxmen sailed to the Kinsale mackerel season, where they were again influenced by the roving Cornish fishermen, as described by Edgar J. March in his monumental *Sailing Drifters*.

The fishing grounds lay thirty to forty miles from land, and the speed and weatherly qualities of the Cornish luggers excited general admiration amongst the Manx fishermen, whose dandies and smacks were outpaced, and soon the well-known St Ives builder, William Paynter, was inundated with orders, so much so that he opened a yard at Kilkeel, Ireland. [His] first boat for the Isle of Man was the *Zenith CT 65*.[8]

Very many Cornish built boats were bought by Manx fishermen, including the *Cedar CT 9*, *Zebra CT 10*, *Lizzie CT 17*, *Zetetic CT 35*, *Dove CT 41*, *Ben my Chree CT 64*, *Zenith CT 65*, *Primrose CT 84* and *Ceres CT 42* for Castletown and the *Meteor PL 59* and *Oracle PL 85* for Peel.[9]

Cornish Lugger, from W. Brabazon's *The Deep Sea and Coast Fisheries of Ireland*, 1848. Brabazon greatly respected the St Ives and Mount's Bay fishermen, their fishing techniques, fishing gear and boats.

In July 1872 the *Kate Rouse* of St Ives shipped a sea which washed three of her crew overboard while running for shelter in Kingstown (Dun Laoghaire) in a storm. Two of them were speedily rescued but the owner's son was drowned.

In May 1893 there were optimistic reports from the Kinsale herring season, with catches of 20,000 a boat.[10] This season was largely worked by the enterprising Manx fishing fleet, many of them Cornish-built luggers.

Robert Henry Toman of St Ives remembered, 'We used to go to Ireland, to Arklow and Wicklow herring catching.' The Cornishmen worked as far north as Ardglass, where in 1876 the fleet was 140 Scots, twenty Manx, forty-two Irish and nineteen Cornish boats.

When the big Cornish luggers became uneconomic, before the Great War, many were sold to Ireland, fourteen from St Ives alone, mainly to Kilkeel and Ardglass at rock bottom prices of £100–150, the *Theophlus SS 1* (*Amela Jane* in Kilkeel), *Lloyd SS 5*, *Peace and Plenty* which fished on until 1952, *Uncle Tom SS 10*, *Snowdrop SS 12*, *Victoria SS 73*, *Branch SS 119* (to Dublin), *Arethusa SS 439*, *Jane SS 536*, *Endeavour SS 568*, *Frank SS 573* (also to Dublin), *Mary Bennetts SS 584* and *Water Lily SS 635*.[11] The *Water Lily* and *Uncle Tom* fished from Kilkeel for another fifty years.

Motors were seen as the salvation of the Cornish fishing fleet and several of the early motor luggers used their newly acquired versatility to head for Ireland. The 38-foot St Ives pilchard boat *Gleaner SS 123* was a regular in the Irish Sea. She was fishing there in June 1908. She was fitted with an engine in November 1909. In 1913 the *Gleaner* spent the spring trawling the Trevose grounds out of Padstow and on 20 May sailed for Howth and fished the summer in Ireland.[12] The first St Ives boat to receive a Government grant for an engine in July 1914 was the Paynter family's *Gratitude SS 626*, which promptly sailed for the Irish herring season, where the new engine gave endless problems. A photograph from the Ulster Museum Picture Library shows the Cornish motor luggers *Bona Fide PZ 339* of Newlyn and *Snowdrop SS 331* of St Ives at Ardglass at this time. The *Bona Fide* was fitted with a Fairbanks petrol motor in 1909, and the elderly *Snowdrop* with a Gardner in June 1911.[13]

The Cornishman reported on 5 July 1917, 'The motor fishing boats *Ben my Chree PZ 545*, *Nellie Jane PZ 130*, *Auld Lang Syne PZ 486* and *Treryn Castle PZ 190* left for Ireland on Tuesday to pursue the herring fishery.' All four of these Mount's Bay boats had a successful season, undeterred by the German submarine campaign.

Cornish motor luggers at Ardglass, Ireland. *Bona Fide PZ 339*, fitted with a Fairbanks petrol motor 1909. *Snowdrop SS 311*, ex *Honor Hain*, built in 1864, fitted with a Gardner engine in 1911, broken up 1917. (National Museums Northern Ireland Collection Ulster Folk and Transport Museum)

The modern motor boats *Ben my Chree* and *Treryn Castle*, and the motor luggers *Nellie Jane* and *Auld Lang Syne* sailed for Ireland in July 1917.

Barney Thomas remembered going to Howth and Kingstown (Dun Laoghaire) in the *Barnabas SS 634*.

> I've bin to Ireland in her, in 1919 to Howth. We parted the tack of the fifty [fifty yard foresail], going to Ireland. We were catched in one of they Baldoorlers what they call them. Storm it was! We had the sail upon her and she parted the tack, where the foot of the sail goes in the thimble. Bre' blowin' it was and she goin'!

The *Barnabas*, which was motorised in 1917, was one of only eight St Ives boats to work the Irish herring in 1919. They all returned safely in September but their season was a failure. The stay at homes had done better in Mount's Bay pilchard driving.[14]

Cornish boats continued to fish the Irish herring until 1961. By the 1930s, the main fishery was at Dunmore East in the autumn. The Cornish motor drifters played an important part in establishing this season. Skipper Tommy Hicks' large Mousehole motor drifter *Ben my Chree PZ 545* was consistently successful at the Isle of Man and Ireland, where she was eventually sold.[15]

The Cornish drifters continued to work at Dunmore during the Second World War. The *Lyonesse PZ 81* and *Internos PZ 46* came home from Dunmore on 18 February 1940 and the *Our Katie PZ 697*, *Renovelle PZ 107*, *Two Boys PZ 214* and *Asthore PZ 182* on the 23rd.

The Cornishman reported on 30 December 1954 that two St Ives drifters were already at Dunmore, the *Renovelle* had left Newlyn and the *Cynthia Yvonne* was nearly ready to go.[16]

In the mid-1950s the *Nazarene SS 114* carried extra nets across for the other St Ives boats already at Dunmore and received a heavy pounding in a storm, not helped by the extra weight she was carrying. When she returned home, she was repaired at Lelant. A veteran vessel, the *Nazarene* was built as a 33-foot pilchard lugger at Porthleven in 1900. In 1920 she was rebuilt as a 44-foot motor boat. When the little *Nazarene* came into Dunmore with a 70-cran shot of herring, famous Lowestoft skipper Jumbo Fiske looked out from the bridge of his of his big new motor drifter *Dick Whittington LT 61* (completed in 1955). '70 crans?' he asked in wonderment, 'in that?'

The *Barnabas SS 634* was one of eight St Ives boats to go to Ireland in 1919. She fished from Howth.

The crew of the Mousehole drifter *Ben my Chree PZ545*.

St Ives fishermen in Ireland, *c*. 1930. (Mrs E. Murrish)

Skipper Tommy Hicks' Mousehole drifter *Ben my Chree PZ 545* was a successful boat at the Irish and Isle of Man herring fishing. She was sold to Ireland in July 1935.

The veteran St Ives drifter *Nazarene SS 114* was damaged in a storm while carrying extra nets across to the other St Ives boats at Dunmore East.

Skipper John Stevens of the *Girl Renee SS 78* remembered being arrested for poaching inside the Irish three mile limit.

We were fishing inside the Irish limit. You had to; that's where the herring were. We were caught by the Bogeyman one night. He put his searchlight on us. We had our nets and catch confiscated. When they landed our herring, they missed a whole lot of fish we had in one wing of the net room. Paddy O'Toole said, 'John, go out and put your herring aboard that klondyker.' There used to be these Dutch luggers there, full up with barrels, buying herring. When our nets were sold, no one would bid. Our fish buyer bought them then he turned around to me and said, 'Go and put your nets back aboard.'

Donald Perkin remembered running to Milford in the *Girl Renee* with 65 crans of herring.

When we looked at the chart, it was sopping wet and fell to pieces. When we got across, we didn't know where we were, so we had to go alongside this lightship and ask them the way into Milford. We didn't get anything out of it. As soon as the buyers in Dunmore heard we'd gone across to Milford to get a better price, they put the price up in Dunmore.

Some of those little old Irish drifters were rough. When you went down in the cabin it was black, full of smoke and they were there eating taties. That's what they had. When we went across in the *Sweet Promise*, my brother Joel collected up all our old damaged oilskins to give to them. You'd think we'd given them gold. We couldn't do anything wrong after that.[17]

Some of the top fishermen in Britain went to fish at Dunmore. The Cornishmen had great respect for the crew of the legendary Peterhead drifter *Star of Bethlehem PD 218*. A Cornish fisherman recalled, 'They ran herring across to Milford one time in a storm. They had some of their wheelhouse windows smashed in. There was this tanker nearby and she called them up, 'Are you in distress?" They answered, 'This is the *Star of Bethlehem*!'

The arrival of the 50-foot Girvan ring netters *Arctic Moon BA 369* and *Elizmor BA 343* and their highly skilled crews in 1955 revolutionised the Dunmore fishery.[18] Their phenomenal success made a big impression on the Cornish fishermen. The last Cornish boats to work the Irish herring were all ring netters though actually the Cornish version of the ring net was a miniature purse seine and the Cornish worked as single boats, unlike the Scots who all worked in pairs, each ring netter fishing with her 'neighbour'.

The Cornish ring net was about 200 metres long and 36 deep. One end, the bunt, was of fine mesh. There were purse rings at the bottom with the 'purse rope' threaded through them. When the skipper found fish on his echo sounder, the net was shot around the fish in a circle. The 'bunt' end was shot first with its flashing light, the 'winkie'. When the fish were encircled, both ends of the purse rope were put on the ring net winch, in front of the wheelhouse, and hauled in. This 'pursed' or closed the bottom of the net so the fish could not escape. The net was hauled in until just the 'bunt' was left enclosing the fish. The fish

Skipper Dick Sampson's *Coeur de Lion PZ 74* was one of five West Cornish boats to go ring netting at Dunmore East.

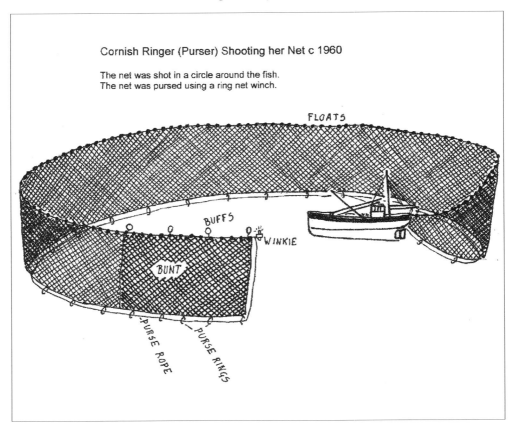

Cornish Ringer (Purser) Shooting her Net c 1960

The net was shot in a circle around the fish.
The net was pursed using a ring net winch.

were dipped out of the net by the brailer, a giant version of a child's shrimp net which was lifted aboard by a derrick in front of the wheelhouse.

Raymond Stevens recalled the last St Ives herring voyage to Ireland.

> I was ringing in Ireland in the *Sweet Promise* in 1960–61. That was the last of it. We had our St Ives number *SS 95* covered over with boards with the Waterford *W 16* number on. They called it a ring net but really it was a purse net with rings along the bottom. The bunt was at one end with four buffs on it to take the weight of the fish. We shot the bunt end first. We pursed the net with the ring net winch in front of the wheelhouse. I hauled one end and John Woolcock hauled the other. After it was pursed, we hauled in the net. That was hard work. Ernie stayed in the wheelhouse with the wheel hard over to starboard and the engine going ahead. That was to keep the boat's stern out of the net.
>
> When we got into Dunmore one day, Paddy O'Toole, the fish buyer, was there. He said, 'Look at your numbers.' We said, 'What do you mean?' He said, 'Look! It says SS.' Somebody had ripped off the Waterford board. We said, 'It's time to go home.'

The Cornish ringers which went to Dunmore were the *Couer de Lion PZ 74*, skipper Dick Sampson, built by Noble of Fraserburgh in 1957; *Girl Renee SS 78*, skipper John Stevens, built by Uphams of Brixham in 1946; *JBS SS 17*, skipper John Maddern Veal, built by Percy Mitchell in 1954; *Renovelle PZ 177*, skipper E. Madron, built by Pearsons of Hull; and *Sweet Promise SS 95*, skipper Ernest Stevens junior, built by Percy Mitchell at

Ernest Stevens' *Sweet Promise* loading a ring net to fish the Irish herring at Dunmore East, December 1960. In front of the wheelhouse is the derrick for the brailer, which emptied the net. She was registered in Waterford so that she could fish in Irish waters. (F. McWilliams)

Porthmellon in 1952. The *Sweet Promise* and *Renovelle* were both outstandingly successful both at Dunmore and the Autumn Cornish pilchard fishery. The *Couer de Lion* famously got herself 'mopped up' in her ring net and had to be towed out. The Scots ringers were purpose built with low bulwarks so they could shoot their nets straight off the stern. The Cornish boats had high bulwarks and worked their ring nets from a platform built at half height beside the wheelhouse.

In April 1962 *World Fishing* magazine published a report on the previous winter's Dunmore East fishing aboard skipper Victor Chambers' Annalong trawler *Green Pastures N 20*. 'A red light coming from the west was the *Sweet Promise*, a Cornish purse seiner bound to Dunmore with 80 cran from three early shoots. 'You'll be in the first division tomorrow," our skipper told him.'[19]

The *Sweet Promise* is remembered for a 100 cran shot at Dunmore, 'She was full right up.'

This was the last Cornish herring voyage to Ireland and the end of a story which endured for a century and a half.

CHAPTER 7

The North Sea Voyage

The fishermen of Newlyn, Mousehole, Porthleven and St Ives sailed away to fish the herring on the coasts of Lothian, Berwickshire, Northumberland, Durham and Yorkshire every summer. This North Sea fishery developed from the Irish herring voyage. The Forth and Clyde Canal opened in 1790. The Cornish luggers headed for Bowling on the Clyde and locked in to the Canal. The fishermen walked all the way across Scotland pulling their luggers behind them and working the lock gates as they went. They emerged into the Firth of Forth at Grangemouth, near Edinburgh. The Cornishmen were certainly fishing the North Sea early in the nineteenth century. On 16 July 1826, Captain Short records in his St Ives Diary, '… Ten of the boats are gone to Wick, in the North of Scotland.' On 19 June 1848, he writes, 'One boat sailed for Whitby and others for Ireland for the herring fisheries.'[1] These early three-masted Cornish luggers were tiny vessels, only 36–40 feet long and entirely open, except for the foredeck where the crew lived.[2] At night they slept wrapped up in their cover-all hooded capes.

They fished the herring off the North East coast from North Berwick, Dunbar, Eyemouth, Berwick on Tweed, Seahouses, North Shields, Whitby and Scarborough. They often sailed for home from Scarborough.

On Sunday the Cornishmen stayed in harbour. Although far away from their chapels in the cobbled streets of Newlyn, Mousehole and St Ives, they often met together for their own services. They praised the Lord in harmony, singing their favourite Methodist hymns, and the local people were moved by their fervent worship and remembered it long afterwards.

When the season ended in September, the Cornish luggers raced each other home, down the North Sea and through the English Channel. The record was held by the *Mary Stevens SS 5* (later renamed *Lloyd*), which sailed the 600 miles from Scarborough to St Ives in fifty hours in 1900. She landed herring in St Ives which had been caught in the North Sea three days before.[3] The *Leading Star SS 615* and *Johanna SS 601* came from Scarborough to St Ives in fifty-five hours and the *Nellie Jane SS 503* in fifty-six hours.

In 1883 100 St Ives boats went to the North Sea. In August 1884 *The Cornishman* reported seventy-two St Ives boats working from Berwick. These included the *Theophilus SS 1, Lord Beaconsfield SS 2, Jane Barber SS 9, Uncle Tom SS 10, Arethusa SS 439, British Workman SS 494, Mary Ann SS 495, Endeavour SS 568, Misty Morn SS 585* and *Waterlily SS 635*. When 400 St Ives men fished the North Sea in 1892, they caught plenty of herring but they were of such poor quality that low prices made the season a failure.[4] 1904 was a bad season and 1905 a failure for the Cornish boats. In 1911, twenty-three St Ives luggers sailed for the Irish herring season but none to the North Sea.

By early July 1894 about forty St Ives boats had left home for the North Sea.[5] On Saturday 25 August 1894, sixty St Ives fishermen working from North Sunderland were entertained by Mr and Mrs Paynter at Bamburgh with a programme of sports and tea.

An early photograph of the Mount's Bay lugger *PE 236 Edwin* at Whitby. *PE* was the original Penzance registration. On 1 January 1869, the *Edwin* was reregistered as *PZ 158*. The 35-foot *Edwin* was owned by James Harvey of Mousehole. She was broken up in 1871. (Leon and Sylvia Pezzack)

St Ives luggers at Spittal, near Berwick, for the weekend. Their outriggers (used for extending the mizzen sail) have been hoisted up the masts and used for drying the footlines of their herring nets and a newly oiled oilskin. *SS 516 Good Templar* 1873–1913, *SS 15 Isabella* 1869–1915 and *SS 514 Hugh Bourne* 1882–1911.

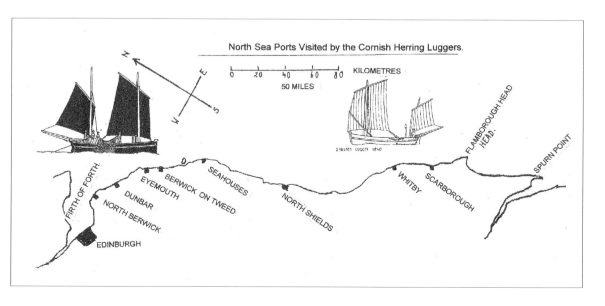

North Sea Ports Visited by the Cornish Herring Luggers.

St Ives mackerel boats returning home from the North Sea.

PZ 455 Monarch and *SS 5 Mary Stevens* at Scarborough, *c.* 1903. The *Mary Stevens* (later renamed *Lloyd*) made one of the fastest passages home from the North Sea in 1900: fifty hours from Scarborough to St Ives. In the background are Cornish and Scots luggers and some new steam drifters, including the *Lord Milner* and one of the Yarmouth Numerical Fleet. On the left is a Scarborough mule.

'After the sports, the fishermen gave much pleasure to the company by singing together several of the songs, hymns and anthems with which they were familiar.' The prize for the 100-yard race was a ham, won by Mr Peters of the *Misty Morn SS 585*. Skipper Harvey of the *Mayflower SS 498* won the skipper's race. Other useful prizes were a leg of mutton and stockings.[6] About forty boats left St Ives for the North in 1895.

Matthew Stevens of the mackerel boat *Jane SS 536* kept a diary of her voyages and landings. She sailed from home at 10.00 a.m. on Wednesday 10 July and called at Kingstown (Dun Laoghaire) and Howth before locking in to the Forth and Clyde Canal at Bowling on the Clyde, on Thursday the 18th. They tied a rope to the *Jane's* foremast and towed her right across Scotland. The *Jane* locked out into the Firth of Forth at Grangemouth on Monday 22nd and went into Granton.

The *Jane's* first shot, of only 2 crans, was 15 miles east of Berwick the following night. They were weather-bound for the rest of the week and spent Sunday 28 July at Berwick. Her landings for the following week were a meagre 1 cran, 2 crans, 2½ baskets, 6½ crans and 6¼ crans. They fished from Berwick until 24 August and then barked their nets before sailing for Scarborough on the 30th. Their top shot was 43 crans on 10 September.

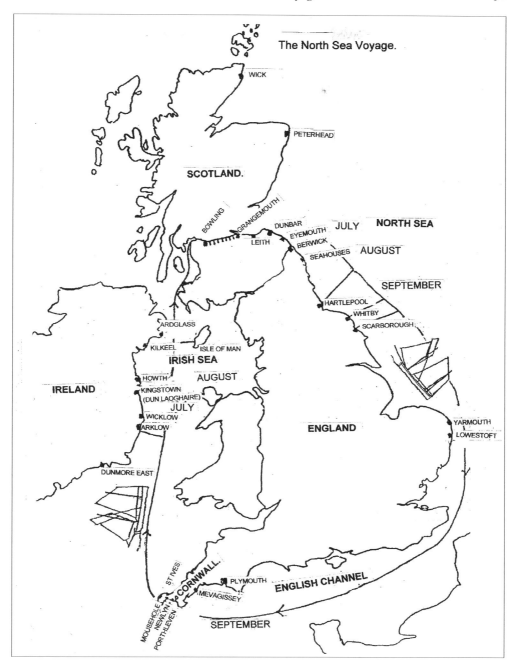

The North Sea Voyage.

They barked their nets again on the 12th and unsuperstitiously sailed for home on Friday 13 September, arriving home a week later. The *Jane* grossed £110 0s 3d for the whole voyage, having shot her nets twenty-six times. Each of her crew earned £5 share plus 18s 6d allowance for the whole North Sea voyage, a total of £5 18s 6d each, about £540 in today's money.[8]

On 17 September 1896, twenty to thirty St Ives luggers were beating about off Lowestoft, held up by contrary winds on their passage home. Four of them, the *Theodore SS 538*, *JMT SS 542*, *Prospect SS 549* and *Sara Stevens SS 599*, put into port. On going to

Above left: The *Endeavour SS 568*.[7] *Above right:* The crew of the *Endeavour SS 568* before leaving for the North Sea, the youngest St Ives crew to sail for the north. From the back: Dan Quick, Joe Murrish, James H. Quick, W. Cocking, Edwin Bottrell, owner, James Cocking and Dick Mills Care. (Private Collection)

The *Jane SS 536* earned £110 0s 3d for her whole 1895 North Sea voyage. She was sold to Ardglass in 1910. (J. Hornsey)

sea the following day, they were stoned by local lads, fortunately without injury. This was in response to the Newlyn Riots of May 1896, when thousands of mackerel were thrown overboard from the Lowestoft drifters in Newlyn Harbour. The *Gyles SS 441* grounded while trying to enter Southwold. She was got off by the Lowestoft Beachmen, who claimed £30 for their services. Her skipper disputed this charge and the boat was arrested. Hearing that the other Cornish boats had been stoned, Skipper James Gyles appealed to the Police and Coastguards for protection and moored his lugger in the middle of the harbour.[9]

The Newlyn luggers *Annie Harvey PZ 102* and *Auld Lang Syne PZ 486* ghosting into Whitby on a quiet summer morning. (National Maritime Museum Cornwall)

Thursday 1 October 1896 must have been a spectacular and emotional day at St Ives when nineteen luggers arrived home from the North Sea: the *Try SS 551*, S. Williams Junior; *Water Lily SS 635*, M. Stevens; *Mary Catherine SS 637*, M. Stevens; *Annie SS 13*, Charles Rowe; *Mary Ann SS 495*, M. Stevens Junior; *Johanna SS 601*, John Care; *Hugh Bourne SS 514*, W. Jennings; *B.H.P SS 304*, John Uren; *Rippling Wave*, T. H. Uren; *Theophilus SS 1*, G. Tanner; *Uncle Tom SS 10*, E. Bottrell; *Isabella SS 15*, W. Mason; *Jane Barber SS 9*, W. Barber; *Jane Lander SS 623*, B. Thomas; *Idea SS 97*, W. Paul; *Mary Jane SS 517*, W. Phillips; *Frank SS 573*, F. Bastian; *Mary Bennetts SS 584*, N. B. Trevorrow; and *Prospect SS 549*, S. Noall. *The Cornishman* commented:

> The return of the St Ives fishing fleet. – Back again safe after many toils – heavy storms; low prices; hard times; rough usage; and hard work to get back. But back again – safe after all, though most have come back with nigh empty pockets, and to poor homes, whose inmates have had to struggle as best they could during the absence of the bread-winner. However, the North season is over, and we must thank God for the preservation of the lives of our fishermen in the past and take courage for the future.[10]

Lowestoft was an ill fated destination for the *Theodore SS 538*, which struck piles and sank there while heading for the North Sea fishing grounds on 21 July 1900.

Although there were differences with the Lowestoft men, they were all fellow fishermen. When the Lowestoft dandy *Faithful* got into difficulties in St Ives Bay in March 1903, the local fishermen immediately went to help and brought her safely into harbour.[11]

In July 1902, the former Mount's Bay lugger *Branch SS 119* collided with a small yacht off Ramsgate while heading for the North Sea.[12] On 3 September, in a Force 6 breeze, the *Jane Lander SS 623*, heavily laden with herring, was being towed into Scarborough by the St Ives steam fishing boat *Rebecca SS 118* when she struck the local yawl *Violet* and sank. Her crew were speedily rescued by the *Rebecca*.[13] In November, the *Alarm* was returning from Scarborough when she was run down and sunk by a schooner. Her crew were rescued by the *Daniel*.

Among the first Mount's Bay boats to leave home for the 1903 season were the *Prima Donna PZ 549*, *Annie Harvey PZ 102* and *Martha Jane*, which sailed on Tuesday 21

July.[14] By the second week of August the top boats were doing well. 'Most of the boats on the North Sea herring fishery did fairly well last week, the *Albania* grossing £25 and the *Auld Lang Syne* and *Annie Harvey*, £20 each. One or two boats caught good quantities of fish, but being of poor quality, they fetched a small price.'[15] Fishing improved during the end of the month, with the top boats like the *Prima Donna*, *Little Clara* and *Annie Harvey* earning from £40–70.[16] But despite the optimism and good shots, *The Cornishman* summed up the 1903 North Sea season from Whitby and Scarborough as 'indifferent'. The last Mount's Bay boats to arrive home were the *Auld Lang Syne* and *Annie Harvey* on Sunday 19 September.[17]

The 1904 season was even worse, as reported on 22 September.

> The luggers *Boy Willie* and *Martha Jane* returned on Friday night and the *Little Clara* on Saturday from the North Sea herring fishery. Only two boats, the *Coronation* and *Annie Harvey*, now remain at Scarborough. The season there has been almost a total failure, some having been unable to earn the expenses connected with the voyage, the best boat having earned only £6 per man. Those boats that have returned from the North are now preparing for the Kinsale mackerel fishery, for which the *Hope* and *Advance* sailed on Friday... [18]

The *Annie Harvey PZ 102* and a Scots Fifie leaving Whitby.

Mount's Bay luggers at Whitby: *Progress PZ 134*, *Prima Donna PZ 594*, *Thomas Harvey PZ 385*. (John Lambourn)

Nicholas Polmeor made a record of his voyages in the *Arethusa SS 439*. She left St Ives for her 1907 North Sea voyage on 10 July. They went south about, sailing up the English Channel instead of the Irish Sea. The *Arethusa* arrived at Lowestoft on the 15th and they had their first shot, 8 crans and 3 baskets, at 21s a cran, off Northumberland, on the 26th. They sailed for home on Saturday 14 September, arriving on the 19th. The *Arethusa* grossed £158 15s for the whole voyage. Each member of her crew shared £6 14s 6d.[19]

The Cornishman was optimistic about the start of the 1907 season.

The herring fishery at Whitby and Scarborough, and other ports further north formerly attracted the entire Mount's Bay fleet, but with a succession of unremunerative seasons, the Bay boats gradually abandoned their fishery till two years ago, only one lugger – a Mousehole craft – ventured on the voyage. This boat doing well, several went North from Newlyn and Mousehole last year and obtained very satisfactory results, while the promise of a good season has this year drawn a number of Mount's Bay and St Ives boats to the North Sea. Newlyn has this year sent ten boats North, the *Bona Fide*, *Annie Harvey*, *Martha Jane*, and *Thomas Harvey* leaving for Whitby on Monday last week, while the following day saw the departure of the *Boy Willie*, *Defiance*, *Lizzie Tonkin*, *Little Clara*, *Mary and Emily* and *Our Lizzie*. They had a good send off from a large crowd of men, women and children on the South Pier on both days. All the luggers arrived safely on Friday and Saturday, although the *Bona Fide* was delayed a few hours at Plymouth getting a new mast, she having been towed there by the *Thomas Harvey*, the *Bona Fide* carrying away her foremast off the Eddystone on Monday night. Mousehole boats arriving at Whitby early in the week made from £22 down, and advices from there state that prospects are excellent.[20]

In July 1909 the Mousehole luggers *Nellie Jane PZ 130*, *Emblem PZ 575* and *Children's Friend PZ 619* sailed from home for Scarborough in company and made a fine passage of 70 hours from the Lizard to Flamborough Head. They would probably have made an even faster voyage except that they had to wait for the slower *Children's Friend*. They hardly touched their sails for the whole passage and arrived on 24 July. They were becalmed by light winds at the start of the voyage but forced to reduce sail by heavy squalls off the Yorkshire coast.[21]

Crew of the St Ives lugger *SS 539 TRC* (Thomas and Richard Clark) in Scotland. 1. Mr Thomas, 2. Thomas Clark, 3. Edward Noall, 4. Mr Ninnis, 5. W. H. Davies *Pard*, 6. Mr Peters, 7. Mr Paynter *Bevins*. The *TRC* returned to St Ives from Peterhead, a distance of 850 miles, in less than 100 hours. (Belinda Ratnayake)

Top left: Arethusa SS 439 landing at Scarborough.

Left: In 1909 the Mousehole lugger *Nellie Jane PZ 130* sailed from the Lizard to Flamborough Head in seventy hours. The Bethel Star on her mizzen sail shows that she does not fish on Sundays.

Bottom: The largely unrecognised heroines of the North Sea Voyage were the women who kept their families afloat, often with very slender means, while the fishermen were absent from July to September. (With permission of the Royal institution of Cornwall – RIC.)

The *Emblem PZ 575* of Mousehole. She lost her foremast returning from the North Sea in 1907 and accidentally sank the *Orlando PZ 495*. (Tony Pawlyn)

The children at home looked forward to their presents of Scarborough rock when dad came home. The fishermen's wives were resourceful people who kept their families going while their men were absent for two months. This must have been a hard task as local school logbooks comment that the boys' conduct deteriorated while their fathers were away.

There are still some souvenirs of the North Sea voyages in West Cornwall: little pink china ornaments and pieces of Whitby jet. George Pearce of St Ives remembered, 'Our Nanny's Dad was a fisherman. No matter how bad a season they had, when the boat came home from the North Sea, she always brought us some Scarborough rock.' It was a remarkable achievement that the fishermen circumnavigated England every year with only the most basic navigational equipment, a compass, a log line to tell them their speed, and a traverse board, marked with the points of the compass, on which they pegged the distance run on each course. The school atlas which the *Jane* took to the North Sea is still treasured by Matthew Stevens' descendants.

The last St Ives voyage was in 1920, when five new motor boats, the *Freeman SS 65*, *Provider SS 49* (later *Francis Stevens*), *James and Edgar SS 163* (later *First PZ 31*), *Mayflower SS 67* (later *PZ 51*) and *White Heather SS 84*, sailed for the North. The venture was a failure. They all came home in debt, except the *White Heather*, which stayed an extra week and paid off her expenses. The high cost of fuel was the main problem.[22]

Many Lowestoft fishermen sailed in local Mount's Bay boats and several of them fished the autumn Home Fishing from Lowestoft between the two world wars. These included the *Efficient FR 242* (*Excellent PZ 513*), *Renovelle PZ 107* of Mousehole, *Lyonesse PZ 81*, *Penlee PZ 85*, *Madeline PZ 88* and *Trevessa PZ 203*.

While fishing out of Lowestoft in October 1938 the *Renovelle* struck it lucky, as reported by *The Cornishman*:

The Mousehole fishing boat *Renovelle* struck a huge shoal of herring. With great difficulty the crew secured half the nets safely inboard with...seventy five crans, the craft being then practically laden to the gunwhales and unable to proceed with hauling the remaining dozen nets.

A flare called a nearby drifter which took over the gear from the *Renovelle*.

Prices were low but the Cornish boats, making trial shots, had landings of from £100 downwards.[23]

After the Second World War, the Mount's Bay boats *Renovelle PZ 107*, *Karenza PZ 85* and *United Friends PZ 297* fished the autumn herring season at Lowestoft, where the *Karenza* and *United Friends* were among the first to land in 1951 with small catches from the Smith's Knoll grounds on 4 October.[24] They were the last Cornish boats at the North Sea herring. Cornish fishermen have continued to go to the North Sea, but not for herring. In recent years, several have worked in the North Sea oil business, crewing and skippering rig supply vessels.

The *Madeline PZ 88* and *Trevessa PZ 203* preparing to leave Newlyn for Lowestoft in 1939. The outbreak of war cut short their voyage.

In October 1938 Skipper Eddie Madron's *Renovelle PZ 107* filled up with 75 crans of herring while fishing from Lowestoft.

Ring netters at Newlyn, 2005: *Resolute FY 119*, *Little Pearl FY 23*, *Pride of Cornwall SS 87* and *Prue Esther PZ 550*. (Francis McWilliams)

The crew of the *Richard and Ann* mending their ring net at Mevagissey, September 2013.

Skipper John Burt's crabber *Bacchus PW 251* at Newlyn, one of many Breton crabbers bought in Cornwall. (Michael Pellowe)

Crabber *Zarvan PW 122* with Cornwall Sea Fishery's *RIB* alongside in November 1998. (Glyn Richards)

The *Kingfisher II FH 529* beaching at Cadgwith, May 2011, one of eight modern fibreglass boats working from the cove.

P. Matthews' *Cornish Lass FY 769* shooting her pots. She is self-shooting through a door in the stern. (Glyn Richards)

Crew of the crabber *Zarvan PW 122* with their parlour pots in 1998. (Glyn Richards)

A bongo of Cornish shellfish. (Glyn Richards)

Above: Stevenson's *PZ 123 Sara Shaun* with her beam trawls in the water. (Glyn Richards)

Right: Like all fishing gear, beam trawls have to be carefully looked after. A good view of the chain mat and heavy groundline of the Belgian beamer *Z 402 Nooitgedacht's* beam trawl.

The veteran Newlyn trawler *Jacqueline PZ 192* towing her trawl in February 1998. (Glyn Richards)

The Looe trawler *Palatine FY 149* towing her trawl in February 1999, one of a fleet of day boats which have built up the port's reputation for high-quality fish. The 33-foot *Palatine*, powered by a 110-hp Volvo Penta engine, was built by C. Toms of Polruan for Skipper Mike Soady in 1985. (Glyn Richards)

Above: The *Southover Scorpio FH 388* hauling her trawl, December 1997. The fishery officer is aboard measuring the meshes of the bag. (Glyn Richards)

Right: The Mevagissey inshore trawler *Lenten Rose FY 43* towing her trawl. (Glyn Richards)

Valhalla of Mevagissey coming in to land her catch, October 2011. Her working deck is covered by a shelter deck.

Trawler *Jolie Brise FY 64* towing. She hauls her trawl with a net drum, which can be seen aft, in front of the gantry. (Glyn Richards)

Mackerel punts at work off Penlee Point, 1998. (Glyn Richards)

Steve Bassett,
David McClary
and David Jones
with crawfish
aboard the
Trazbar SS 104.
(Steve Bassett)

The *Lamorna SS 28* was built by John Moor at Mevagissey for Ron Eglington of Newquay in 1986. She has since had a long career fishing from Newlyn. (Glyn Richards)

Skipper Chris Hill's netter *Ar Bageergan PZ 287*. (Collection Treizour Douarnenez, copyright Christian Signor)

Skipper Barney Thomas' *Ygraine SS 284* alongside at Douarnenez with a good catch aboard. (Collection Treizour Douarnenez, copyright Christian Signor)

Nigel Hill's *Clairvoyant M 126* of Newlyn hauling 5-inch cod nets in 1999. (Glyn Richards)

The ex-French *Boy Anthony PZ 498* was replaced by the steel-built *Silver Dawn PZ 1196* in 2002. (Collection Treizour Douarnenez, copyright Christian Signor)

Hauling nets in David McClary's St Ives netter *Celtic Lass PZ 459* in 1999. (Glyn Richards)

Stelissa II, bought from Lorient for Newlyn in 2012.

Netter *Mordros FY 523*, 1999. Many smaller netters use these blue plastic net bins. Her hauler is a hefty piece of kit compared with the pedestal haulers of a previous generation. (Glyn Richards)

Dredges full of scallops, and some starfish, aboard the *Neptune*. (Glyn Richards)

The Troon-registered scalloper *Philomena TN 32* at Newlyn, July 2009, one of many large scallopers from the west of Scotland to visit Cornwall during the summer.

Skipper Steven Long's Falmouth scalloper *Morel Margh FH 12* getting ready to tip her dredges, July 1999. (Glyn Richards)

The scalloper *Golden Fleece FH 206*, August 1999. (Glyn Richards)

The *Jacoba* of Newlyn tows seventeen dredges from each side, 2010.

The little *Charlotta PW 362* of Mevagissey tows three dredges off her stern and works single-handed.

CHAPTER 8

Longlining

Using baited hooks and lines must be one of the oldest kinds of fishing. A long line is a very long rope with short pieces of cord called 'orsels' or 'snoods' branching off, each with a hook on the end. A piece of bait is threaded onto each hook as the line is thrown out to rest on the sea bed.

In the days of sail, only small boats could work lines as they usually had to be rowed along the line. They worked small lines which the Cornishmen called 'tayckle' (tackle). Tayckle was baited into and later shot from three-sided boxes called 'rips'. The usual bait for shore lining in St Ives was sand eels or 'linsees' (lance) which were caught in miniature seines called draw bait nets. Each St Ives long liner had its own draw bait gig. At St Ives the gigs worked the lines but they were sometimes towed off to their fishing grounds by the luggers, if there was enough wind. Barney Thomas described such a trip.

They used to go Summers Raying; that's tayckling [lining] in the summer time, after these rays, down the Brisons [fishing ground] before they had engines. Father has been in the *Barnabas* [the lugger] and had to sail her round the gig by himself all night. The gig was working the gear. She was the *Boy Phillip SS 146*, 28 feet long,

Two old fellows baiting up boxes of small lines called rips. The line is kept tidy in a vertical grooved stick called a claw, seen on top of the barrel. Each hook slid into the groove. The line is carefully coiled into the rip, the baited hooks placed in order along the back. (St Ives Museum)

and when she was built, the men said, 'Which way are ee goin to row her Barney?' She was the biggest gig that was built then and had four rooms foreside of the net room.

They left here one morning and rowed to the [Hayle] Bar. Caught their [sand eel] bait and rowed home. They came ashore and had a cup of tea; came down with their bags [of food] and went aboard. They cast the *Barney* off and towed her with the gig out to the New Pier Buoy; got her under way with the sails. It was fine weather in those days, brother. By the time they got between the Hor and Clodgy, the tayckle was all baited. Granda said to father, 'Phillip, if you want to shut this gear tonight, you'll have to get in the gig.' In the gig they got; put in all the stones [chain weights] that were wanted, buoy ropes and everything and their canteen of water. They rowed to the Longships, down to Mill Bay; that's further than the Longships; shot the tayckle, zig zagged them. In the morning, when the tayckle was all in, the *Barney* was up to the Shark's Fin [rock]. They rowed up to the *Barney*, got aboard and had a cup of tea. Now that's a long row, from Mill Bay up to the Shark's Fin. They came to have a bit of a smoke and Grandfer said to Father, 'Phillip, if you want to land these rays today, you've got to get in the gig.'

There was another boat there, the *Perseverance SS 140*. They had a gig called the *Naomi*, I believe. Father and they had four oars and the other gig had five. Johnny Bassett said, 'Phillip, I'd rather I died to the oar than they beat we today.' Father said, 'Johnny, they're bound to beat ee. They've got an extra oar.' My Uncle Paul and old Cork-an-Barber were in her and they were the only ones spelling one another. Father had the helm first and his watch on the thwart. Ten minutes, and he hopped afora'd and took the bow oar. They worked like that all the way home. When they were rounding the Head [the Island], they couldn't see the other one coming to Clodgy. They beat her!

A pound a man they got out of that brother. And they had their hats cocked to one side. Big money! With all that work and they reckon they rowed sixty miles.[1]

The shore grounds worked by the St Ives men had picturesque names: The Pill, Nowan Noweth, The White Spot, The Klondyke, the Brisons and The Ladner and Stone.

Overhauling a draw-bait net from its draw-bait gig. (St Ives Archive)

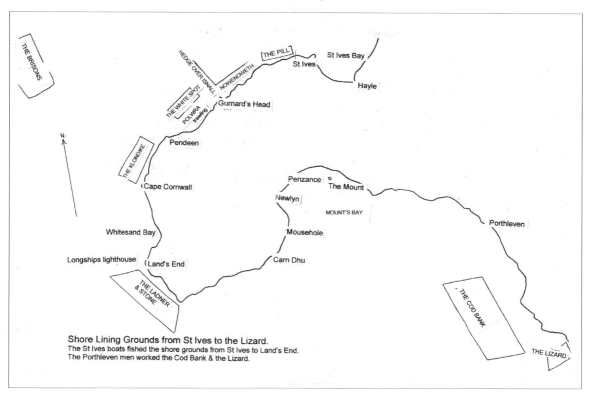

Shore Lining Grounds from St Ives to the Lizard.
The St Ives boats fished the shore grounds from St Ives to Land's End.
The Porthleven men worked the Cod Bank & the Lizard.

Until the Great War, most of the Cornish fishing fleet was involved with the seasonal mackerel, pilchard and herring fisheries and most of the white fish landed at Newlyn was from the visiting Brixham, Plymouth and Lowestoft sailing smacks and, during the spring seasons for soles on the Trevose grounds, increasing numbers of Lowestoft steam drifter trawlers. So dominant were the mackerel and pilchard fisheries that Newlyn's trawl fish market was not opened until 1907.

Engines were fitted into some Cornish boats like the *Ailsa Craig*, *Phyllis* and *Bona Fide* of Mount's Bay in the early years of the twentieth century and a few purpose-built motor boats like the *Treryn Castle PZ 190*, *Ben my Chree PZ 545* and *Lamorna PZ 169* were built.[2] There were also the miniature steam boats *Pioneer* and *Adventure*, run by the Hendy family and known colloquially as *White Hendy* and *Black Hendy*. Long lining became an important season for these early Cornish powered vessels. They may well have taken inspiration from the little French steam liners from Boulogne which frequently visited Plymouth and Newlyn for bait and coal when they worked the grounds off the Start and the Lizard and between the Longships and St Ives.[3] Indeed, the *Treryn Castle* was built by Henry Peake of Newlyn in 1910 specifically with lining in mind. A square-sterned boat 53 feet long, she was later lengthened by the addition of a counter stern, probably to provide more room for her line baskets.

In January 1911 there were nineteen motor fishing boats in Cornwall. Five Alpha engines, two Ailsa Craigs and four Gardners had been fitted. A successful pilchard season in East Cornwall saw up to thirty of the very popular Kelvins installed at Mevagissey. These engines started on petrol and switched over to the cheaper paraffin. Cornwall County Council saw motors as the salvation of the ailing West Cornwall fishing industry and resolved to request £10,000 from the Development Commissioners to provide motor loans.

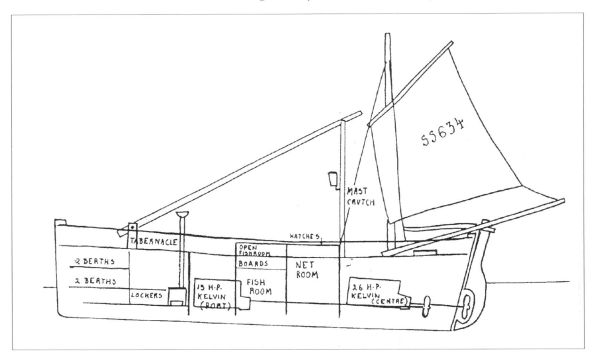

The motor lugger *Barnabas* SS 634, fitted with her first engine in 1917.

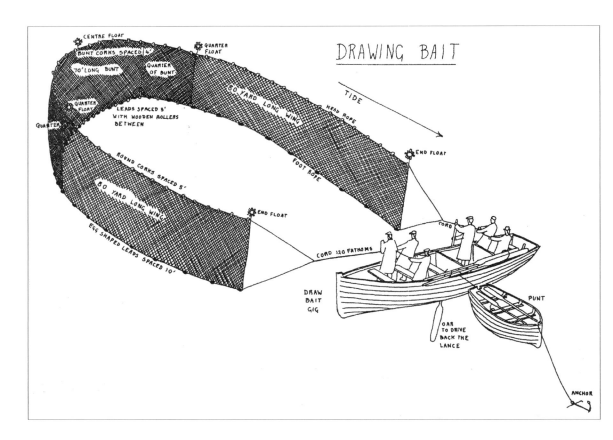

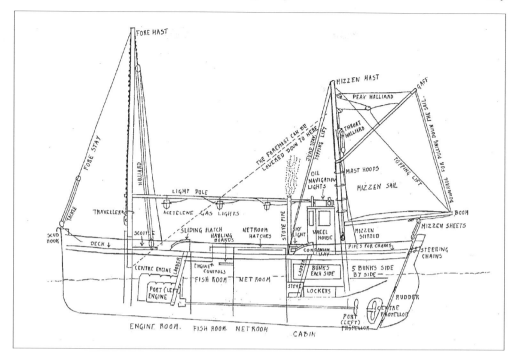

Our John SS 64, a typical West Cornish motor boat, built in 1926.

During the First World War, paraffin engines were fitted in the sailing luggers, with the help of the Motor Loans Committee of the Ministry of Agriculture and Fisheries. Some St Ives motor luggers worked out of Padstow and caught their sand eel bait in the Camel estuary. They had to get permission for this bait fishing so as not to infringe the local salmon fishery laws.[4]

In the post-War optimism of the early 1920s, many fine big motor fishing boats were built in West Cornwall. Some were constructed at Newlyn and Looe but the majority were from the highly reputed shipwrights of Porthleven. These new boats included the *Snowdrop PZ 144*, *Penrose PZ 105*, and *Energetic PZ 114* for Porthleven; the *Two Boys PZ 214*, *Our Katie PZ 697*, *Ocean Pride PZ 134*, *Emblem PZ 26*, *Heather Glen PZ 262*, *Internos PZ 46*, *Penzer PZ 324* and *Lyonesse PZ 81* for Mousehole; the *Rosebud PZ 87*, *Asthore PZ 182*, *Peel Castle PZ 17*, *United Boys PZ 18*, *Penlee PZ 85*, *Mayon Castle PZ 123*, *Valiant PZ 142* and *Cornishman PZ 120* for Newlyn; and the *Our Lizzie SS 41*, *Provider SS 49*, *Freeman SS 65*, *Mayflower SS 67*, *Iverna SS 41*, *White Heather SS 84*, *James and Edgar SS 163*, *Pioneer SS 57*, *Nellie SS 101*, *Our John SS 64*, *Sheerness SS 10*, *Peaceful SS 90* and *Amelia SS 93* for St Ives.

Many of these big motor boats were built with counter sterns, probably in imitation of the much-admired Yorkie steam drifters. St Ives was also built over thirty shallow draught motor gigs, adapted for its tidal and groundswell-ridden harbour, mainly with the seasonal herring and crabbing seasons in mind.

In East Cornwall, the *Forget Me Not FY 269*, *Our Daddy FY 7*, *Seagull FY 408*, *Janie FY 227*, *I.R.I.S. FY 357* and *Swift FY405* were built for Looe and the *Westward FY 229* and *Ibis FY 119* for Mevagissey. The Ministry of Agriculture and Fisheries gave the Cornish fisheries a shot in the arm by building the five little counter-sterned motor drifters *Golden Sunset PZ 178*, *Carn Du PZ 193*, *Our Girlie PZ 265*, *Memento PZ 243* and *Twin Boys SS 115*.[5]

Our Daddy FY 7, built for the Pengelly family of Looe in 1921.

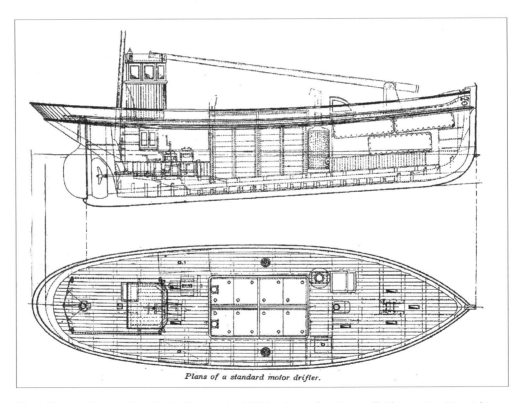

Plans of a standard motor drifter.

The Ministry of Agriculture built five standard fishing boats for Cornwall. Skipper Joe Murrish's *Twin Boys SS115* was lost while longlining in May 1924.

Several of these Cornish motor boats, built in the 1920s, soldiered on until the 1960s. Initially, many of these new boats joined the spring mackerel season each year but as they found they could not compete with the powerful Lowestoft and Yarmouth steam drifters, they switched over to long lining for white fish.

The motor long liners usually worked their lines far from land, 30 to 100 or more miles away. This deep-water lining began during the First World War and continued from Newlyn into the 1970s, when it was replaced by netting for white fish.

Each boat carried about twenty-five to thirty-five or more baskets of line. Each basket had 150 hooks with a space of 2 fathoms between each hook. A large fleet of long lines stretched for about 9 miles along the sea bed. The baskets were beautifully made, with open sides to allow the rope to ventilate and slabs of cork tied around the rim where the hooks were carefully stuck in order. Mount's Bay hooks were stuck in rope instead of cork. The lengths of rope was specially spun for the purpose and filled with grease to preserve the hooks.

To shoot the lines, first the 'dan' buoy and buoy rope with its anchor were shot. The long line was tied to the anchor. The basket of long line was put on a stand called the 'shooting plat' to raise it to a convenient working height. Three men stood around it. Each fisherman in turn picked a hook out of the corked rim of the basket, baited the hook with a piece of mackerel and threw it over the side. A fourth man, the 'shooter', stood behind the basket, threw out the line, pausing now and again to pull it tight. As each basket was emptied, another was tied on and took its place on the shooting plat. The lines were joined to make one long line. Each end of the line was anchored and buoyed with a dan (a float with a pole and flag) and there were one or two middle dans at intervals along the line.

Shooting lines was dangerous work as the hooks flew through the air. Depending on their highly skilled crews, some liners shot their gear at considerable speed. Many liner men had hooks through their hands and one St Ives skipper, famously, through his nose. There were usually several razor sharp knives in leather straps on the side of the wheelhouse. If someone was hooked, the orsel was quickly cut so they would not be dragged overboard. Hooks could often be removed on board. The hook was pushed through until the barb appeared. The barb was then pinched off with a pair of pliers and the hook pulled out. The

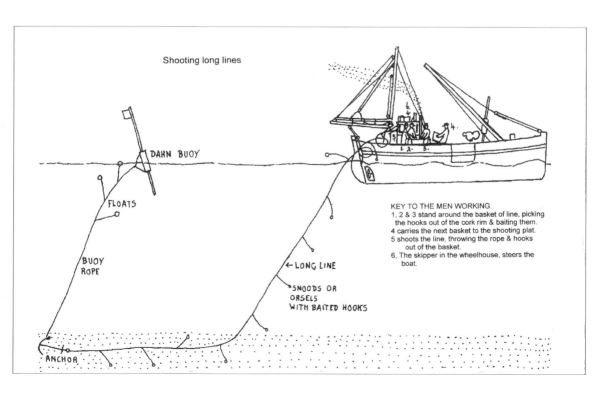

Shooting long lines

DAHN BUOY

FLOATS

BUOY ROPE

← LONG LINE

SNOODS OR ORSELS WITH BAITED HOOKS

ANCHOR

KEY TO THE MEN WORKING.
1, 2 & 3 stand around the basket of line, picking the hooks out of the cork rim & baiting them.
4 carries the next basket to the shooting plat.
5 shoots the line, throwing the rope & hooks out of the basket.
6, The skipper in the wheelhouse, steers the boat.

Rose of Sharon SS 118 had a hammer, cold chisel and half hundred weight in her cabin. Barbs were speedily cut off by putting the hook on the half hundred and giving it a whack with the hammer and cold chisel. No doubt speedy, but not a lot of fun with the hook through your finger. More serious hookings led to a visit to the surgery or local hospital.

There were local differences. When the St Ives men worked their shore grounds, they baited all their lines first, using sand eels or lance, known as linsees. The idea was to shoot as much gear as possible on the very limited grounds. The lines were shot first across the tide, then before it, then back across the tide, and so on. Each turn in the lines was weighted with two weights of old chain, known as 'stones'. At Looe and Polperro, boxes were used for the lines instead of baskets. At Mevagissey, special small 'dog lines', with smaller hooks, fastened closer together, were used for dog fish. Ordinary Mevagissey line baskets were smaller than Mount's Bay and St Ives baskets, to fit their miniature luggers. In East Cornwall, long lines were sometimes called 'boulters'.

The Looe men called their inshore lining grounds the 'Quat'. During the 1930s they developed a very successful class of half-decked boats with steering shelters, or 'canopies', forward, at the break of the foredeck. They called these boats 'quatters'. Perhaps the first was the 32-foot *Dessie*, built in 1925 for Luther Pengelly with her engines and cabin forward.[6] These were the forerunners of dozens of boats built in Cornwall in the post-War years.

There were also the everyday dangers of being at sea. The Newlyn long liner *Goodwill PZ 12* was hauling her lines on the Wolf grounds on the night of Monday 5 March 1934 when a sudden lurch threw skipper Fred Hichens overboard. Though hampered by his sea boots and oilskins, fortunately he was able to grab the lines in the darkness and the crew hauled him back aboard.[7] A similar accident resulted in the loss of Robert Harvey of the *Girl Lillian PZ 319* as she was returning to Newlyn from the Wolf grounds early on Saturday 4 August 1934. As he came aft to relieve the watch at 4.45, he missed his hold on the wheelhouse and was lost overboard. His body was recovered on the following Wednesday night by the Brixham trawler *Servabo BM 77*.[8] In July 1938 the *Asthore PZ182* was shooting her lines 84 miles off Lamorna when she was struck by a heavy sea which damaged her bulwarks and washed overboard two of her crew, 28 year old Archie James and Joseph Johns. Joseph hung on to Archie, a non-swimmer, for 10 minutes but tragically, he was lost in the darkness.[9]

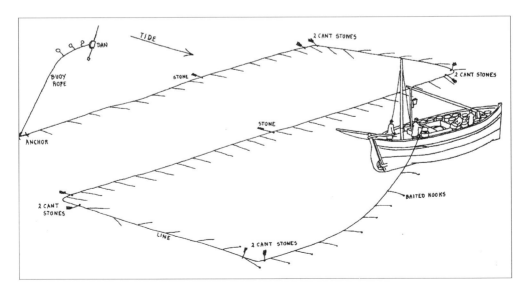

A St Ives boat shooting lines on the shore grounds.

Overhauling lines at Polperro, 1937.
At Looe and Polperro, longlines
were worked from boxes. (Wilkinson
Collection, Vol. 1, St Ives Museum)

The lines were hauled with the aid of a petrol engined line-hauler called the 'jinny'. This consisted of two grooved wheels, one behind the other. The long line came in over the top of the first wheel and was hauled out under the second. The first line jinny was the hand-powered 'iron man'. Several of the big mackerel boats which already had steam boilers in their cabins to power their capstans fitted steam-driven jinnies. In the 1950s, the St Ives long liner *Sweet Promise SS 95* took 2 hours to shoot her 9 miles of line but 9 hours to haul them.[10]

The dan, buoy rope and anchor were hauled in, then the anchor was cast off and they started to pull in the lines. One man stood behind the line hauler, facing aft, and hauled the line off the jinny. Another, beside him, roughly coiled the rope back into its basket. A third, in the starboard waterway, gaffed each fish as it came up and gutted them. In heavy fishing, this could take two crew. It was not usually necessary for anyone to steer the boat. The rest of the crew overhauled or 'clawed' the roughly coiled lines. Each basket was tipped out and carefully re-coiled, first remembering to leave the end hanging over the edge of the basket so it could be tied on to its neighbour when shooting. Tangles were unscrambled and the hooks carefully placed in order around the corked rim of the basket. The fish, ray, skate, turbot, dogfish and ling were unhooked using a T-hook called a 'jumper', gutted and put on ice in the fishroom. The crook at the base of the T was put into each hook, which was twisted out of the fish's mouth. In Newlyn boats, each man hauled and coiled a basket, then took it away to clear.

The strong link between the installation of motors and the introduction of long lining is illustrated by the loss of the ancient (1876) motor mackerel boat *Result SS 567* in May 1915. Skipper William Barber's *Result* had just had an engine installed. With the rest of the St Ives fleet, she sailed for the mackerel grounds 36 miles NNW of St Ives Head on Monday 29 May and first shot her long lines and then her mackerel nets. The motor was not needed for the mackerel nets, which were hauled with the aid of her steam capstan. When the nets were all in, on Tuesday morning, they attempted to start the engine so they

Skipper Tommy Toman's *Nellie SS 101* hauling her longlines, *c.* 1930.

could get their long lines. Immediately, the magneto exploded, filling the engine room with flames. Skipper Barber got four hands to launch the punt while two vainly tried to smother the flames with buckets of water, which only spread the burning fuel. It was too late to save the *Result*. They rowed towards the nearby *Gratitude SS 626*, which speedily buoyed her lines and came to their rescue.[11]

The increasing importance of lining is shown by a local press report about Newlyn of March 1919. 'Lining was the chief occupation of the local boats, one of which had £450 for a day's landing, others making from £250 to £50.' There were also thirty-four steam and motor mackerel drifters working from the port. The mackerel boats and the liners were all working the Wolf grounds.[12]

The liners often fished many miles from land. Navigation was by compass, watch, and log line which gave the distance run. In those days, before the advent of radar, radio, Decca or GPS, fog was a constant hazard and several long liners came to grief while making their landfall.

The new year of 1924 began well for the little Newlyn liner *Bethel*, which was returning from a successful day working the Wolf grounds on the evening of Thursday 3 January. But heavy rain squalls reduced visibility to zero for skipper Sidney Thomas, and the former St Ives pilchard boat struck the rocks on the Lamorna side of Carn Dhu and quickly sank. Skipper Thomas and his three crew, including the skipper's 72 year old father, John, scrambled ashore and scaled the steep cliffs in the dark. They found their way to a nearby house, where Mr Bert Waters looked after them and later drove them home to Newlyn in his pony and trap.[13]

On 10 May 1924, the St Ives long liner *Twin Boys SS 115* struck the Three Stone Ore rock, north of Pendeen, while coming in from lining 35 miles NW of St Ives in thick weather. She was under a temporary skipper, her experienced owner Joe Murrish being ashore ill. This was a very dicey piece of navigation as the boy, William Ninnes, 'Leggar', had spotted that they were right under Pendeen light just a short while before. Fortunately, after some scary adventures, they all got into their punt and landed near Zennor cliffs, from where they walked home to St Ives.[14]

As they were open boats, it might be thought that the large fleet of new St Ives motor gigs of 30–40 feet length might not be very suitable for lining far from land. However, many of them went lining quite successfully, including the *Glorious Peace SS 37*, *Guide*

Me SS 106, Cutty Sark SS 117, Our Boys SS 150, Blush Rose SS 152 and *Eden SS 85*. Skipper William Stevens of the *Eden* did well on the shore grounds and at Scilly, and often worked from Newlyn.

It was remembered: 'He'd be in against the quay, landing rays when everyone else had herring nets in.' Some of the more boisterous of the gig men tempted providence by boasting, 'We're going to drive the liners out of the Channel.' Their aspirations were badly shaken up by the first gale. John Peake Murt remembered being caught out in the Channel in skipper Edward Bassett's *Blush Rose*: 'We had to bail out with the biscuit tins we took our croust in.' The gigs were lucky to get in safely but the decked liners made their trips with no problems. In October 1923, Skipper Mike Peters' gig *Cutty Sark* lost her whole fleet of lines.[15] She was unique among the St Ives gigs in having been rebuilt from the old seine boat *Harmony*. Initially the gigs were fitted with 'iron man' hand-powered line-haulers. When the Britt petrol-engined jinny arrived in 1926, several of the gigs fitted them.

The crew of the Hart family's gig *Guide Me SS 106* overhauling their longlines. The *Guide Me* was built in 1921 and sold from St Ives in 1936.

Eden SS 85, a successful longlining gig.

In May 1925 the St Ives fishermen were struggling with low fish prices and high expenses. Line fish were plentiful but as the *Western Echo* reported, 'Working expenses are very high, the cost of bait and fuel sometimes absorbing the whole price of the catch,' a dispiriting experience for the fishermen. Two years later, at St Ives, 'fair catches of long-line fish' were fetching the following prices: rays 2s 11d, and 5s per stone; skate 1s 5d–1s 7d; large flake (spur dog) 6s per score; ling from 2s to 4s 6d each; conger from 30s per lot downwards; turbot from 19s 6d per lot; and cod from 13s per lot down.[16]

Barney Thomas remembered lining in the *Young John SS 18*: 'We were dependent on dogs all the time.' The marketing of spur dogfish as 'flake' or 'rock salmon' by the fish and chip shops was a help to the Cornish line fishermen but, at 6s per score, they needed to catch boatloads of them to get a living.

In June 1928, Cornwall's Fishery Officer reported,

> These boats, when travelling to and from the fishing grounds, often cover a distance of from 120–150 miles. Few people outside the industry realise the immense amount of labour entailed in baiting, shooting, hauling and clearing a line, consisting of from 3000 to 5000 hooks, and extending from five to nine miles in length.
>
> On many occasions, several of these boats have returned to port with catches that have not realised sufficient money to meet the heavy expenses incurred. Many of the men engaged have not earned 10s per week per man for the season's fishing ... a great number of boats have been laid up.[17]

Another problem for the liners was the increasing numbers of trawlers on the fishing grounds. It has always been difficult for static gear boats, liners, netters or crabbers to coexist with trawlers, which have to tow their gear along to fish. Between the world wars there were many trawlers from Brixham, Lowestoft, Milford Haven, Ostend, Heist and Boulogne on the West Country grounds. The Cornish fishermen were generally slow to adopt trawling, and sometimes complained of their lines being towed away by trawlers. In September 1931, the *Western Echo* reported,

> Foreign trawlers had given the local liners considerable trouble through fouling their gear and seriously interfering with their fishing operations ... Foreign trawlers

Longline fishermen and dogfish.

Skinning
and cleaning
dogfish at
Looe. (Raddy
and Son)

continued to land good catches at Newlyn which usually realised fair prices. There were about 120 of these vessels fishing around the coast.[18]

The Newlyn longliner *First PZ 31* put to sea on Wednesday 9 March 1927 and shot her lines 20 miles south of the Bishop Rock. They were about halfway through hauling when their engine stopped. They cut their lines and marked the end with a dan. After restarting the engine, they picked up their middle dan but, unfortunately, the line parted. They headed for the end dan and were about to pick it up the when the dan light blew out. After a further search, in heavy seas with a strong wind, Skipper Richard Cattran decided to shelter at Scilly, and they arrived in St Mary's at about 8.00 on the Thursday night. The *First* put to sea on Friday morning and headed back for her gear, where they spoke to the crew of the Porthleven liner *Snowdrop PZ 144*. Their misfortunes were not over, as the *First* sprang a leak. Although both her steam and handpumps were used, she could not be saved. In response to their shouts, Skipper Wesley Hosking took the *Snowdrop* alongside, and the *First*'s crew jumped for safety with their decks already awash. Skipper Hosking later said,

> It was a very lucky job for them that our boat was at hand. Had it been dark, or had it been the day before, when they were alone, then all hands would have gone down with the *First*. We heard their shouts but did not think they were in such a plight until we got there then. On getting within reach, we got them all on board without mishap, although there was a big sea running at the time, and the decks of the *First* were awash.[19]

The *First* had been built for St Ives as the steamboat *James and Edgar SS 163* in 1918. With four other St Ives boats, she made an unsuccessful herring voyage to the North Sea in 1920. At the time of her loss, she was fitted with 55-hp Gardner and 26-hp Kelvin engines. She carried no punt so, but for the arrival of the *Snowdrop*, they would have been lost. After a long career from Porthleven, Newlyn and Mevagissey, her rescuer the *Snowdrop* (PZ 144/FY 104) is still afloat, rigged as a lugger.

There were other hazards. On a fine summer day in 1930, the Mousehole longliner *Emblem PZ 26* was heading for the lining grounds west of the Bishop Light. Mr Leslie

Hicks, the 'driver', had just checked the engines and emerged on deck into the sunshine. At that instant, a feed pipe to the engines broke and, within seconds, the engine room was full of flames. The blaze quickly devoured the cabin bulkhead, driving the crew on deck, with the last man, Jack Humphries, escaping through the skylight. Fortunately Skipper Nicholas Thomas Humphries was nearby in the *Orion*, and he rescued them and their dog Peter from the blazing wreck. Skipper Hicks said, 'If it was not for Necky Tommy we should have drowned. Our punt was leaky as a basket.'[20]

In June 1931 the Pender family's Mousehole longliner *Lyonesse PZ 81* came into Newlyn with a staggering shot of 2,050 stones, made up of 1,000 stones of ray, 550 stones of dogfish, 200 stones of skate and 300 stones of ling, cod and conger, which earned £180.[21]

The St Ives longliner *Iverna SS 41*, skipper John Stevens, left Newlyn for the Wolf grounds at 4.00 a.m. on Thursday 17 September 1931. They shot their lines twice. On the second haul, they were enveloped in thick fog and were surrounded by coasters all sounding their foghorns. They got under way at about 1.00 on Friday morning, and slowly headed for Newlyn. They spotted the outline of the Runnelstone buoy and shortly afterwards struck the rocks at Porthcurnow. The crew tried to attract attention by burning their bed sacks, but she was hidden from Treen coastguard station by the high cliffs. After waiting two hours for the tide to ebb, the crew got ashore in their punt, climbed the cliffs and walked to the coastguard station. The *Iverna* quickly broke up in the heavy groundswell.[22]

Rodda Williams and Ben Batten's Newlyn longliner *Peel Castle PZ 17* had better luck when coming in from lining on Tuesday 22 September 1936. In dense fog, she struck the ledges at Carn Dhu about 10 o'clock at night. Fortunately she was sailing dead slow and the sea was quiet. They went astern and got off safely, with some damage to the bows and keel.[23]

In August 1932, over seventy Mount's Bay and St Ives boats were pilchard driving out of Newlyn, but eighteen of them persisted with the more arduous longlining.

Two St Ives mackerel drivers and the longliners put to sea on Monday 1 May 1933. While they were hauling their lines during the night, a strong south-easterly gale sprang up and strengthened into a severe storm during Tuesday. Their lining grounds were 60 miles north-west of St Ives Head. Not until Wednesday were all the boats safely back on their

Skipper Leslie Hicks' Mousehole longliner *Emblem PZ 26* was lost by fire in 1930. (T. H. Victor)

moorings. While none of them were damaged, there were heavy and expensive losses of gear. Skipper Tommy Toman's *Nellie SS 101* lost seventeen baskets of lines, and Skipper Matthew Stevens' (*Gentry*) *Sheerness SS 10* ten baskets. Skipper Philip Thomas' large motor lugger *Young John SS 18* had her mizzen sail blown out. The Mount's Bay liners, 'The Baymen' in St Ives speak, were caught out in the same blow and, while most of the bigger boats made it safely back to Newlyn, the smaller craft ran for shelter at Scilly.[24]

Expensive losses of lines could be crippling, but there were sometimes happy endings. The Newlyn longliner *Asthore PZ 182* was caught in the storm of Friday 17 May 1935 and had to run for home, leaving her lines on the fishing grounds. She put to sea on the Sunday, set her log just off Mousehole and towed it for 40 miles. After a brief search, they spotted their dan and hauled in a shot of ray, skate and round fish, which fetched £31 on Monday's market. The *Penlee PZ 85* was less lucky. She was so badly damaged that she needed expensive repairs. The *Penlee* and *Asthore* were among the smallest liners in the Newlyn fleet.[25]

In July 1934, the magazine *The Motor Boat* published a record of a lining trip in the *Boy George PZ 576* of Porthleven, which was 40 feet 9 inches long, with a beam of 11 feet 5 inchess and draught of 4 feet 8 inches, powered by a Ruston & Hornsby 27-hp diesel and a paraffin engine on the port quarter. The Porthleven and many East Cornish liners caught their own bait in pilchard nets, a system sometimes called 'Faith, Hope and Charity': Faith that the nets would provide enough bait, Hope that the lines would catch a worthwhile shot and Charity that the buyer would pay an economic price for it.

The *Boy George* left Porthleven at 8.45 p.m. and shot her fifteen 50-yard-long pilchard nets 10 miles off the Lizard. After drifting to the nets, they started to haul just after 10.00 and had enough pilchards to bait their lines. 'The real labour then began. *Boy George* was carrying 19 baskets of line with hooks attached every 10 feet. There were 2,400 hooks, and each had to be baited, 800 of the catch of pilchards being cut up and used for this purpose.' They started to shoot at 12.50, and the gear was all out by 2.10. They started to haul at 3.30.

A small petrol engine in a casing against the starboard bulwark was started up. This motor drives through a clutch, a jenny wheel for hauling in the line … One man

Newlyn longliners *Asthore PZ 182*, *Penlee PZ 85* and *Peel Castle PZ 17* at work.

operates the jenny; another stands with hook in hand, peering over the side into the depths. When a fish appears on the line, he helps it over the side with the hook; with a jab and a twist of the same instrument he releases the hook from its mouth and then heaves it over the coaming into the fish hold. The other members of the crew debait the hooks as the line comes inboard, coiling the latter up neatly in the baskets. Round one side of each basket, at the top is a piece of cork, into which each hook is pressed.

As I stood and watched the work proceeding, I marvelled at the way in which the fishermen kept their hands out of the way of the hooks. The line came over the wheel with hooks flying, but was handled almost casually. The line was in by 6.15 and they headed for Newlyn. There, the writer reports, a catch of 112 ray, 37 conger, one skate and about 800 pilchards, the result of 20 hours work on the part of five men, being sold to a group of (apparently) uninterested buyers at Newlyn for a little over £5.[26]

Three Newlyn longliners, the *Trevessa PZ 203*, *Penlee PZ 85* and *Two Boys PZ 214*, had a narrow escape from being run down by the Cunard liner *Berengaria* in thick fog on the morning of Thursday 21 March 1935. They were fishing 15 miles south-west of the Bishop. The skipper of the *Trevessa* saw the outward-bound *Berengaria* heading straight for them. He ordered full speed ahead and they just managed to clear the liner's bows. They were so close that they were able to read her name and hear her lookout call, 'Small craft ahead, sir,' and the huge liner's siren sounded.[27] The Brixham smack *Compeer BM 21* was enveloped in the same thick fog 6 miles west of the Lizard when she was struck by the steamer *Vinemoor*, and sunk with all three crew.

The St Ives liners took another battering in April 1937. They left home at about 1.30 on Monday 19th and steamed for five hours north-north-west to their ground 36 miles off in the Channel, where they shot their lines. On Tuesday the wind veered to north-westerly and increased to storm force. In Bassett's Bay, Skipper William Barber's *Our John SS 64* was swept by a wave, which damaged her wheelhouse and rudder and swept her punt on to the rail. The *Sheerness SS 10*, which had her mizzen sail blown out, entered harbour near low tide and grounded at the end of Smeaton's Pier. She put a rope ashore, and over 100 local and Breton fishermen dragged her into safety, where five Camaret crabbers were already sheltering. Skipper Edward Toman's *Nazarene SS 114* had to cut away a basket of lines with its buoy rope and dan. She was the last to arrive home on Tuesday evening.[28]

On Sunday 9 May Skipper Billy Capps' *Forget Me Not PZ 47* was hauling her lines in the Channel when they saw the crew of Skipper Jack Williams' longliner *Betty INS 198*, burning a *flambeau*. The *Betty*'s Bolinder engine had broken down. After hauling her lines, the *Forget Me Not* towed the *Betty* into Newlyn.[29] The *Betty* was towed in from another lining trip by the *Cornishman PZ 120*. Unfortunately the problems persisted and she was laid up in Newlyn Old Harbour, where she eventually disintegrated.

During the Second World War, most of the large West Cornish motor boats were requisitioned by the Royal Navy, and many of them served far from home. Admiralty regulations limited deep-water longlining. Their place was taken by a fleet of modern, efficient refugee Belgian trawlers at Newlyn, where the only large local boats remaining were the *Mayflower PZ 51* and *Acacia PZ 319*, until the *Renovelle PZ 107* and *Mayon Castle PZ 123* were released from the Navy. Local legend credits Skipper Dick Worth of the *Mayflower* with some very risky lining trips. In view of the dangers of lining, the *Renovelle* was fitted with a winch and coiler, and went seining for white fish very successfully, landing at Brixham, Plymouth, Mevagissey and Newlyn. Her skipper, Eddie Madron, was helped by Ted Yallop of Lowestoft who had pioneered seine netting in the steam drifter *Nelson LT 516*.[30] The *Renovelle* was one of very few Cornish boats to try seining, which requires clean, unobstructed grounds. Some of the refugee French boats at Newlyn were longliners, including the *Espérance* of Le Portel

(Boulogne), remembered as 'crewed by old men', and Skipper Prosper Couillandre's auxiliary sloop *Ruanez ar Mor Au 1074* from the Île de Sein. Prosper was a very talented fisherman whose landings earned him the respectful title of 'The Turbot King'. He returned to Cornwall after the war in the new motor liner *Marie Edith Au 2451*.[31]

The war years had allowed the depleted fishing grounds to restock, and with peace in Europe the Cornish boats got back into their traditional fisheries, often with good landings at controlled prices.

The Newlyn liner *Goodwill PZ 12* had not long resumed her peacetime career when, on 21 May 1946, an explosion blew the 'driver', Fred Hitchens, out of the engine room and set fire to her. Penzance fire brigade speedily extinguished the blaze and pumped out the *Goodwill*, which was badly damaged.[32]

Despite the very great success of the Belgian trawler fleet during the war, lining continued to be the main way of catching white fish in the early post-war years until the Stevenson company began to build up its fleet of ex-Admiralty 75-foot-long motor fishing vessels (MFVs). In January 1949, the *Cornishman* commented on the changing scene:

> Deep sea trawling is taking the place of long lining, pilchard, herring and mackerel fishing, which had been the main types of fishing for many years.
>
> Pioneers of deep sea trawling at Newlyn have been Messrs W. Stevenson and Sons who have five former MFVs converted into trawlers, while several others are in private ownership; their craft have all done well, in the new venture, comparing favourably with the Belgian and French trawlers which visit the port.[33]

However, the liners were by no means done with, and they continued to make their mark in the Cornish ports. Conditions had certainly improved from the penurious interwar years. In September, the *Cornishman* reported, 'LONG LINING SEASON BEST FOR YEARS.'[34]

Longlining got off to a slow start in 1949, with difficulty in finding bait in July, but most boats made a successful season, although complaining about the increasing numbers of foreign trawlers on their grounds. They were fishing well on dogfish in September 1950,

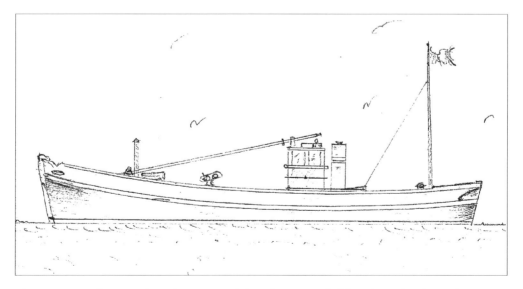

The *Espérance* of Le Portel, Boulogne, one of the refugee French fishing boats longlining from Newlyn during the Second World War. (Raymond Peake, Newlyn)

Lining in the *Sweet Promise* of St Ives. (Dan Uren and Donald Williams, courtesy of Carole Catteral)

The *Cynthia Yvonne PZ 87* landed 1,000 stones at Newlyn.

several catching their own bait in pilchard nets, and others buying squid bait from the trawlers, when the *Asthore PZ 182* had the misfortune to lose seven baskets of line, towed away by a large steamer.[35]

Fishing was a dangerous business. In April 1950, Arthur Sampson of the Newlyn liner *Snowdrop PZ 144* was taken to West Cornwall hospital to have a hook removed from his hand. Newlyn Mission was looking after injured fishermen from the East Coast drifters *Lord Hood LT 20*, *Olivia* and *Playmates LT 180*, the Brixham trawler *Roger Bushell BM 76*, which had three crew struck by a wire after her trawl 'came fast' on the Wolf grounds, and several French fishermen.[36]

As always, the top fishermen broke records. In August 1962, Skipper Sidney Thomas' Newlyn liner *Cynthia Yvonne PZ 87* (ex *Rosebud*) landed a 1,000-stone shot, of which 700 stones were ling. This fine haul came from only fifteen baskets of line.[37] On Tuesday 25 September, Skipper Ernest Stevens Junior brought the St Ives liner *Sweet Promise SS 80* home with a shot of 573 stones, including 364 stones of ray, 203 stones of turbot and 6 stones of conger, which fetched £555[38]. This shot probably came from the shore grounds where the St Ives men used sand eel bait caught by their 'linsee' gigs. The *Cynthia Yvonne* landed other excellent shots of 1,200 stones on 28 June 1963, and over 700 stones in July after a slack start to the lining season.[39]

At St Ives, the fish was punted to the shore and carted to the lifeboat slipway, where it was spread out for sale. Dan Uren, James 'Maffis' Perkin and Skipper Ernest Stevens with the *Sweet Promise*'s punt, and Ben Phillips with his horse and cart, one of the most photographed characters in Cornwall. (Carole Catteral)

Skipper Ernest Stevens' new *Rose of Sharon SS 118* running the traditional trip for local children on her arrival from Forbes of Sandhaven in April 1964. (Shelldrake Collection, St Ives Archive)

In April 1964, Skipper Ernest Stevens Junior showed his faith in the future of the industry by the arrival of his new 54-foot longliner *Rose of Sharon SS 118* from Forbes of Sandhaven, near Fraserburgh.[40] In 1968, she was followed by the 57-foot liner trawler *Spaven Mor PZ 47* for Ron Jenkin and Ian Downing from the newly revived Porthleven Shipyard,[41] and two years later the slightly beefier *Girl Pat PZ 87* for Skipper T. Thomas.[42] These two fine craft, the first large vessels built at Porthleven for forty years, replaced the Newlyn veterans *Asthore* and *Cynthia Yvonne*. Not to be outdone, Ernest Stevens built a new *Rose of Sharon FR 23* in 1969.[43] Too big for her home port of St Ives, the *Rose of Sharon FR 23* had a long and successful career from Newlyn until finally being sold in 2003. The *Spaven Mor*, *Girl Pat* and *Rose of Sharon* (2) were all liner/trawlers, a sign of the current trend. Pilchard driving was no longer a serious alternative to lining.

Raymond Stevens remembers lining in the first *Rose of Sharon SS 118*: 'There was a big tide so we went upalong and shut for dogs. Ernie said, "We'll go into Newquay for fish and chips." Half a crown they cost. When we hauled, we had 500 stone on the first 15 baskets, one on every hook. And we had one basket full for all the rest.'

In 1978, Skipper Tommy Thomas also took another step up, building the 84-foot steel trawler/liner *Girl Pat III PZ 87* at the McTay yard on Merseyside.[44] Michael Hosking of Porthleven had skippered the 47-foot liner *Heather Armorel PZ 155*, then the larger ex-

Longline baskets at Newlyn. (Michael Pellowe)

Ron Jenkin's and Ian Downing's *Spaven Mor PZ 47*, built by Porthleven shipyard in 1968, one of a new generation of liner/trawlers. (Michael Pellowe, 1973)

Scots boat *Kilravock BS 18*. In January 1975, his 86-foot steel *Dew Genen Ny PZ 185* arrived from John Lewis of Aberdeen. After an excellent start on the Cornish mackerel, she went lining. In 1977 she made a record shot of 2,600 stones of ling, which grossed £6,153, while fishing 80 miles west of Scilly.[45]

On 21 June 1978, skipper Godfrey Hicks' 62-foot-long Newlyn longliner *Karenza PZ 85* was working 50 miles north of St Ives when the diesel cooking stove caught fire, filling the cabin with smoke and driving her crew on deck. Their 'Mayday' distress call was answered by Skipper David Williams of Porthleven in the *Gamrie Bay BF 141*, who plucked all seven crew from their life raft. The blazing *Karenza* was sunk by HMS *Shoulton* as a danger to navigation.[46] Skipper Hicks was the nephew of Jack Hicks, who had escaped through the skylight of the burning *Emblem PZ 26* thirty-eight years before.

During the 1970s there were dramatic changes in the Cornish fishing industry. Massive shoals of overwintering mackerel attracted palaegic vessels from Scotland, the Humber, Holland, Scandinavia and the Eastern Bloc countries. The short-lived boom in crawfish netting developed into netting for dogfish, hake and wreck netting. Beam trawling and deep-water netting, using miles of nets, developed during the 1980s.

Lining could not remain unaffected by these new fisheries. Despite a very successful swansong, working new deep-water grounds, in much bigger, abler boats than the little old 1920s liner/drifters, longlining faded away. Probably the last large Cornish boat to go lining was Skipper John Turtle's Newlyn netter *Ben Loyal WK 3*, which in the 1990s was spending the last three months of each year lining for conger as an alternative to netting.[47] Cornwall's static-gear white fish boats are now netters, not longliners.

CHAPTER 9

Crabbing: Fishing for Lobsters, Crabs and Crawfish

A century ago, little sailing boats, usually miniature luggers, fished with crab pots for lobsters, crabs and crawfish all around the Cornish coast.

Most of these crabbers fished from coves like Port Isaac, Sennen, Penberth, Prussia Cove, Cadgwith, Coverack, Mullion and Portloe. The bigger ports of St Ives, Mousehole, Newlyn, Porthleven, Mevagissey and Looe usually concentrated on the more expensive but more profitable drift net fisheries, though Porthleven and Mousehole had their fleets of crabbers.

CRAWFISH. LOBSTER. CRAB.

Crabbers hauled up at Porthgwarra, c. 1900.

The boats sailed out to their crab pots but the actual fishing was done using oars. Each crab pot was fastened by a short rope, called the 'leg' or 'strop', to the 'backrope' to make a tier. The space between each pot was 10 fathoms. The number of pots in a tier depended on the size of the boat; in these early times, up to ten or a dozen.

Each tier has a buoy rope and dan float at each end. Every day the crab pots are pulled in, the lobsters, crabs or crawfish removed, and new bait, usually salt mackerel or gurnards, fastened inside the entrance. Until recent times, this was the main use for gurnard, but its excellent flavour has become better known and it is now popular with restaurants.

Crab pots were usually shot on rocky ground, where lobsters, crabs and crawfish live. Little crabbers could often be seen working right under the cliffs along rocky shores. The fishermen knew when they were on sandy ground, as the sand stuck to the back rope when the gear was hauled.

When the pots are hauled, they are carefully stacked, each in its right place around the deck. When shooting the gear, first the dan and buoy rope are shot. The back rope begins to fly overboard as the boat goes ahead. Each pot is thrown over in turn. The fisherman must always know which pot goes next, before the back rope pulls it out. A mistake is dangerous.

The back rope was hauled over a roller, which fitted over the stem post, or in later years over the starboard bow. This was a simple pulley wheel, which revolved in the end of a stout piece of wood. There were local names for this rope roller; it was called the 'bulljowler' in St Ives and the 'timmynoggy' in parts of Mount's Bay.

During the fifteenth century, piers were built at some of the coves by the local landowners, but this really took off from the nineteenth century, and coves like Mullion, Portloe and Sennen were provided with more shelter.

A lively picture of the Cornish shellfish industry in 1876 is provided by the Parliamentary Report on the Crab and Lobster Fisheries, compiled by Frank Buckland and Spencer Walpole and published the following year. It discusses overfishing, the impact of rail transport on marketing, minimum landing sizes, closed seasons, and how the fishery might

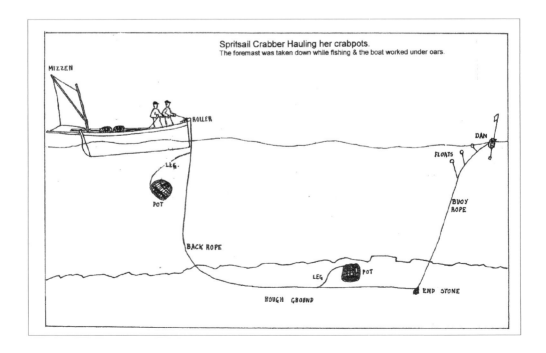

Spritsail Crabber Hauling her crabpots.
The foremast was taken down while fishing & the boat worked under oars.

Crabbers getting ready at Cadgwith. The buoy ropes and dans are on the beach. This card was posted in 1913.

be regulated. Several well-known Cornish personalities of the time gave evidence: James Pawlyn and Matthias Dunn of Mevagissey; Cadgwith lifeboat coxswain Edward Rutter; Penzance Mayor W. Rodd; Edward Pengelly of Looe; and Richard Nicholas of Sennen. The Sennen fishermen said they were doing fine and simply wanted to be left alone to get on with their work. No interfering legislation for them! Sennen was a vibrant fishing community, its twenty-two boats and sixty–seventy fishermen working from Scilly to Padstow and beyond. The Report gives the numbers of crabbing boats working from each port in 1876:

Mevagissey 7
Gorran 24
Portloe 26
Fowey 6
Looe 20
Portscatho 6
St Mawes 13
Sennen 22
Porthgwarra 6
Prussia Cove 9
Cadgwith 10
Mullion 4
Porthallow 9
Durgan 10
Polperro 7

The numbers of crabbing boats had risen from six at Gorran in 1836, seven at Sennen in 1826, five at Cadgwith and seven at Looe in 1856. Some witnesses were concerned about declining catches. James Jane of Durgan said more boats meant less fish.

There were some general, and perhaps predictable, grouses about lack of fish, too many boats, low prices and obtaining bait. At St Mawes, Durgan, Penzance, Looe and Polperro, the crabbers complained that they could not work during the drift net fishing. Drift nets and crab pot buoys would tangle up. There was little crabbing at St Ives, which then had a summer pilchard drift fishery. It could be that the development of potting there only happened after its pilchard boats started going to 'round land' Newlyn to fish.

Boats seemed to have averaged about forty crab pots. The St Mawes boats carried forty-five; at Prussia Cove, there were forty-five pots in three strings of fifteen; and at Cadgwith forty pots in six strings of six–seven, set 10–15 fathoms apart. Shellfish were kept for market in store pots, big versions of withy pots, at Cadgwith, and in 'cruives' at Prussia Cove. Cruives were floating wooden boxes 9 feet long, 3 feet wide and 1 foot 6 inches deep. At Cadgwith, well smacks ('vivier' smacks) came about every nine days to buy shellfish. Other ports sent their shellfish away by train or by the Hayle–Bristol steamers to obtain better prices. Big crabs fetched up to 1s 3d each. Smaller crabs counted as two for one.

Trammel nets were set to catch bait. They could also catch up to a third of a crabber's shellfish. Skate, ray, wrasse, gurnard and mackerel were used for bait, and often salted down. More controversially, small or soft crabs were broken up for bait or to bait wrasse pots, although many witnesses said this was penny wise.[1] 'On the Cornish coast and in the Scilly isles a small pot of withies finer than in the crab and lobster pots is used for the capture of wrasse.'[2]

Lobster smacks played an important role in the shellfish industry. Robert Scovell, fish merchant, owned eight of the twenty-two lobster smacks sailing from the Hamble River. He bought crabs and lobsters from Start to Scilly and at Sennen, from France and in Ireland from Cape Clear to Bantry Bay. In 1875, his smacks brought home 108,499 crabs and crayfish and 88,296 lobsters.

The numbers of crabbers had increased at the start of the twentieth century. About 300 boats and 600 fishermen worked from Cornwall's coves, most of them shellfishing. Gorran Haven, near Mevagissey, had the most, with thirty sprit-rigged boats of about 16-foot length. Sennen Cove is more exposed than Gorran, so its twenty-four luggers were larger, at 18–22 feet long. There were twenty-one at Cadgwith; twenty at St Mawes, soon to be entirely devoted to tourism; twenty between Port Isaac and nearby Porth Gaverne; eighteen at Portloe, all clinker built; and sixteen at Porthleven harbour,[3] which also had a bustling fleet of mackerel boats, pilchard drivers and 'half and halfers', which were a cross

The Cornish Maritime Trust's Gorran Haven crabber *Ellen*. Thirty sprit-rigged sailing crabbers worked from Gorran Haven. (Sylvia Pezzack)

Oneida PZ 284 of Sennen, built at St Ives for Nicholas of Sennen, 1903.

between the two. St Ives also had a large fleet of narrow clinker-built gigs, very different craft from the stocky cove boats, which went crabbing during the summer before getting stuck into their autumn herring season.

The Sennen fishermen were unusual for working away from home in the Isles of Scilly and even at Lundy Island in the Bristol Channel, where in 1869 they were encountered by the eccentric yachtsman Empson Middleton. Middleton, who was making a single-handed circuit of England in his 23-foot yawl *Kate*, was loud in his praise of the Sennen men, who moved with their families to Lundy during the crabbing season. A coaster collected their shellfish every ten days for sale on the London market.[4]

Middleton was not the only yachtsman to admire the seamanship of the Cornish crabbers. In 1906 Herbert Warington Smyth wrote of the spritsail crabbers found off South Cornwall,

> They are a very smart class of neatly built little vessel, and with one or two men are handled in any weather ... One of them I once met outside, running in before a strong sou'wester, with the peculiar sprit mainsail which the western men like ... with her two hands in their oilies standing up looking out for their crab-pot buoys. How they kept their feet as the tiny craft, with scarcely 16 inches freeboard, rolled and lurched top-heavy before that wind and sea was a mystery, and we watched them with admiration.[5]

He also gave an affectionate tribute to the cove fishermen:

> I doubt if any finer boatmen are to be met with than the crabbers ... whose little open boats may be seen hauled up inaccessible cliff paths in the rough exposed coves among the cliffs, or ranging wide at sea twenty or thirty miles from their capstans in any weather that a boat may live in.

In the spring of 1902 the first Breton crabber, Skipper Pierre Douguet's *Aventurier C 896* of Camaret, arrived to fish the crawfish in the Isles of Scilly, and immediately struck gold. On his first day, he caught a phenomenal ninety-six large crawfish and thirty-two lobsters. Pierre Douguet had been told about the rich grounds around the Seven Stones by the crew of the English well smack *Welcome* when she visited Camaret on her way to buy shellfish at the Île de Sein. The *Aventurier* was soon followed by a large fleet of *langoustiers* (crawfishers) from Camaret, Loguivy and Le Conquet.[6] Despite their generally cavalier attitude to the British 3-mile limit bordering territorial waters, many of the Bretons established good relationships with the locals at Scilly, St Ives and Newlyn.

In April 1903, the *Cornishman* reported the Bretons poaching at Scilly and commented,

> It is true the Scillonians rarely visit the Seven Stones now for the purpose of fishing, though the Cornish fishermen sometimes do so; and it is equally true the Frenchmen seem to be greatly superior to us in their modes of fishing, and in the gear they use. They also tell us that if Scilly belonged to them, there would be a population of something like ten thousand people, living entirely on the fishing industry.[7]

While the Bretons were fishing a bonanza, Mr Pezzack, Cornwall's Fishery Officer, reported in November that crabbing in Cornwall had been very unsuccessful due to two months of bad weather and heavy losses of fishing gear.

Not surprisingly, there were sometimes problems with the French visitors. When Cornish crab pots were lost, as sometimes happened in the normal course of events, the foreigners were blamed, as in August 1907 at St Ives.[8] Further allegations were made there in June 1910, when the pilchard boat *Geen* lost 1½ dozen pots and the gig *Lily John* 2½ dozen in fine weather.[9] Some Mousehole fishermen also made complaints about the Bretons fishing on the Seven Stones.[10]

The Cornish cove boats had to be shallow draught to be easily hauled up and launched. This could affect their sailing qualities, and some were fitted with centreboards, as were some St Ives gigs, an unusual feature for sailing fishing boats.

The St Ives pilchard boat *Golden Lily 14 SS* going to sea crabbing. Built in 1896, she was fitted with a motor in October 1912.

In the 1913 Harmsworth Report on fitting engines to Cornish boats, far-sighted Fishery Officer Stephen Reynolds wrote,

> The western Cornishmen, with their pride in their big deep sea boats, describe the East Cornishmen as 'fishers in their own puddle'. At all events, the East Cornishmen have succeeded in fishing a living out of their puddle, and it is possible that the western Cornishmen will, sooner or later, be driven to withdraw from competition with steam, and to develop in smaller boats the mixed and shellfishing resources of their puddles.

Events were to prove him right.[11]

As in all fishing, marketing the catch was the key to success. Shellfish buyers' smacks visited Cornwall and the Isles of Scilly, from Hamble and Plymouth, throughout the nineteenth century. These smacks were all fitted with wet wells (viviers) in which their shellfish were kept alive. They continued to visit until the 1930s.

In the twentieth century they were joined by vivier smacks from Roscoff in Brittany, which bought crawfish at Newlyn. In April 1905 the *Cornishman* reported from Newlyn, 'The French lobster smack Jean Baptiste arrived on Monday, this being her first visit for the year, for the purpose of buying shellfish.'[12] Recently Skipper Robert George recalled, 'When the French lobster smack anchored in Penberth to buy my Grandpa's shellfish, the skipper came ashore. The mousse [cabin boy] brought him ashore in the punt. My Granny always made apple pie and cream for the little boy. He loved it!' The schooner *Madeleine Charles* came in the 1920s. She was followed by M. Alexandre Oulhen's Dundee (ketch) *Lutin* in the 1930s, the *Maryannic* and *Rosko* in the 1950s, and in the 1960s the *Plomarch*, which bought crawfish from local merchants W. Harvey & Sons. The arrival of the Roscoff Ferry service in 1973 made the shellfish carriers redundant. Vivier lorries took over shellfish exports.

Like the rest of the Cornish fishing fleet, the crabbers were fitted with motors during the First World War. These were often 7-hp or 3½-hp Kelvins, which were started on petrol

St Ives fishermen with their wire crab pots, 1920s.
(Shore Shelter Collection)

and then changed over to cheaper paraffin. To prevent their spark plugs getting damp between trips, some thorough fishermen took them home and put them in the oven. The fitting of motors reduced the size of the cove fleet to 220 boats, crewed by 460 men, by the early 1930s.

In February 1919, despite the high cost of gear, the crabbers were encouraged by good shellfish prices to put out their crab pots early. Unfortunately, heavy gales destroyed many of these pots and ruined the rest of the season.[13] In June 1924 the Fishery Officer reported that shellfish were so scarce that sometimes 100 pots were hauled for no catch. Shellfish sent to Billingsgate had failed to cover the cost of its transport.[14] There were more heavy gear losses in March 1925. In September 1930 Tommy Stevens's ('Blue') St Ives crabbing gig *Lead Me SS 50* lost eight dozen pots.[15]

Motors did not always provide security. In May 1925, the St Ives crabbing fleet was caught out in a south-east gale and many boats struggled to reach port. One with engine trouble was towed in by another crabber. Yet another also had motor problems and lost her mizzen mast. She was towed in by a French sailing crabber. No doubt the old salts shook their heads at the sight of a motor boat being rescued by a pure sailing craft.[16]

From the mid-1930s the crabbers were fitted with 'dollies', mechanical haulers. These were improvised using old lorry back axles. A drive shaft came forward from the front of the engine under the bottom boards. The back axle was used to turn the corner, to create a vertical shaft on which the capstan was fitted. Many early capstans were made of wood, which gave a good grip on the rope.[17] These back axle capstans survived until the introduction of hydraulic drives from the 1960s.

The most popular Cornish crab pot was undoubtedly the dome-shaped 'withy pot', which was also used in Devon, Ireland and, in earlier times, in Normandy and Brittany. A crabbing crew would make about 150 crab pots over the winter, together with four or five withy store pots where the catch was kept alive.[18] Large floating wooden storepots were also used. Withy pots were made at about one per man per day. There was also much extra work in cutting and trimming the withies. The willows were cut in November and December. Many fishermen had their own withy gardens.[19]

The north coast of Cornwall is afflicted by shallow water and heavy groundswell, which could quickly destroy the effective but vulnerable withy pots, so St Ives and Newquay fishermen made their pots out of strong wire supported by several hoops around the

The St Ives gig *Endeavour SS 23* going to sea to shoot her crab pots. (Andy Smith, courtesy of Nigel Stevens)

Above left: Mullion motor crabber hauling her withy pots. The dolly (winch) can be seen just to the left of the forward fisherman.

Above right: Making withy crab pots at Porthgwarra.

Right: Making St Ives wire crab pots, 1930s. Skipper Nicholas Polmeor, R. C. Berriman and Phillip Noall 'Sparrowhawk' of the gig *Silver Spray SS 28*. (David Berriman)

circumference. These would last two seasons in contrast to the withy's one, but perhaps did not fish so well. Port Isaac later adopted these wire pots for the same reason.

The pots were baited using 'skivvers', sharpened pieces of wood. The skivver was passed through the bait then firmly inserted into the inside of the woven mouth of the pot. Skivvers were often lost, so other crabbers used bait strops, lengths of cord with a running loop. The bait went into the loop, which was pulled tight. The bait was placed inside the mouth, and the strop was passed through the mouth and made fast on the outside of the pot. Baiting with skivvers was much quicker. Each pot had two baits, one either side of the mouth.

Shellfishing was largely brought to a halt by the Second World War, as the British population was in desperate need of food, and shellfish were regarded as a luxury. After the war, it took off again and, despite low prices, was initially very successful, as stocks had regenerated. Fishing materials were in short supply, and this supply was controlled.

Shooting crab pots in Nicholas Polmeor's *Silver Spray SS 28*, 1930s. (David Berriman)

Excellent PW 102, a typical South Devon crabber, built for the job. (Port of Lowestoft Research Society)

Skipper George Stevens of the *May SS47* recalled, 'You couldn't get rope for crabpot backrope, as shellfish was a luxury, but you could get miles of it, as much as you liked, as long as it was for trawl warps.'

With the increase of tourism during the 1950s and the reduction in catches after the post-war boom, the Cornish crabbing fleet declined in numbers, but there were other developments. Next door in Devon, Browse brothers of Paignton were developing their own specialised crabbing business and fishing fleet.[20] Unlike the multipurpose Cornish boats, which might be crabbing one summer and pilchard catching another, the Devon crabbers, many of them built by Dixons of Exmouth, were purpose-built for crabbing. They were fully decked with a low freeboard and graceful sheer, high bulwarks, broad gunwales and a capstan forward at the break of the foredeck. Their decks were completely unobstructed, unlike the Cornish drifters, whose decks were full of net room and fishroom hatches for working drift nets. They were excellent modern boats, ideal for the job, and crabbing took off in South Devon. The Devon crabbers also improved the fishing gear. More rugged versions of the traditional withy pot were made of metal frames covered with net. They were very effective.

In the early 1960s, skin divers discovered that they could dive and collect crawfish in a sack. Shellfish divers were quickly recognised as bona fide fishermen by the Cornwall Sea

Fisheries Committee, despite the misgivings of the traditional potters. Their boats were registered as fishing vessels, and many sailed from Hayle and other Cornish ports. Within a short time, the skin divers accounted for half the Cornish crawfish catch.[21] However, as was discovered a decade later, the crawfish was not an inexhaustible stock.

At the same time, there was a revival of shellfishing on the north coast. Several Mount's Bay crabbers – including Cecil Hosking's *Provider PZ 19*, Charlie Laity's *Robert and John PZ 100* and the *Morning Star PZ 31* from Porthleven, W. Harvey & Sons' *Gillian Claire PZ 404* and *Dos Amigos PZ 60*, Ed Downing's *Ocean Pride PZ 134*, Dick 'Johnnie Conger' Sampson's *Ibis PZ 146* and Dick 'Glasses' Samson's *Coeur de Lion PZ 74* – came to work from St Ives and Hayle. The French market had improved the demand for crawfish, and many of these boats used cylindrical French-style crab pots very succesfully. These were introduced by Barlow Richards of Ashton who, after a career driving a traction engine and threshing machine, became a successful crawfisherman.

In the 1950s, the elderly Breton motorised sailing crabbers were replaced by fine modern motor boats, which made a big impression in Cornwall. The Audierne boats that arrived

Skipper Ed Downing's *Ocean Pride PZ 134*, with French-type pots aboard at St Ives, 1963, one of many Newlyn and Porthleven boats to fish from St Ives and Hayle.

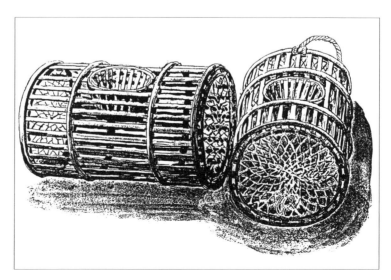

During the 1960s, French-style crab pots were worked by many Cornish boats.

from the late 1950s were all fitted with echo sounders and radios, and manned by go ahead and progressive fishermen. All the Breton crabbers had a vivier shellfish tank in the bottom of the hold to keep the catch alive. The water could flow freely through the vivier through slots cut in the bottom of the boat. (Modern large crabbers have pumped vivier tanks, which can be pumped empty to access the catch.) In 1964, British territorial waters were extended from the traditional 3-mile limit to 12 miles, 6 miles for those with traditional rights to fish. This effectively barred the Bretons from most of their fishing grounds around Cornwall.

Many of their boats were soon for sale, and were bought in Cornwall. Probably the first was the crabber *Nicole Au 2422*, which was wrecked on the island of Beniguet while running shellfish to Audierne in November 1965. Fortunately, Skipper Frank Newell, Barlow and David Richards, Jo Saly and Jason Weare got ashore safely.[22] In 1966, John Burt of Newquay bought the *Bacchus Cm 3027* of Camaret and registered her as *PW 251*. John and his crew worked her in the same way as the Bretons. They returned to Camaret for engine refits and to buy the very successful 'Crystal' crab pot rope. In 1968, Jim Richards of Marazion bought the Audierne sardiner/crabber *François and Jeanette Au 2322* and registered her as *PZ 22*. Jim told Pat Crockford of Falmouth that the *Étoile du Marin Au 2293* was for sale and she became *FH 4*.[23] In 1977, Pat Crockford replaced the *Étoile du Marin* with the fine new French-style wooden vivier crabber *Celtic Mor FH 403*, built by Hinks of Appledore. Other French crabbers bought in Cornwall were the *Mez Creiz Cm 3150* (*PZ 105*) in 1969, *Notre Dame de Rosaire Au 2287* (*PZ 379*) in 1971, *Kalon Breizh Cm 3165* and the *Dom Bosco* (*Celtic Crusader PW 78*) in 1987. In 2007 the *Dom Bosco* was extensively refitted, and sailed from Newlyn for Rowse Fishing under skipper Mario Perry.

In 1961, Porthleven harbour was bought by Wykeham & Co., who were determined to revive the port and its activities.[24] They invested heavily in Porthleven shipyard, which was to turn out many high-quality vessels. They also built their own fishing vessels, the very traditional *Sadie Whykeham PZ 287* (fitted with drift net hatches at a time when pilchard driving was in sharp decline), and the open crabber *Audrey*. Ahead of their time were their high-speed crabbers *Priscilla PZ 347* and *Anna PZ 248*. These were of hard-chine hull

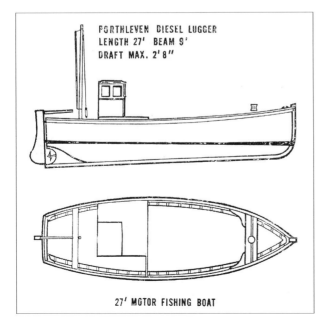

PORTHLEVEN DIESEL LUGGER
LENGTH 27' BEAM 9'
DRAFT MAX. 2'8"

27' MOTOR FISHING BOAT

Porthleven shipyard's traditional Porthleven crabber *Audrey PZ 234*. (Porthleven shipyard)

design, with wheelhouses forward. They were fitted with pot davits, which raised the crab pots to working height as they were hauled. This did away with the chore of 'boating' pots, lifting them over the side.

During the 1970s the crawfish stocks were decimated by netting. Crawfish and lobsters had been the mainstay of the crabbing fleet, with low-value crabs taking a lesser role. However, from now on, the fleet depended largely on crabs. This resulted in much more gear being worked. In the 1960s a large crabber worked seven tiers of thirty crab pots. By the end of the twentieth century, this would be 1,000 pots in tiers as long as 100. There were technical changes to achieve this. The 'slave hauler' or 'V wheel' hauls the backrope by itself. No one is needed to haul the rope off the capstan. Hydraulic drives mean that machinery can be sited anywhere in the boat. Crab pots are now factory made and covered with netting. 'Parlour pots' are escape proof; once shellfish get in, there is no getting out. Bait is now fitted in elastic bands or bait bags. Baiting is much quicker now that there are no bait strops to tie. A tier of 100 pots can now be worked almost as fast as a tier of thirty could forty years ago.

In 1987, Newlyn shellfish merchants W. Harvey & Sons bought the *Enfant d'Arvor Cm 3080* and renamed her *Julian Paul PZ 245*. After a long and successful career from Newlyn

Porthleven Fisheries' traditional Cornish crabber *Audrey PZ 234*, foreground, and the high-speed crabbers *Priscilla PZ 347* and *Anna PZ 248*, 1964.

W. Harvey & Sons of Newlyn's crabber *Michael and David PZ 436*, skipper Robert Jones, shooting her gear. (Susie Jones)

she was lost in May 2004 at Le Deben near Roscoff, after landing her catch to Viviers de la Meloine. Fortunately, Skipper Stuart Trembath and his four crew were speedily rescued.[25] Harvey's acquired a little fleet of French boats, which were named after members of the family: the *Michael and David PZ 436*, *Matthew Harvey PZ 190*, *William Harvey PZ75* and the *Rachel Harvey*, ex *Le Cap AD 279014*, which sadly was lost at Scilly and replaced in 2003[26] by the *Vagabonde des Mers J 612*. Like the *Dom Bosco*, the *Vagabonde* had been fitted with a shelter deck and completely modernised. In August 1996, Harvey's Newlyn crabber *Rachel and Daniel PZ 243* was lost off the north Brittany coast after a fire in her engine room, while running 6 tonnes of crabs to Le Deben. After a four-hour search in thick weather, the Île de Batz lifeboat rescued her four crew from their life raft.[27]

Skipper Rowse bought the Camaret crabber *Stereden va Bro*, which as *TO 5* fished very successfully until halted by a fire aboard in 2003. In 2010, Rowse Fishing, led by Mark Rowse, worked the large shelter deck crabbers *Intuition TO 40*, *Dom Bosco TO 60* and the 25-metre former beam trawler *Emma Louise TO 50* from Newlyn. All three crabbers were registered in Truro. In 2012, the *Emma Louise* was replaced by a new state-of-the-art steel crabber of the same name, built by Toms of Polruan.[28] Since all undersized shellfish are returned to the sea, a crabber's baited gear feeds the local shellfish stock until it is big enough to be caught.

Of all the Cornish ports and coves that sent crabbers to sea at the start of the twentieth century, only a minority are still active, often with just a few mackerel punts working part-

Skipper Rowse's *Stereden Va Bro TO 5* working her gear. (Glyn Richards)

Rowse Fishing converted the steel beamer *ABS PZ 203* to the crabber *Emma Louise TO 50* in 2007. She is pumping water through her vivier tank to keep her shellfish catch alive.

Fast crabbers at Port Isaac, June 2007. Port Isaac reinvented itself as a shellfishing port.

PW 104 running into Port Isaac, April 2011. There are several of these Cygnus Cyclone class boats in Cornwall.

time. Newquay which was a commercial port in the nineteenth century, and welcomed fleets of Porthleven herring boats in the early twentieth, before taking off as a fishing port in the 1980s with big investment in a modern fleet of netters, which it retains.

Port Isaac, whose fishing fleet had declined since the big herring landings of the 1920s, built a fleet of modern high-speed potters during the 1970s and 1980s, several of them the well-known Lochin 38-footers capable of steaming off to the Lundy grounds at 15 knots.[29] By 1980, the port's shellfish landings had risen to over £100,000.

In Penwith, Penberth and Boat Cove near St Just built up fleets of modern mackerel punts and ran their fish to Newlyn by road each evening. Cadgwith built fine wooden traditional crabbers like the 28-foot *Cornish Light* and 23-foot *Princess* in the mid-1970s,[30] and has more recently adopted modern fibreglass boats, fitted with every electronic aid, eight of which at present work from the cove.

There are still many small crabbers working in Cornwall. Most of these work 'self-shooting'. Instead of each crab pot being manually shot from the rail, each tier is carefully lined up in order on the deck. Once the dan and buoy rope have been shot, the backrope pulls each pot out through a door in the stern as the boat steams ahead. For this, it is important that the backrope and crew are quite separate. Economic pressures have forced many fishermen to work single-handed. Safety is paramount. If an accident happens, there is no one else to help.

Many Cornish resorts have become famous for the high quality of their award-winning restaurants. The continued landing of high-quality shellfish is part of this success story.

CHAPTER 10

Trawling

A trawl is a stocking-shaped net that is towed along the bottom of the sea to catch the fish that live there, white fish or *demersal* fish like cod, ray, turbot, haddock, pollack and soles.

The traditional Cornish way of catching these fish was with longlines. In the past, Cornish fishermen hated trawling because they said it caught small fish and destroyed their spawn. They were angry that their longlines were cut by trawlers towing over them.

Brixham fishermen probably invented trawling in Britain. They were certainly the most successful in developing it, and opened up new trawling grounds in the English Channel, North Sea and Bristol Channel early in the nineteenth century. They were probably the first to trawl the Trevose ground off the north coast of Cornwall, near Padstow. The main catch from the Trevose was high-value sole. In the early days, Brixham did not yet have its own *BM* registration, and its boats were registered in Dartmouth with the letters *DH*. The Brixham trawlers were joined on the Cornish grounds by vessels from Plymouth, Lowestoft and Ramsgate. By the mid-1870s, 60–100 Plymouth and Brixham sailing trawlers were at work off West Cornwall from February to April, landing their catches at Newlyn, which then possessed neither an adequate harbour nor a white fish market, for transhipment by rail.[1]

Sailing trawlers, known as smacks, used a 'beam trawl'. It was kept open by a long pole called a 'beam'. On each end of the beam were metal frames called 'trawl heads', which lifted it 3 or 4 feet off the seabed. These trawl heads slid over the sand as the smack towed along. The trawl net was fastened to the beam and trawl heads. The bottom of the trawl was fastened to the ground rope, which stretched along the seabed in a curve from one trawl head to the other.

Smacks towed their trawls with one large rope called the 'warp'. Near the net, two ropes, the 'bridles', went from the warp to the trawl heads at each end of the beam. From the late 1880s, smacks hauled their trawls with a steam capstan, powered by a boiler below decks. Before then, a hand winch was used. Soles bury themselves in the sand. The fishermen put chains called 'ticklers' across the mouth of the net to dig the soles out of the sand.

At the end of each tow, the beam was hauled alongside by the capstan. The iron trawl heads were lifted up with tackles until the beam was on the smack's rail. Next the net was hauled up by hand until they got to the end, the 'cod end' which held the fish. This was hoisted aboard with a tackle, the cod end knot released and the catch spilled on to the deck where it was sorted and gutted before being put below in the fish room.[2] Since, at the end of their days, Brixham smacks had only three crew, there was an immense amount of hard physical work involved, even with the help of the steam capstan.

Padstow's Doom Bar was a dangerous place, and the local lifeboats went to many smacks. In April 1900, both Padstow lifeboats – the *Arab* and the steam-powered *James Stevens No. 4* – were wrecked going to the Lowestoft smack *Peace and Plenty LT 387*,

Lowestoft smack
Excelsior LT 472.
(Steve Martin)

which was also wrecked with the loss of three of her crew. The *James Stevens* was driven ashore with the tragic loss of her two stokers and two engineers, who were trapped below. The second *Arab* lifeboat saved the Milford steam trawler *Birda* in March 1903. In February 1904 she saved the four crew of the Brixham smack *Annie*. In January 1906 she brought in another 'Brickie', the *Hadassah*. In February 1911 she escorted in the *Sunflower* and *Crimson Rose* of Lowestoft.[3]

In February 1910 the Lowestoft smack *Vigilant LT601* disappeared with her five crew while fishing from Padstow. It was thought that she had been sunk in collision. A relief fund for the crew's dependants was started in her home port.[4]

Although they were among the most seaworthy craft ever to sail, the Brixham smacks were not immune to the power of the sea. During the storm of 16 December 1910, four of them – the *Eva, Marjorie BM 246, Speedwell BM 213* and *Vigilance BM 218* – were lost with all hands in the Bristol Channel. The *Friendship BM 244* lost two of her crew overboard off Lundy, and the smack and two survivors were only saved by the efforts of Skipper Albert Gempton of the *Gratitude BM 25* and his crew. Altogether eighteen Brixham fishermen were lost in this disaster.[5]

In February 1911 the smacks were fishing well, with several landing 250 pairs of soles from the Bristol Channel at Newlyn and others landing 150 pairs from the Wolf grounds. Prices were £3 18s–£4 16s per fifty pairs. A year later, in April 1912, the *Cornishman* reported landings of 2,000 pairs of soles from ten Brixham smacks at prices of £3 16s–£4 per fifty pairs.[6]

Research on the 1911 Census by Tony Pawlyn shows the massive impact of the Lowestoft, Brixham and Ramsgate smacks on Cornwall. On 2 April 1911, two steam trawlers, ninety-three Lowestoft smacks, twenty-four from Brixham and twenty-one from Ramsgate (total 138) were based at Padstow, and another eleven Brixham vessels worked from Newlyn. There were also forty-one Lowestoft steam drifters and two from Yarmouth, twenty-four at Newlyn, fourteen in Penzance Dock and five at Scilly.[7] It might be argued that the Cornish fishing fleet had become almost irrelevant on its own grounds. T. C. Lethbridge recalled, 'As a boy at Falmouth before the 1914 War, I remember seeing over a hundred Brixham trawlers in the harbour at one time.'[8]

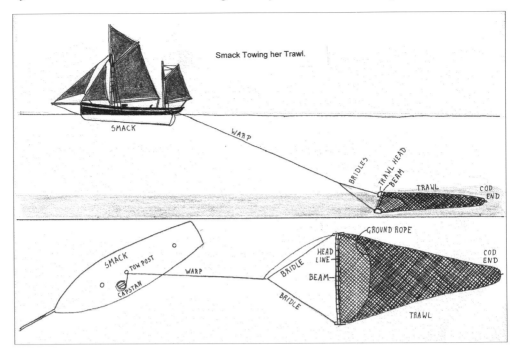

Smack Towing her Trawl.

Lowestoft smacks
LT 1693 and
LT 134 Zercon
leaving Padstow.
The *Zercon* was
sunk by a German
U-boat on 13
February 1916.

    While fishing in Mount's Bay in the early morning of 11 April 1911, the *Sabrina BM 210* struck the *Wingrove BM 152* amidships. The *Sabrina*'s stem was driven in and she sank half an hour later. Her crew were rescued by the *Wingrove*.[9]

    Steam trawling took off in Grimsby and Hull from the 1880s. The first English steam drifter was built in 1897, and soon some of these vessels were fitted for trawling, when they were not chasing the herring and mackerel shoals. In the early 1900s, steam drifter/trawlers from Lowestoft and Yarmouth began to join, and then gradually to replace the fleet of smacks working the Trevose grounds each spring. The Yorkies, as the Cornish called them, arrived in Padstow each January, straight after the Plymouth herring season, and worked there until May. Many of the Lowestoft fishermen liked to enjoy Padstow Mayday and see the hobbyhorse. The London & South Western Railway arrived at Padstow in 1899 and greatly improved fish selling opportunities. In 1911 work began on a large trawl dock alongside the fish market.

Plymouth's first steam trawler, the *Reginald PH 75*, recently built of iron by Cochrane of Selby, was registered in October 1901. On 5 July 1902 she went ashore in fog at Clapper Rocks, St Mary's, Isles of Scilly. Her eight crew picnicked on the nearby rocks while waiting for the flood tide to float her off.[10]

In April 1904 the local paper recorded steam trawlers from Hull and Milford sheltering in St Ives Bay as well as local, Lowestoft, Dutch and French mackerel drifters.[11] Two years later, the *Cornishman* reported Brixham and Lowestoft smacks on the local grounds, together with 150 Lowestoft and Yarmouth drifters.

Nearly all the trawl landings in Cornwall were made by non-Cornish boats, as the Cornish fishermen still concentrated on the traditional mackerel, pilchard and herring drift fisheries, but several local fish merchants invested in smacks. Benjamin Ridge of Newlyn acquired the *Budget PZ 10* and the *Try PH 14*, which was sunk by a German submarine while trawling south of the Wolf in March 1916. Her crew were rescued from their punt by the patrol boat *Sunbeam II*. Fish merchants T. A. Pawlyn of Mevagissey and G. F. Pawlyn of Plymouth and Padstow were involved in the ownership of the smacks *Godrevy LT 475* built in 1909, *Brissons LT 351* built in 1914, *Pentire LT 742* built in 1910 (all three built at Rye), *Hepatica BM 29* and *Peto BM 297*, largely with the profitable spring trawling from Padstow in mind.[12] On 12 March 1917, eleven smacks were sunk by a German submarine on the Trevose grounds. The Royal Navy responded by fitting several vessels with motors and guns.

On 29 November 1920 the French five-masted schooner *Capitan* was in sinking condition 14 miles off the Lizard, and her thirty-eight crew took to their three boats. The Brixham smack *Vigilant BM 273* stood by the derelict, and rescued the French seamen in worsening weather.[13] In contrast to the powerful smacks, the St Ives miniature trawler, converted from a lug-rigged 'jumbo', was remembered as not going very far: 'She was out there in the Bay, tied fast by the ass, going nowhere.'[14]

Plymouth steam trawler *Reginald PH 75* aground at St Mary's. (Gibson of Scilly)

The smack *Godrevy LT 475*, built at Rye for T. A. Pawlyn of Mevagissey in 1909. Pawlyn's were much involved in the development of Padstow fish market. (Tony Pawlyn)

Lowestoft drifter trawlers at Newlyn: *Hosanna LT 167*, *Lord Collingwood LT 183*, *Pêcheur LT 228*, *BTB LT 1153* and *Lord St Vincent LT 79*. (Penzance Morrab Library)

Lowestoft drifter/trawler *Smiling Thru LT 1274* wrecked in fog while heading for Padstow, 20 April 1924.

Unlike the smacks with their beam trawls, steam and motor trawlers used the 'otter trawl', which was kept open laterally by 'trawl doors'. The otter trawl has two wire warps instead of one rope one. A warp goes to each trawl door, which is attached to the side of the net called the 'wing'. The warps are fastened to special brackets on the trawl doors, which keeps them towing at an angle. This angle makes the water push the doors apart to keep the net open laterally. Nowadays, instead of being attached straight on to the net, the doors are attached to the net by long wires called 'bridles'. These bridles travel over the sand and drive the fish in front of the net. This enables the trawl to fish a much wider space. There is a lot of slate, which can rip open trawls, on the Trevose grounds. The men were kept busy mending nets.

The steam drifter/trawlers made a success of the annual voyage to Padstow but, in later years, many of them sailed from Milford Haven and Fleetwood, where operating costs were cheaper.[15] On 20 April 1924 the Yarmouth drifter trawler *Smiling Thru* was lost after striking rocks in Trevone Bay while heading for Padstow in thick fog.[16] She had been built as the 'standard drifter' HMS *Neaptide* in 1920. In February 1937 the Lowestoft drifter/trawler *Beacon Star LT 770*, which was well known in Newlyn, was lost with all hands while heading for Padstow.[17]

There were very few Cornish steam trawlers in the early twentieth century: the *Rebecca SS 118*, *Edgar SS 66*, *Gleaner SS 89*, *Adventure PZ 655* and *Pioneer PZ 277* (which is still afloat, having been rebuilt by Jim Richards). These were all small vessels 45–55 feet long. Raymond Peake recalls how the *Pioneer* hauled her trawl with an 'iron man' hand winch: 'I used to go aboard her when I was a little boy of 9 or 10 (c 1932). She only had two crew and the iron man forward. The iron man was used for hauling the trawl.'[18]

The fitting of motors to the Cornish fleet enabled a few of them to go trawling. As described earlier, the 38-foot pilchard boat *Gleaner SS 123* was fitted with an engine in November 1909. In 1913 she spent from January to May trawling the Trevose grounds out of Padstow.[19]

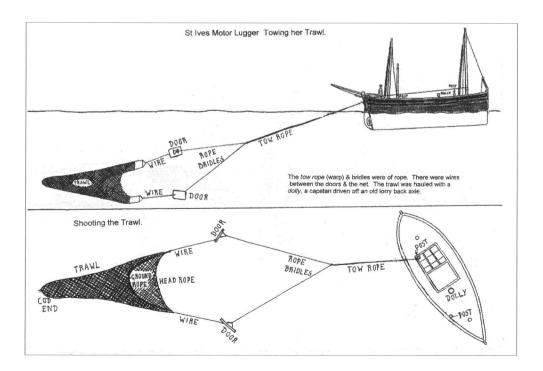

The little steam trawler *Pioneer PZ 277* at St Ives, 1930s. She hauled her trawl, which is hanging up to dry, with the iron man line hauler on the bow.

There were no large trawlers owned in Cornwall, just some small gigs and pilchard boats which hauled their trawls by hand, until capstans, powered from the engine through old lorry back axles, arrived from 1936. On 24 May 1920, Skipper James Penberthy's pilchard boat trawler *Joseph SS 77* struck a rock off Hor Point while heading for St Ives after trawling off the Brisons. She was salvaged and continued her trawling career.[20] The following month, a similar fate befell the little *Sea Bird SS 68*, wrecked on the western side of St Ives Island while returning from trawling.[21]

During the 1930s the modern Belgian motor trawlers from Zeebrugge, Heist, Ostend and Nieuport extended their fishing around Cornwall and the West Country. With their diesel engines and cheaper fuel, these vessels were much more economical to run than the coal-burning drifter/trawlers. They began to land very profitably at Newlyn, where their agents were the Stevenson company, landing catches worth £15,000 in 1930. The *Western Morning News* whipped itself into a frenzy about this development, reporting on 18 May 1931, with the headline 'THE BELGIAN INVASION, BLOW TO WESTERN FISHERIES':

> The invasion of the Channel fishing grounds from Portland to the Isles of Scilly by the fleet of Belgian motor trawlers has perturbed the Westcountry trawlermen, who fear that intensive operations with trawls of a much smaller mesh ... will have a devastating effect on the western grounds.[22]

In a previous article, it wrote of a 'War' between the Cornish fishermen and the 'powerful fleet of Ostend trawlers', which were reaching the early morning markets at Newlyn before the local boats. This was quickly contradicted by local fish salesman Mr Stevenson, who denied that the Belgian landings at Newlyn affected the local longliners, which were catching different species. He said that the Belgians shopped in the village and got on well with the locals.[23]

In September 1931 it was alleged that foreign trawlers towed over the Cornish longliners' gear. There were said to be 120 foreign trawlers around the coast. They were landing good catches at Newlyn for fair prices.[24]

Right: Inshore trawler *Boy James SS 77*, ex *Joseph*, 1930s. She has a back-axle capstan and two posts for shooting the rope tow rope and bridles.

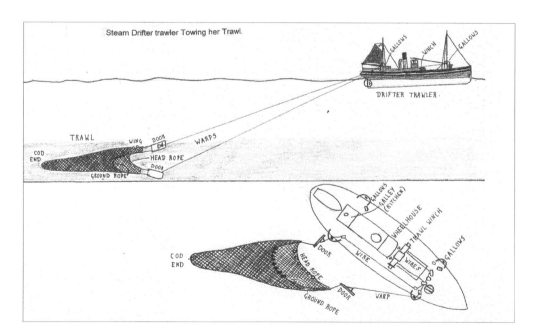

Many other trawlers from Lowestoft, Milford Haven, Fleetwood, Grimsby, Hull, Boulogne and Dieppe visited and sometimes landed at Newlyn. All these steam trawlers were powered by coal, and they frequently called at Newlyn and Penzance for bunkers. A drifter or drifter/trawler needed more than 10 tons of coal a week. In 1903, 1,500 tons of coal was shipped into Newlyn every week to bunker the steam boats.

On 2 April 1927 the Cardiff steam trawler *Miura CF 45*, returning from trawling off Scilly, was lost ashore at Morwenstow with only one survivor from her eight crew.[25] In

The Ostend trawler *Jeanine O 278*, built at Vlaardingen in 1913, regularly fished around Cornwall and landed her catches at Newlyn. She was owned by Gonzales.

Belgian trawlers at Brixham during the Second World War. Each has the Belgian flag and *Belgie* painted on the bows. *O 348 J Van Merlant, O 270 Rafael Gabrielle* and *O 265 Victoire Roger*. With the preparations for D-Day, the Belgian fleet moved to Newlyn.

1931, fifty or sixty steam drifter/trawlers were expected at Padstow after a good season the previous year.[26]

There were declining numbers of the graceful Brixham sailing smacks, which had found their home grounds much more difficult to work due to the large number of wrecks of ships torpedoed during the First World War. In 1926 there had been over 100 Brixham smacks fishing around Cornwall. On Sunday 6 May 1934 Skipper Marshall's smack *Eureka BM 374*, which had been anchored off Newlyn North Pier, was driven ashore near the Bolitho Gardens. Her crew of three, including seventy-one-year-old John King, who was unperturbed by the incident, got ashore in their punt, but their trawler was smashed to pieces.[27] One of her crew was summoned for debt at Torquay the following day. His wife explained to the judge that his previous month's share was four pence!

On 18 May 1935 Skipper Alf Lovis and the crew of the *Torbay Lass BM 163* performed one of the most remarkable acts of seamanship ever, when they towed in to Newlyn the disabled Appledore schooner *Welcome*. The *Torbay Lass* had no engine, and the wind was right in her teeth. The same gale damaged the *Valerian BM 161*, which was fishing off the Wolf, and Skipper John Pillar's *Lucetta BM 331* off Trevose.[28]

In 1940 the Nazis invaded the West, and Holland, Belgium and most of France were quickly overrun. Much of the Belgian fishing fleet escaped to the UK and fished throughout the war years from Fleetwood, Brixham and Newlyn, where nearly all the larger boats had been called up as naval auxiliaries. Despite the dangers of mines, enemy aircraft and E-boats, the progressive Belgian fishermen kept Newlyn and Brixham afloat as fishing ports during the war years.[29]

As during the First World War, most of the East Coast grounds became unsafe for fishing and many of the trawlers that were not requisitioned came to work from Fleetwood and Milford Haven. Several Lowestoft trawlers worked from Padstow, including the pioneer motor trawlers *Togo LT 69* and *J.A.P. LT 245* and the motor smacks *Pilot Jack LT 1212*, *Flag Jack LT 1224*, *Boy Clifford LT 1202*, *Helping Hand LT 1239* and *Holkar LT 18*.[30] Although built as pure sailing vessels, the smacks were relatively new ships, dating from the 1920s. These vessels were owned by Diesel Trawlers and Podds of Lowestoft.[31]

After the Second World War, the Stevenson company of Newlyn acquired many of the 75-foot-long wooden MFVs (motor fishing vessels) built as naval auxiliaries during the

The Lowestoft motor smack *Pilot Jack LT 1212* and drifter trawler *Togo LT 69* landing at Padstow, 1940. (G. Ellis)

PZ 196 Trewarveneth, one of a fleet of wooden trawlers acquired by Stevensons of Newlyn in the post-war years. (Michael Pellowe)

war. These rugged vessels were refitted as trawlers, and Newlyn began the move away from the traditional line and drift net fisheries towards trawling. These sturdy craft included the *Jacqueline PZ 192*, *WandS PZ 193*, *Roseland PZ 194*, *William Stevenson PZ 195*, *Trewarveneth PZ 196*, *Sara A Stevenson PZ 253* and *Anthony Stevenson PZ 331*. At this time, many Cornish fishermen had no experience of trawling, and several Newlyn trawler skippers originated from Belgium and Lowestoft. The trawl was still pulled in mainly by manpower and these vessels usually had crews of six. These changes were noted by the *Cornishman* in January 1949:

> Deep sea trawling is taking the place of long lining, pilchard, herring and mackerel fishing, which had been the main types of fishing for many years.
>
> Pioneers of deep sea trawling at Newlyn have been Messrs W. Stevenson and Sons who have five former MFVs converted into trawlers ... their craft have all done well in the new venture comparing favourably with the Belgian and French trawlers which visit the port.[32]

Trawling was also becoming more important for small boats. William Stevens of St Ives remembered, 'The gigs used to go out trawling on the Two Hour ground when it was fine weather in the summer. It used to take them three hours to get up there, they didn't have much power. When I was a boy, I used to help Father aboard the White Heather SS 8.' When the gig *Boy Richard SS 148* needed more power for trawling, they simply added a third engine. (It was explained to a boy who asked, 'Why 3 engines?' 'Well, one is to drive the boat ahead, the other one is for when we shut the net and the other one is to boil the kettle.') In October 1947 several pilchard boats shipped trawls when the pilchard shoals failed.[33]

In April 1950 three crew from the Brixham motor trawler *Roger Bushell BM 76* were injured when she 'came fast' on the Wolf grounds and a wire parted.[34]

Despite the expansion of trawling, the Breton fishermen wryly asserted in the late 1950s that 'fish die of old age around Cornwall'! Mevagissey had only one trawler, the aged (1904) *Chrystobel FY 3*, and St Ives two, the *Girl Renee SS 78* and *Francis Stevens SS 49*, and the gigs *Trevose SS 63* and *Our Boys SS 150*, which hauled their trawls with back axle dollies. There were no trawlers at Looe, which is now second to Newlyn as a

Skipper Tommy Toman, centre, and Tom Pearce, left, mending the trawl aboard the St Ives gig *Nellie SS 25*, 1950s. (Penlee House Museum, Penzance)

In the early 1960s, Mevagissey had only one trawler, the veteran *Chrystobel FY 3*. The first artificial fibre trawls used in Cornwall were made of orange courlene. They did not need hanging up to dry. (J. Salmon Ltd, Sevenoaks, Kent)

Cornish trawling port. In November 1952 the veteran Newlyn trawler *Our Katie PZ 697* caught such a large bag of dogfish on the Pits ground that it could not be got aboard, and the bag split while she was trying to tow it home to Newlyn. Current rules forbid the landing of dogfish.

It was often foreign trawlers which led the way, as in November 1950: 'A spate of trawlers, local, French and Belgian, have landed at Newlyn, many dispatching fairly large catches of ray. One Belgian, last Thursday landed about 1,000 stone.'[35]

In 1957 the Stevenson company began buying larger vessels, starting with the 90-foot former MFV *St Clair*, which quickly established a reputation for staying at sea when the weather had driven smaller vessels into port. In March 1961, she landed a record 1,400-stone catch, which earned £1,000, then a record, on Newlyn market.[36] Skipper George Lacey also famously caught the submarine HMS *Teredo* off the Seven Stones. Six years later three similar wooden ex-MFVs were bought from Torbay Trawlers of Brixham. Between 1969 and 1972 Stevensons bought four steel 'Sputnik'-type 22-metre-long pocket trawlers which had been built for Aberdeen during the 1960s: the *Sara Shaun PZ 123*, *ABS PZ 203*, *Karen PZ 193*, and *Bervie Braes PZ 253*. These vessels were adapted at Newlyn for fishing off both sides.[37] At that time, practically all trawlers were side-winders, working their nets off the side in the traditional way.

From 1968 to 1970, as described earlier, three large modern boats were built for West Cornwall: the *Spaven Mor PZ 47* for Ron Jenkin and Ian Downing, the *Rose of Sharon FR 23* for Ernest Stevens, and the *Girl Pat PZ 87* for Tommy Thomas.[38] Although they were longliners, all three were also fitted for trawling. The traditional drift net fishery could not pay for such expensive boats. Other boats like Michael Hosking's *Kilravock BS 18* and Bobby Jewell's *Galilean PZ 131* were bought for trawling.

Meanwhile, in 1969 an event had happened in Brixham that would revolutionise trawling in the West Country. Brothers Tony and Quentin Rae had bought from Holland the twin beam trawlers *Scaldis* and *Sara Lena BM 30*.[39] These vessels worked two beam trawls, one on each side, hoisted out and towed from long derricks. These were updated versions of the nets once used by smacks. The beams were made of steel and there was a

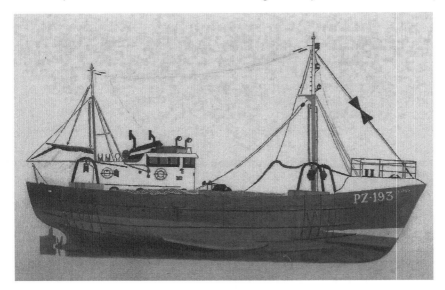

One of four Sputnik trawlers bought by Stevensons, the *Karen PZ 193* at Newlyn, May 1972. (Michael Pellowe)

Skipper Bobby Jewell's *Galilean PZ 131*, ex *French Bijyma*. (Michael Pellowe, Newlyn, 1973)

grid of chains on the bottom of each trawl. The chain mat reduced the number of stones entering the trawl. This gear caught high-value flatfish and was immensely successful. Beaming for shrimps had only started in Ostend in 1961 (though it had been used in Germany for many years) but the method very quickly proved a success for catching white fish too. From the 1970s, many large beam trawlers, all originally built in Holland, were bought for Newlyn, Plymouth and Brixham. While fishing, the beamer does not bring her nets aboard. At the end of each tow, the winch brings both trawls up to the ends of the derricks, alongside the trawler. Only the ends of the nets, the cod ends, are brought aboard and emptied. Many modern beamers have wheels at the end of their beams to reduce friction, rather than the traditional trawl heads.

Tragically, the great success of beaming has not been cost free. In October 1990 the Brixham trawler *Dionne Marie BM 275* capsized and sank while beam trawling.

Fortunately her crew were rescued 15 miles east of the Lizard by the yacht *Jazrah*. In November 1995 the small beamer *Provider FH 6* went missing with her skipper Peter Smith and Paul and Tim Bennett, north of Lundy in the Bristol Channel. In November 1997 Trelawney Fish's 70-foot Newlyn beamer *Margaretha Maria BM 148* was lost with Skipper Robbie Holmes of Newlyn, John and Kerry Todd of Penberth and Vinnie Marshall of Penzance, while fishing 70 miles south of her home port.[40]

Visiting trawlers continued to fish around Cornwall. Padstow lifeboats had numerous 'shouts' to the rugged Belgian vessels working the Trevose grounds, the *Apollo* in February 1973, the *Twilight* in September 1974, the *Okeanos* and *Nautilus* in 1976 and the *Coudekercke* in January 1978. These were all medical calls to help injured fishermen.

With the arrival of beaming, and the mackerel boom of the 1970s, several top Cornish skippers upgraded to bigger vessels. In January 1975 the *Dew Genen Ny PZ 185* arrived from shipbuilders John Lewis of Aberdeen for Skipper Michael Hosking of Porthleven and partners. She began a very successful twenty-five-year career, trawling for mackerel. Three years later Michael Hosking took over the ex-Dutch beamer *Silver Harvester PZ 622*, and Robert George skippered the *Dew Genen Ny*. Both vessels pair-trawled for mackerel off the west coast of Scotland. In 1980 the *Dew Genen Ny* was fitted with rope reels for seining off the south of Ireland and in the North Sea working out of Aberdeen.[41] A well-known Cornish anecdote concerns the *Dew Genen Ny*'s name. When she arrived at Newlyn, an old salt asked what the name meant. When it was explained that it was Cornish for 'God with Us' he said, 'Well I suppose that's another share has got to be took out.'

In 1968 Ron Jenkin, Ian Downing and Stevenson's bought the Dutch beamer *Mariene* from Urk.[42] In August 1978 the Thomas family of Newlyn upgraded again with the 83-foot longliner/trawler *Girl Pat III* from McTay Marine of Merseyside at a cost of £480,000.

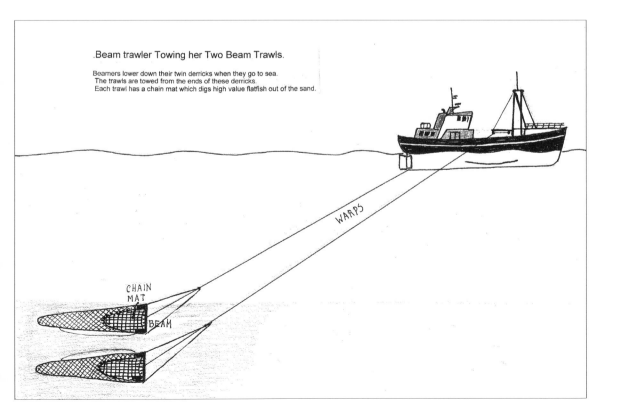

Beam trawler Towing her Two Beam Trawls.

Beamers lower down their twin derricks when they go to sea. The trawls are towed from the ends of these derricks. Each trawl has a chain mat which digs high value flatfish out of the sand.

The beamer *Algrie PZ 199* in Mount's Bay. (Glyn Richards)

Fitted with refrigerated seawater tanks, with the mackerel fishery in mind, the *Girl Pat III* was later converted for beaming.

The Stevenson company also went into beaming big time, acquiring many former Dutch beamers, including the *Aalteje Adriaantje (AA)*, *PZ 198*, *Algrie PZ 199*, *Basil St Clair Stevenson PZ 99*, *Billy Rowney*, *Bryan D Stevenson PZ 290*, *Cornishman PZ 512*, *Daisy Christiane PZ 1172*, *Filadelfia PZ 542*, *Lisa Jacqueline Stevenson PZ 476*, *Sara Cathryn Stevenson*, *St Georges PZ 1053*, *Trevessa IV PZ 193* and *Twilight III PZ 137*. The company also enterprisingly converted the veteran wooden MFVs *Elizabeth Caroline PZ 293*, *Elizabeth Ann Webster* and *Marie Claire PZ 295*, and the steel 'Sputnik' trawlers *Sara Shaun PZ 123* and *ABS PZ 243*, for beaming. Many other beamers have worked from Newlyn, including the *Chloe T PZ 1186*, the Nowell family's *Semper Allegro PZ 100*, *Elizabeth N PZ 100* and *Louisa N PZ 101* and the Corin family's *Sapphire PZ 66*, recently replaced by the larger *Sapphire II*. These vessels have been the mainstay of Newlyn, some of them landing record shots. In April 1986 the *James RH Stevenson* broke the port record with £26,500 for a seven-day trip, landing 150 kits including eighty of soles. She was skippered by her engineer Peter Elsworth. This broke Skipper Robert George's £25,000 record landed by the *Dew Genen Ny* the previous year.

More records were broken by the Stevenson beamers in 2011. On 3 January, Skipper George Stevens and the crew of the *Twilight III PZ 137* landed 420 boxes for £51,648. The next day, Skipper Don Liddicoat's *Filadelfia PZ 542* made £52,377. This was followed by Skipper Peter Elsworth's *Cornishman PZ 512*, with 440 boxes realising £52,802. Cuttlefish were an important part of these successes.[43]

In a recent 'Through the Gaps' Newlyn blog, Laurence Hartwell listed the large number of side trawlers working from Newlyn during the late 1970s and 1980s, including the *Ben my Chree*, *Pathfinder*, *Gamrie Bay*, *Scarlet Thread*, *Keriolet*, *Galilean*, *Ocean Harvester*, *Girl Patricia*, *Confide*, *La Critique*, *Defiant*, *Wyre Star*, *Fern*, *Green Cormorant*, *Nicola Marie*, *Three Lads*, *Rose of Sharon*, *Lia G* and *Marina* as well as Stevensons' *Excellent*, *Jacqueline*, *Trewarveneth*, *Anthony Stevenson*, and *Bervie Braes*. Newlyn had certainly become a trawler port.[44] The majority of these vessels originated from Scotland, though some, like the *Keriolet*, *Galilean*, *Ocean Harvester*, *Ben my Chree* and *La Critique*, came from France, mainly from Brittany. Several French boats were bought for trawling and scalloping in Falmouth and East Cornwall. Some were past their sell-by date. Like the beamers, the number of conventional trawlers at Newlyn had dramatically reduced by 2011.

Skipper Bobby Jewell of the *Galilean* was a popular local preacher, much in demand at Harvests of the Sea. A sermon on Faith included, 'We were down off the Lizard one day and we trawled up a mine. We had a boy aboard with us and he ran away and hid behind the wheelhouse. Now he had Faith. He had Faith that if the mine blew up, the wheelhouse would save him!'

Conventional trawling was also being modernised. Since the trawl was towed astern of the trawler, it might seem logical to work it over the stern instead of off the side, as in the sailing smacks. The first British stern factory trawler, the *Fairtry LH 8*, began work in 1955. She was followed during the 1960s by many large factory stern trawlers for Hull. These big industrial ships hauled their trawls up ramps fitted at the stern. During the 1970s the Bretons began to replace their sidewinder *classiques* by stern trawlers fitted with 'shelter decks' so their crews could work under cover. These vessels were often seen at Newlyn. Soon the sidewinder became a thing of the past, and practically all trawlers were adapted to work over the stern.

The mackerel boom of the 1970s was a shot in the arm for Looe, which became a busy winter mackerel harbour. However, with the destruction of the mackerel shoals by the industrial fleet, Looe did not lose its way as a fishing port, investing in a whole series of inshore stern trawlers including the *Paravel FY 369* in January 1980, *Bilander* in June 1981, *Galatea FY 97* in July 1984, *Danvic of Looe FY 444*, *Maxine's Pride FY 38*, *Innisfallen FY 46*, *Palatine FY 149*, *Cachalot FY 587*, *Kingfisher*, *Genesis* and *Cazadora*. Several were built at the local Pearn yard, and others by Toms at nearby Polruan. Some, like Skipper Hocking's 38-foot *Natalie FY 602*, were built of fibreglass by Cygnus Marine of Penryn. Typical of this new generation of Looe trawlers was the 40-foot-long *Paravel FY 369*, built of Iroko by Pearn for Skipper Mike Soady. She had 15-foot beam and 6-foot draft, and was powered by a 290-hp Volvo Penta diesel. Her cabin and wheelhouse were forward; next came the engine room and the insulated fishroom was aft. She was fitted with a 2½-ton trawl winch and a 3-ton net drum aft. Her modern fit out of electronics included a Redifon radar, Koden echo sounder, Neco autopilot, Decca navigator and plotter and Sailor radio.[45] The Looe trawler men also went pair trawling with some good landings of pilchards. At Christmas 1990 the pair trawlers *Cazadora FY 614* and *Briagha Mara FY 293* landed a massive 10 tons of bass for £66,000. The Looe trawler fleet has been progressively modernised, and fitted with shelter decks, although some are now showing their age. In recent years the number of trawlers at the port has declined from thirty to ten. Looe has recently been overtaken as Cornwall's second fishing port by Mevagissey's diverse fleet of trawlers, netters and sardine ringers, which landed fish worth £2.25 million in the year to April 2012.[46] This compares with about £19 million at Newlyn, which is now the West Country's second port after Brixham.

The next big change in trawling was developed by the Danes during the 1980s, and quickly picked up by the Scots fishing alongside them in the North Sea. This was 'twin rigging'. Two trawls are towed from three warps. The trawls are spread by two doors, one on each side of the rig. The middle wire goes to the 'clump', a weight towed between the two nets. Twin rigging is a very efficient form of trawling adopted by several Cornish boats. Consistently successful has been the Stevens family's *Crystal Sea SS 118*, worked by skippers David and Alec Stevens, which lands at Newlyn and sends her catches to Plymouth.[47] Crucial to her success has been the purchase of enough fish quota to keep her running. The fleet is increasingly regulated, e.g. the fruitful Trevose grounds are closed for part of the year as a cod conservation measure.

The Stevens family's twin rigger *Crystal Sea SS 118* at Newlyn, January 2011.

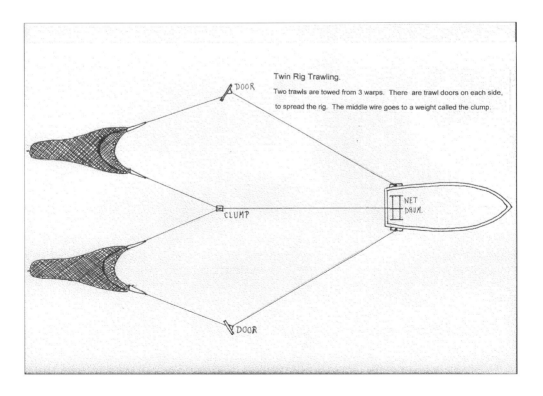

Twin Rig Trawling.

Two trawls are towed from 3 warps. There are trawl doors on each side, to spread the rig. The middle wire goes to a weight called the clump.

While these changes were happening, the boats were being modified to make their work much more efficient. Deck machinery was formerly driven by direct drives like belts and shafts. Since the introduction of hydraulic power, machinery of all kinds can be located almost anywhere in the boat. Sidewinders hauled in their nets mainly by manpower. With stern trawling, the net drum, a giant reel which winds in the trawl, appeared. The catch used to cascade on to the deck, where it was picked up to be gutted and sorted into baskets. Now it is likely to fall into a hopper and be cleaned and sorted at waist height, probably under cover, since all but the smallest stern trawlers are covered over by shelter decks.

The catch is iced and boxed, and often kept in a chilled fishroom. The emphasis is on quality. This emphasis has certainly paid off, as Cornish fish has earned a reputation for high quality and is sought after by some of the country's top chefs. (It is remembered that, until after the Second World War, the fishrooms of Cornish boats were tarred. When fish merchants Suttons of Newlyn protested, the only paint that would effectively cover tar was found to be silver!) All these changes have halved the crews since the 1950s, when a 75-foot-long trawler probably had six crew, but safer shelter-decked boats often fish in much worse weather than was thought possible or safe.

The trawlers have diversified their catches and profited from the TV chefs' campaigns to educate the public about other kinds of fish than cod. This is a success. Hake, monkfish, gurnard (once used exclusively for crab pot bait), pollack, and cuttlefish (destined for Spain and Italy and now landed in such quantities in the winter that it has earnt the title 'black gold') have become more popular.

Cornish fishermen of an earlier generation knew nothing of trawling and loathed it, but their descendants have shown themselves to be highly adaptable, and mastered stern trawling, beam trawling, twin rigging and in some cases prawn trawling, pair trawling for white fish and palaegic trawling for pilchards and mackerel. They have proved themselves to be highly skillful. With the huge reductions in the fishing fleet, many fish stocks have regenerated, and modern Cornish trawlers are landing good catches.

CHAPTER 11

Mackerel Hand Lines and the Industrial Fishery of the 1970s

Until the Second World War, the main mackerel fishing was by the visiting steam drifters, with drift nets, but little boats also fished with hand lines. This was called 'whiffing'. Originally the lines were baited with thin strips of mackerel cut off the side of a fish. Between the world wars, bright metal lures called 'spinners' were used. A spinner could only catch one mackerel at a time, but a boat might tow four lines using poles.[1] Trippers, out for an afternoon's sail, often caught mackerel on spinners.

At Mevagissey, a fleet of little motor sailing boats called 'toshers' was built for 'plummeting', as they called it in the 1920s. Mevagissey toshers were fitted with 3-hp Kelvin petrol/paraffin engines and boomless gaff sails.[2] They were one-man boats, all just under 20 feet long because higher harbour dues were charged for boats of 20 feet and over. These cheap boats with their low expenses enabled fishermen to earn a living when the more expensive motor luggers could not.

After the Second World War, a survey vessel was working off St Ives. One of her crew, a Scots fisherman, is believed to have introduced mackerel feathering to Cornwall. These lines had been used to catch herring in Loch Fyne. Coloured feathers are fastened to the hooks. There can be ten–thirty hooks on a line. This made it possible for hand lines to catch many more fish, up to thirty at a time instead of one.

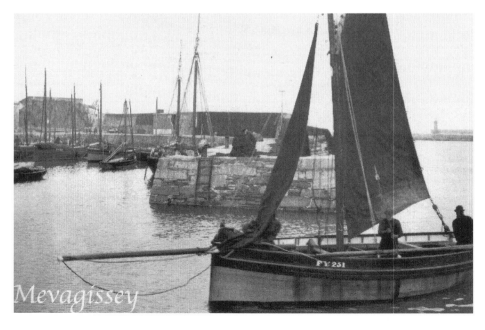

Mevagissey tosher *FY 251*. (With permission of the Royal Institution of Cornwall – RIC.)

Spinning for mackerel. Spinners caught one mackerel at a time.

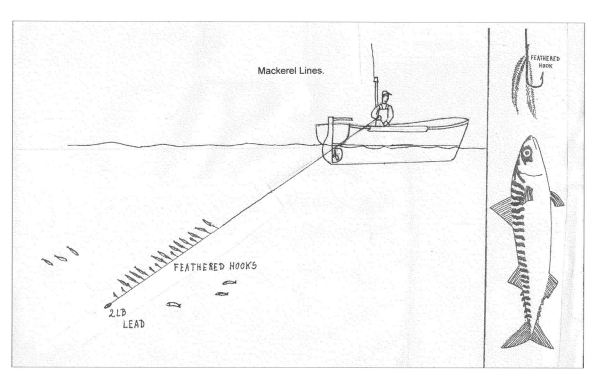

To begin with, feathering or whiffing was carried on only from small boats, usually by part-time fishermen who worked at other jobs during the day and fished before and after work. Feathering was mainly during the summer. Many full-time fishermen scorned whiffing, not seeing it as proper fishing. Others, who began to get a living from it, complained bitterly about part-timers. There was, perhaps, an element of humbug in this. It was said of one vociferous complainer to the local paper, 'He'd take a paint brush out of anyone's hand during the winter!'

Mackerel
handline
boats at
Mousehole,
1964.
(Margaret
Perry)

John Cock's
Bri Al En
FH 234 of
Flushing,
one of
the very
popular
Cygnus
GM32
boats
designed
by Gary
Mitchell.

In March 1949, when the French drifters were landing shots of up to 4,000 stones at Newlyn, handline catches of up to 30 stones were thought remarkable.[3] Before long, much more mackerel was caught by hand lines than by nets. The need for longline bait contributed to demand, but most handline catches were landed in the summer when the market could very quickly be oversupplied, as in July 1963 when gluts caused the whiffers to remain in harbour. In October 1964, the Newlyn hand liners had an unusual end of season bonus of a good run of whiting.[4] In June 1969 the Newlyn mackerel toshers were ignoring the unsettled weather to round Land's End and fish off Pendeen, where they were rewarded with good catches of up to 150 stones.[5]

In the late 1960s, a whole new winter hand line fishery was built up from Looe, Falmouth and Newlyn. There were also some good summer landings, as in July 1974, when 40,000 stones of hand line mackerel valued at £22,000 were landed at Newlyn.

For the first time for many years, young men went fishing for a living. In 1970, 926 tons of handline mackerel were landed at Newlyn. Many new boats were built during the 1970s, among them the Cygnus 32-foot boats, designed by Gary Mitchell and built of fibreglass by Cygnus Marine of Penryn, including the *Crimson Arrow PW 185* for Boscastle, the *Bri Al En FH 234* for John Cock of Flushing, the *Tyak Mor* for the Plummer family of St Ives, the *Kendore SS 245* for Ken and David Brian of St Ives, the *Southern Comfort FY 276*, *Emma Goody FY 276* and the *Rockhopper FH 328* for Robbie Curtis, who promptly brought her in with a record hand line landing of 1,060 stones of mackerel. Typical equipment was a Ford Sabre 100-hp diesel with a 2:1 reduction gear, Seawinch capstan, Graphete echo-sounder, Westminster VHF radio and Decca Mk 21 navigator. Pedestal net haulers had yet to arrive.[6] These very successful boats were developed from the *Trazbar SS 104*, for Andrew *Traz* Treloar and Barney Thomas, and *Louise Johanne SS 106* for Nickey Lander, designed and built for St Ives by Gary Mitchell at Portmellon, near Mevagissey. These two boats were fully decked, unlike the half-decked boats built before then. They were the forerunners of a whole generation of successful Cornish inshore boats.[7]

The Toms boatyard at Polruan developed a very popular class of wooden half-decked 32-foot boats fitted with steering shelters forward, including the *Sea Prince*, *Compass Rose*,

Boy Anthony PZ 511 coming into Newlyn to land her mackerel, October 1976.

Halcyon and *My Partner SS 148* for St Ives, the *Valency FY 262* for Polruan, *Huntress FY 424* for Mevagissey, and Derek Soulsby's *Scath Ros PZ 138* and Thomas and Rogers' *Treryn Castle PZ 182* for Newlyn. In December 1974 Porthleven shipyard completed the 34-foot *Kim Bill PZ 511* for Bill Tonkin of Newlyn, followed by the *Frances Jane PZ 500* of Porthleven for Ricky Stacey. These boats were all designed for hand lining in the winter and crawfish netting during the summer.[8]

Small feathering boats had fished near the land in shallow water. When the winter mackerel fishery developed, the boats went much further from land, often 20 miles from port, in deep water. That was far enough for a half-decked boat in winter. Concerns were raised for their safety, with headlines like 'Mackerel Madness'! Hand-wound reels called 'gurdies' were introduced to wind up the heavy lines full of mackerel from these greater depths.

The Cornish fishermen prospered with mackerel fishing in the winter, and tangle netting for shellfish in the summer. St Ives, which had faded away as a fishing port, became a thriving harbour, and sent twenty-one boats round land to the 1973/4 winter mackerel season. Much of the catch was exported by the Roscoff ferry.

Then, like the steam drifters seventy years before, large industrial ships came to Cornwall. The Scots pair trawlers and purse seiners that had wiped out their own herring stocks on the west coast of Scotland came to fish the mackerel

In 1976 the purse seiners *Gallic May BCK 108* and *Gallic Rose BCK 109* came to Penzance. These ships could load 250 tons of mackerel. In January 1976 the *Gallic Rose*, under Skipper 'Bert' Andrew of Maidens (a Clyde fishing village), landed her maiden shot of 115 tons at Penzance.[9] The purser *Quo Vadis A 778* had already started landing at Plymouth. When the pursers caught more fish than they could handle, it was alleged that they released them, and soon the whole seabed off South Cornwall was carpeted with

Peter Freeman hauling a string of mackerel, using a gurdy. (Andrew Besley)

Above: St Ives handline boats working from Newlyn and Falmouth, winter 1973/4.

Right: Handline boats landing at Newlyn, 1976.

rotting dead mackerel, an ecological crime that went on unrestrained. The Scots blamed the Humber freezer trawlers, alleging that, if they caught more than the 40–50 tons they could process, the excess was slipped. Former Cornwall Fishery Officers Eddy Downing and Glyn Richards discussed this question: 'We don't remember the pursers slipping mackerel. The freezer trawlers certainly did and masses of it.'[10]

The Scots pair trawlers fished in groups. Most famous were the 'Big Three', the *Star Crest PD 114*, *Faithful PD 67* and *Accord PD 90*, which often landed at Penzance, and

The *Gallic Rose BCK 109* landing mackerel, Penzance Dock, January 1977.

The Peterhead Big Three *Faithful PD 67, Star Crest PD 114* and *Accord PD 90,* Penzance Dock, October 1975.

the 'Big Five', the *Fairweather V PD 157, Juneve III PD 215, Shemara PD 78, Sparkling Star* and *Ugievale II PD 105* of Peterhead, which had earned a big reputation for herring fishing. The Big Five worked from Plymouth from October 1975. These boats searched for the mackerel together, their skippers keeping in touch by radio. When they found a mark, one boat shot her trawl. Her partner came and took one side of the net and they both towed as a pair. The other boats carried on searching. When the tow was over, one boat hauled the net and her partner joined another to make a new pair. No time was wasted.

Several large Cornish boats went midwater trawling for mackerel, including Bobbie Jewell's *Galilean PZ 131,* David and Paul Stevens' *Rose of Sharon FR 23,* and Ronnie and

Ian Downing's *Spaven Mor PZ 47*. In 1976 they were fitted with net drums for midwater fishing.[11] Michael Hosking's *Dew Genen Ny PZ185* arrived in January 1975. She was fitted with a net drum and a Karmoy fish pump to pump her mackerel aboard, instead of the traditional process of bagging up the net and taking the catch aboard a lift at a time. Skipper John Day of Brixham refitted and re-engined the battered Sputnik trawler *Crannoch* for midwater trawling, and began a very successful career in the renamed *Pescoso II BF 197*.[12]

In a far-sighted article of August 1976, *Fishing News* reported,

> The big question facing fishermen in Devon and Cornwall is not how much can be caught, but how much can be sold? … Last winter, south west fishermen had their first taste of high capacity Scottish vessels hitting the mackerel and oversupplying the market … As rumours of a threatened invasion by Scottish purse seiners, plus middle water and distant water trawlers from Humberside, grow, the hundreds of small line crews know that this can only mean one thing – a price war in which the only winner will be the processor … Some line fishermen have already been told to expect no more than 40p a stone. Many boats were sold last year when mackerel was fetching 50p, and if present forecasts prove correct then boats could go out of business in droves.[13]

The article described talks between the Ministry of Agriculture and Fisheries and fishermen's Producer Organisations as 'a charade' and demanded Government action on fishing quotas.

A year later, *Commercial Fishing*'s article was headed 'The South West Mackerel. All set for the slaughter?' and captioned its photo of Scots pursers with the question, 'How long can the stock stand up to the catching power of vessels such as these?' It quoted Skipper Donal McAlinden of the top purse seiner *Quo Vadis A 778*, which fished from Plymouth: 'We noticed last season just how the shoals had been hammered. If this happens again this year, I don't think we'll see the mackerel there again.'[14]

The Rumanian factory trawler *Rarau* was lost on the Seven Stones on a fine morning in September 1976. (Gibson of Scilly)

There was also an international fleet of Russian, Polish, Bulgarian, Rumanian and Dutch factory trawlers. In September 1976 the Romanian factory trawler *Rarau* was lost on the Seven Stones.[15] The local folklore was that she had mistaken the reef for a shoal of mackerel and vainly tried to trawl it up. The Dutch ships from Scheveningen and Katwijk came with their own hospital church ship, the *de Hoop*. They fished at night and often anchored in Mount's Bay and St Ives Bay to process their catches. On Sundays, they kept the Sabbath and remained at anchor. The Eastern Bloc ships soon found it more economic to buy their catches from the Scots.

At the start of the 1977 season it was proposed that industrial vessels should be limited to landings of 3½ tons per man per day. Cornwall Sea Fisheries Committee appealed for a ban on all vessels over 80 feet in length fishing inside 6 miles, except for named local vessels.

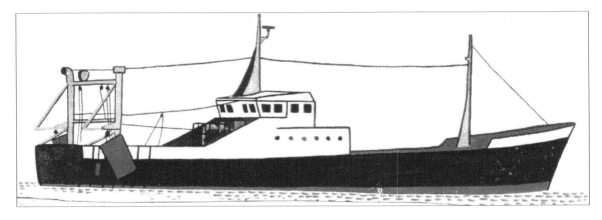

Dutch freezer trawler *Jacob van der Zwan* of Scheveningen.

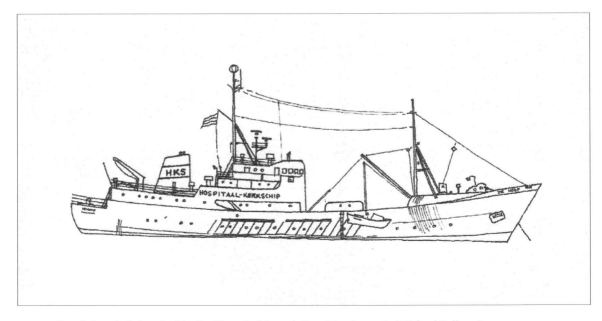

Dutch hospital church ship *De Hoop* in Mount's Bay, March 1976. (Michael Pellowe)

Boston Sea Knight LT 319 heading in to Penzance Dock to land her mackerel on a rainy day in January 1978.

The *Conqueror GY 1364* aground on Penzer Point, December 1977. (Michael Pellowe)

In December 1977 it was reported that British purse seiners and trawlers supplying factory ships from Russia, East Germany and Bulgaria had already earned £400,000, which could be exceeded by the end of the season.[16] Many Scots boats were fitted with chilled seawater tanks, which kept their catch in prime condition.

Like the drifters of an earlier generation, the Lowestoft men returned to fish the mackerel. Several modern stern trawlers, the *Boston Sea Stallion*, *Boston Sea Knight* and *Boston Sea Ranger*, worked from Penzance Dock. On 5 December 1977, the *Boston Sea Ranger LT 328*, fishing her second Cornish season, was lost while fishing on the Epsom Shoal, 3 miles south of the Runnelstone. Tragically only three of her eight crew were rescued from life rafts by Sennen lifeboat. She took on seawater, which flooded her hold and caused her to capsize within seven–eight minutes.

The large modern Hull freezer factory trawlers were banned from Iceland's coastal waters, so they came to Cornwall too. On 27 December 1977 the Grimsby freezer trawler *Conqueror GY 1364* was heading for Mount's Bay to process her catch when she grounded near Penzer Point, south of Mousehole. The officer of the watch had left the bridge unattended.[17]

In his *Lands End Radio Book 1*, William Hocking described the scene at Falmouth:

> I stepped out onto the battlements of Pendennis Castle to be met by the tang of salt air heavily laden with the smell of fish. It was a rare crystal clear day in November 1979. The low sun's rays bounced fiercely off the sea's surface fractured minutely by a light breeze. Squinting against this intense glare, I made out the silhouettes of an impressive array of vessels, the like of which had not been seen here at Falmouth since the preparations for the D-Day landings in 1944.
>
> There were no less than thirty three fish factory ships from seven different countries, receiving and processing fish from a wide variety of catchers. Attendant upon this fleet were fish carriers and supply vessels. There were trawlers and purse seiners lying quietly at anchor in Carrick Roads and alongside the Docks. Others, deep laden, furrowed their way in from deep sea.
>
> They were all here for one thing. Mackerel.[18]

In October 1978 Clenham Management set up a landing facility for the industrial vessels at Falmouth Docks. Weekly limits were imposed on landings, 145 tons for trawlers of 55–90 feet in length, 225 tons for pursers of 120–140 feet, and 390 tons for freezers. The industrials stopped fishing on 10 March 1979, after filling their quota, but there were complaints that the Dutch freezers and the Norwegian pursers *Varberg* and *Radek* were continuing to fish.

On 30 December 1978, the trawler *Ben Asdale A 328* was driven ashore and capsized at Maenporth, Falmouth, after attempting to repair defective steering gear alongside the Russian klondiker *Antarktika*. In freezing blizzard conditions, most of her crew were saved by the courage and professionalism of the Sea King helicopter crew from Culdrose. Sadly three were lost.[19]

Hull freezer trawler *Arctic Freebooter H 362* alongside a Russian factory ship. (Glyn Richards)

Brailing mackerel aboard a Russian factory ship. (Glyn Richards)

Marr's *Glen Rushen FD 221* converted from a stern trawler to a purser in Norway in 1979. (Glyn Richards)

The Boyd line's Hull factory freezer trawler *Arctic Buccaneer H 188*. There was no way the Cornish hand liners could compete with these vessels. (Glyn Richards)

Gary Leach's catamaran hand liner, *Bethshan SS 252*, 2012.

In November 1979 four small trawlers from Buckie in Scotland, the *Loranthus BCK 133*, *Bounteous BCK 337*, *Heather Sprig BCK 153* and *Wave Crest BCK 217*, arrived at Penzance to pair trawl for mackerel.[20] They were struck by tragedy just a few weeks later on 4 January 1980 when the 50-foot *Bounteous* was pair trawling with her partner *Loranthus* west of Mousehole. They were bagging up the catch when she suddenly sank with the loss of three of her six crew, despite an extensive search.[21]

In February 1980 the *Sparkling Star* towed her partner *Fairweather V* into Newlyn after she was 'mopped up' when a purser shot her net ahead of the pair when they were towing. Local divers cleared her propeller after several hours' work in poor visibility.[22]

In November 1979 a fleet of eleven Dutch freezer trawlers anchored in St Ives Bay to process their catches. Skipper J. Pronk of the *Franziska SCH 54* told journalist Andrew Besley that they were working 50 miles north-north-west of St Ives.[23]

In the 1978/9 winter mackerel season it was estimated that over 450,000 tons of mackerel were caught and sold to Nigeria, the Soviet Union, East Germany, France, Bulgaria, Norway, Romania and Egypt. A quarter of this total went for fishmeal and fertiliser. This kind of fishing was not sustainable, and by 1981 the fishery was in decline.[24]

The 1979–80 season closed to British vessels on 16 February, but the fleet of eleven massive Norwegian pursers that sheltered in St Ives Bay in January was entitled to fish on outside the British 12-mile limit.[25]

Within a few years, these ships had destroyed the Cornish winter handline mackerel fishery. Most of the handline boats were sold. It was no longer possible to earn a living handlining in the winter. The industrial ships were banned from an area known as the 'mackerel box' but this provision was too late. Former Fishery Officer Glyn Richards commented, 'Once they brought in the Mackerel Box, that made our life a lot more straightforward.'[26] The pursers continued to hammer the declining fishery. In February 1988 the pursers *Accord, Alert, Aquarius II, Cornelia, Crystal Sea, Eschol, Gratitude, Krossfjord, Polarfisk, Radiant Star, Radiant Way, Serene, Star Crest*, and *Stella Nova* were at work in the South West, and the *Courage, Heritage, Julianne, Prowess* and *Westward* were expected. The Eastern Bloc klondikers were still hard at work at Falmouth.

Handlining for mackerel still goes on all around the coast of Cornwall, mainly in small open fibreglass 'punts', but not on the same scale as the boom years of the early 1970s when every port in Cornwall thrived on the Mackerel Boom, which brought short-lived prosperity to Cornish fishermen. However, like pilchards (alias sardines), mackerel have gone upmarket, and punt fisherman are likely to be better rewarded than the whiffers of the past.

CHAPTER 12

Cornish Netters

From the nineteenth century, if not earlier, tangle nets were used to catch shellfish: crabs, crawfish, lobsters and big flatfish, like ray and turbot, which live on the seabed. These were large mesh nets with floats at the top and leads on the bottom, and were moored on the seabed in rows called tiers.

The first Camaret crabber, the *Aventurier*, came from Brittany to fish at Scilly in the spring of 1902.[1] After Christmas, four Douarnenez luggers came to try fishing with craw nets at Scilly. Only one lugger was decked, and the crews of the other three camped under their sails, wrapped up against the rain in their hooded capes. Their voyage was a failure and the local authorities were concerned for their safety until a break in the vile weather allowed them to sail for home.[2] A Camaret crabber had another try around the Seven Stones in December 1910. She had seven crew to handle her nets instead of the four that was customary in those days.[3]

In August 1910 Cornwall Sea Fisheries Committee reported,

An important feature of the crayfish industry in the western part of the district has been the development in building motor boats, using nets instead of pots, which has been attended with fairly satisfactory results. The demand for crayfish has been good with substantial prices.

This was followed in November by

The crayfish industry has been very successful from the western shore of Mount's Bay, around the Land's End district, as far as Padstow, but possibly the large landings are accounted for by the motor boats engaged prosecuting this industry. The prices have been unusually high on account of the keen competition by buyers from France and Belgium.[4]

On August Bank Holiday 1912, the St Ives gigs went away to work their crawfish nets. On their return, the wind died right away, and they had to take down their sails and row. The gig *Young Tom*, with the very experienced fishermen brothers James and Thomas Hodge, was last seen at 5.30, about 4 miles off St Ives. She was thought to be a victim of the strong squalls that later swept over the area.[5]

The early Cornish steamboat *Pioneer PZ 277* fished with crawfish nets and is remembered 'unmeshing craws over the roller like herring' early in her career, before the First World War.

Crawfish nets, also known as crab nets or ray nets, were very successful, but, because they were made out of cotton, which rots, and were worked on rocky ground, were often ripped. The fishermen could not mend the nets fast enough to keep them working. A

Hauling
crab nets
in the gig
*Caronia SS
70*, 1930s.
(James,
Richard,
Edward
and Mike
Peters)

Mending
crab nets on
Smeaton's
Pier, St Ives,
1930s. Left,
Skipper
Henry
Murley
Andrews of
the *Ocean
Gift SS* 60.

schoolboy remembered that he had to fill up the window with crab net before going out
to play.[6] Nevertheless cotton craw nets were widely used in the interwar years.

Another kind of set net was 'the trammel', consisting of three parallel walls of net. The
mesh of the inner net, which was set very slack, was of about 1 inch between knots. The
two outer walls were of large mesh, about 6 inches between knots. When a fish swam into
the net, it pushed the centre small-meshed net through one of the outside meshes to make
an escape-proof bag. Trammels were used in ancient times and are recorded in Carew's
Survey of Cornwall of 1602. They were used to catch red mullet and also bass, plaice and
even lobsters. They were usually shot on rough ground and left overnight. In more recent
times, they were often used to catch crab pot bait.[7]

Tangle nets were very successfully revived in the late 1960s. Some ancient barked cotton
nets were discovered in a St Ives loft, where the 'shore captain' assured his skipper, 'My

Unloading crab nets from Skipper Tommy Bassett's *Blush Rose SS 152*, 1930s.

Overhauling nets aboard Nicky Lander's St Ives netter *Argosy*, May 1969.

boy, these nets are suffering from "loft fever". They won't earn you enough to get bran for ducks!' The new nets were made out of artificial fibre, much stronger than cotton, and rot proof. To begin with, the nets were still hauled by hand but the hydraulic 'pedestal hauler' came in during the 1970s. The boats fished with tangle nets during the summer and mackerel handlines in the winter.

As described in the previous chapter, many new boats were built in Cornwall for handlining and netting, by the Toms yard at Polruan; Cygnus Marine with its popular GRP GM 32-footer; Porthleven shipyard; Percy Mitchell at Portmellon; John Moore at Mevagissey; Gerald Pearn at Looe and other yards.

The new nets were so efficient that each season more had to be worked to produce an economic catch. Within a few years, they fished out the grounds near the shore. Crawfish and ray became rare.

Crawfish coming up to the hauler aboard John Stevens' *Sweet Promise SS 192*, 1970s. Douglas Stevens, left; John Stevens, right. (W. Stevens, courtesy of St Ives Archive)

St Ives harbour master Steve Bassett remembered how more gear was worked each season:

> When I was with Father in the *Heather Armorel*, we worked 8 tiers of crab nets. That was in '69 or '70. We hauled four tiers a day. We hauled each Monday and Tuesday then left them lie on the Wednesday then worked them again on the Thursday and Friday. We hauled everything by hand, buoy ropes and anchors too. I used to haul with *Boy William Bennetts*. We were young and strong then. Over the spring tides, we put our gear up to the eastward; there was less tide there. Then I worked with Father in the *Girl Sharon*; she was a lovely little boat.
>
> By the time I finished up with *Traz* in the Trazbar we were working 35 tiers. We were all young men with *Traz*. We used to come down in the morning and they'd all be looking at the weather, over the back of the Quay. We just got in the punt, went aboard and went to sea and worked our gear. When the grounds got fished out here, we tried a trip out of Milford.

Other kinds of nets were used for catching dogfish and the fish which live in old shipwrecks. In the late 1970s and early 1980s, large shoals of dogfish appeared to scavenge on the massive mackerel shoals. Dogfish had formerly been targeted by the longliners, but now, very large shots were caught by the netters, and sometimes, piles of fish stretched along the new Mary Williams Pier at Newlyn.

Steve remembers how netting diversified: 'Skipper Goddard of the Fern had a good shot of hake out here. Geoff Bullis was wreck netting in the *Wave Dancer* of Nunney. We tried sole nets in the CKS and had a big shot.'[8]

Newlyn netter
CKS PZ 425.
(Steve Bassett)

Turbot nets are used to catch turbot, monkfish and crawfish. They have the biggest mesh: 30 cm². Hake nets have the smallest mesh: 4⅞ inches. Wreck nets are used from January to March to catch pollack, ling and cod, which often live in old shipwrecks. Wreck nets with a mesh of 16 cm² are used in small groups. Netters can not work during strong tides. They work during the weaker neaps. This means that their crews have to earn two weeks' wages from one week at sea.

All netters have a powered rubber-covered roller, the hauler, forward on the starboard side. This hauler pulls in the nets. As the nets come off the hauler, the fish are taken out by the crew. The deck is divided by wooden boards into pounds, where the nets are kept. The main net pound is a high one right at the stern of the boat. Over this net pound is the net stacker, another powered device which pulls the nets aft and drops them in place. The position of the net stacker can be altered. Before the arrival of the net stacker, it took two crew to haul the nets aft, ready for shooting again. Often the nets get to the pound through a special metal channel beside the wheelhouse. This was often a large piece of plastic drainpipe. (This can be seen in the photos of the *Trevose, Poul Neilsen* and *Ygraine*.)

When a netter shoots her gear, the dan float, buoy rope and anchor go over first, then, as the netter steams ahead, the nets run out over the stern. There are anchors, buoy ropes and dans at the end of each tier (row) of nets. The dans, with their brightly coloured flags, are kept beside the wheelhouse. The anchors are often hooked over the rail, near the stern.

The Decca navigator and, at present, satnavs help skippers to pinpoint the position of wrecks. Wreck nets took over from longlines at wreck fishing.

Hake netting became an important part of the netters' work, and miles of hake nets are shot on the grounds. Much of the catch is exported to Europe, particularly Spain, in large freezer lorries, which are often seen at Newlyn.

As the crawfish were fished out, many skippers gave up. For example, the St Ives fleet, which flourished during the 1970s, very quickly shrank during the 1980s. Others diversified into other kinds of netting. and built fine new boats like J. Thomas's *Boy Gary PZ 576* in 1978, the 38-foot wreck netter *Blenjan Ehre FY 527* for Graham Mills of Mevagissey in 1979, the 38-foot *Berlewen PZ 711* for Kenneth Thomas and Ian Johns in January 1982, Ben Kirby's 44-foot *Heart of Oak of Helford FH 96* in March 1983, and Clive Hosking's second *Boy Anthony PZ 518* in 1984.[9]

Newquay, which had not had a serious fishing industry since the decline of seining in Victorian times, invested heavily in a fleet of fine Cornish-built netters, the 38-foot *Celtic Mor* for Frank Dungey, the 38-foot *Trelawney of Cornwall SS 83* for Arthur Cain, the 38-foot *Guiding Light PW 377* for Phil Trebilcock, the 40-foot *Lamorna SS 28* for Ron Eglington, the *Regina Maris PW 57* for Barry Ball in 1985, the *Pearn Pride PW 62* for David Glades in 1986, the 40-foot *Atlanta PW 182* for John Bennett in 1988 and the 40-foot *Trevose of Newquay*, built by Cann & Pender of Brixham for John and Michael Burt in 1986. The *Trevose* completed £1.5 million of investment in boats for Newquay.[10] In 1988 the Toms yard completed the 41-foot netter *Trevas FY 620* for a partnership of Polperro fishermen. Designed by Gary Mitchell, she was similar to the *Trevose*. The many new boats built for Cornwall in the 1970s and 1980s were a shot in the arm for the local economy. Such Cornish boatbuilding had not been seen since the 1920s.

In May 1974 Derek Soulsby's *Scath Ros PZ 138* sank in Mount's Bay while heavily laden with nets. After three weeks on the seabed she was successfully raised and put back to work.[11] On 26 January 1982 the *Lamorna SS 28* was towed into port by the Padstow lifeboat after getting mopped up on the fishing grounds with a rope around her propeller. Skipper Ben Kirby's sturdy Helford netter *First Light of Helford FH 194* was swamped and sunk in heavy seas 36 miles south-south-east of the Lizard on 6 April 1990. Her four crew took to their life raft, which drifted before a strong-easterly wind until they were rescued by the French fishing vessel *Jean Germaine*. On 21 September 1991 the Padstow lifeboat *James Burrough* rescued the three crew of the *Pearn Pride*.[12]

Soon many of these handy sized craft were replaced by large decked boats, most of them second hand. Several 20-metre-long vessels were bought from Scotland and some from France, to be converted for deep water netting. Often the former Scots boats kept their original registration letters and numbers so *WK* for Wick, *BCK* for Buckie, *FR* for Fraserburgh, *LH* for Leith, *AH* for Arbroath and *KY* for Kirkaldy could be seen painted on the sides of boats which fished in Cornwall for decades. Recent legislation has seen boats registered in their home districts. In 1985 Skipper Henry Altenberg of Falmouth bought

The *Trevose PW 64* coming into port, laden down with a good shot. (Collection Treizour Douarnenez, copyright Christian Signor)

Left: Pearn Pride PW 62, Newquay, April 1986.

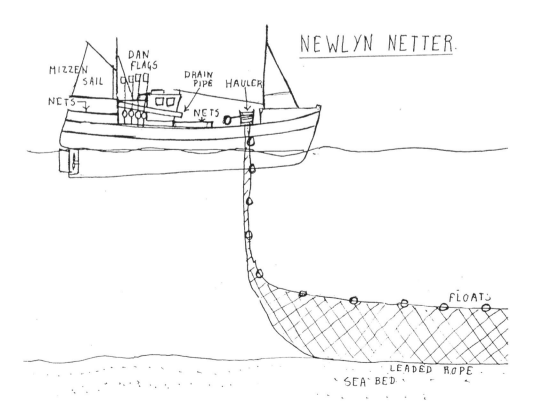

the 40-foot *Harvester FH198*, built in 1974 by Nobles of Fraserburgh, and fitted her with a Danish Grenaa hauler.[13] In 1987 Skipper Kenny Thomas replaced the 38-foot *Berlewen* with the 54-foot *Pilot Star PZ 188*, which was refitted to work up to 7,500 yards of hake gear in the southern Celtic Sea.[14]

A very successful netter was Skipper Chris Hill's 54-foot *Ar Bageergan PZ 287*, bought from St Guenole in Brittany and familiarly known as the *Bag of Rags*. (*Ar bageergan* is Breton for *barcarole*, a Venetian boating song.) In March 1988 she landed a record wreck net shot of 3,700 stones of pollack and ling, which grossed about £12,000.[15] This was followed by a similar shot from Skipper Dave Hibbert's *Sharon Corinna*, originally built as the anchor seiner *Kia Ora BCK 125* in 1960. She had been bought from Kilkeel in 1986.

Another very successful former Scots boat is the *Ajax AH 32*, bought from Newlyn by St Ives skipper Barney Thomas in 1990 and still going strong, now owned by the Pascoe family. One of a dozen netters at present working from Newlyn, the *Ajax* works up to six tiers of thirty-two hake nets with a mesh of 4⅞ inches and forty-five meshes deep. She works trips of nine days.[16]

In 1988 Skipper Frank Dungey of Padstow bought the forty-eight-year-old Danish seiner *Poul Nielsen GY 370* from Grimsby and had her extensively refitted for netting.[17] She was renamed *Chrisande PW 108*. Her four crew were rescued when she was lost 19 miles north of Padstow in November 1994.[18]

Several trawlers, including Geoff Davies' *La Critique*, Skipper Hicks' *Ben my Chree PZ 645* and Andrew Treloar's *Keriolet SS 114*, were converted for netting.[19]

Although most large Cornish netters were second-hand, some fine new boats were built for the fishery. The immaculately varnished 50-foot *Britannia V FH 121* was completed by Alexander Noble of Girvan for John Leach and Freddie Turner. She returned to her builders in 1989, 2½ years after her completion, to be fitted with a shelter deck.[20] In April 1990 Skipper Ian Mitchell accepted the 60-foot GRP netter *Sowenna PZ 14* (Cornish for 'success') from her builder, Halfish.[21] In June the Toms yard at Polruan delivered the Gary Mitchell-designed *Ocean Spray PZ 41* for owner Skipper Janner Thomas. Skipper Thomas

The ex-Danish seiner *Poul Neilsen GY 370* refitted for netting from Padstow in 1988. Her dans with their flags are stacked around the wheelhouse. (J. Paynter)

said that bigger boats were needed to carry 10,000 yards of hake nets and even longer fleets for turbot.[22]

Cornish netters worked as far away as Baltimore, in south-west Ireland, on grounds 200 miles from Newlyn. This was a very long voyage for a 20-metre wooden boat built in Scotland thirty years ago. The Spanish and French boats working the same grounds were much bigger and more modern. Sometimes Cornish netters landed their catches at Dunmore East in Ireland or Roscoff, Douarnenez or Le Guilvinec in France.

Netting brought prosperity to many Cornish ports, but sometimes at a tragic cost. On 4 September 1991 the 36-foot Newlyn netter *Margaret and William SU 96* was fishing 50 miles west-north-west of Ushant when she was struck in daylight by the Dutch chemical tanker *Jacobus Broere*. Three of her crew, Skipper Malcolm Nicholls, Ian Hagues and Terry Freeman, were rescued from their life raft by a Culdrose helicopter. Tragically, Denis Nicholls and Alex Howes were lost.[23] On 11 March 1997 the small St Ives netter *Gorah Lass SE 94*, laden with nets, was lost in Bassett's Bay with her three crew, Philip Benny, William Pirie and Steve Cooper.[24] In October, Chris Cripps was lost from the Newlyn netter *Ocean Spray PZ 41*, skipper Malcolm Nicholls, while she was shooting her gear.[25] On Saturday 13 March 2004 the 32-foot Newlyn netter *Sabre PW 5* was swamped and sank 19 miles off the Lizard with the loss of forty-two-year-old Mark Jose. Her skipper Carl Thomas and Malcolm Nicholls were rescued, after twelve desperate hours in their life raft, by Penlee lifeboat.

Several Danish netters arrived off Cornish waters in the late 1980s and showed what could be done. These included the pale-blue-painted *Svalbarde L 352* and *Asta Ruby L 310* of Thorsmunde, and the bright red *Cornwall L 416* of Lemvig, which netted some eye-watering shots of turbot.

During the 1980s, the netting fleets in both Cornwall and Brittany expanded. Newlyn became the premier netting port in the UK. Miles of nets were shot on the grounds for hake, pollack and ling. Inevitably, there were conflicts between these static gear boats and trawlers, which have to tow their nets along to fish.

Danish netters *Svalbarde L 352* and *Asta Ruby L 310* at Penzance. (Michael Pellowe)

In June 1992 a fishing conflict off the Isles of Scilly between the Cornish netters *St Uny*, *Britannia IV* and *Sardia Louise* and the large French industrial stern trawlers *L'Arche* and *Rhapsody*, from Concarneau, hit the national headlines in both France and the UK. *L'Arche* was boarded by officers from HMS *Brecon* and questions were asked in Parliament.[26] In August there was another conflict between the Le Guilvinec trawler *Damocles* and the Newquay netter *Aquarius*. The Breton netters also had problems with French industrial trawlers towing over their gear. Gentlemen's agreements between netters and trawlers are needed for them to work in harmony.

The generally harmonious relationship between the skippers of Breton trawlers and Cornish netters again came unstuck on 29 April 2004 when a large group of Cornish boats was kept in port by poor weather. When they returned to their gear off the Lizard, they found that many nets had been destroyed by St Brieuc trawlers. *Fishing News* reported that Skipper Andrew Pascoe's *Lamorna* lost thirty-seven nets, Rolly Kirby's *Heart of Oak* twenty-two, Kizzy Beesley's *Tracey Claire* seventeen and Patrick Harvey's *Matthew Harvey* seven nets. Urgent talks were planned between the Cornish and French producer organisations to resolve the problems.

Chris 'Bish' Care, who runs a net setting business in St Ives, recalled,

> I was netting with Traz in the *Keriolet SS 114* in the 90s. There were about forty netters in Newlyn in those days. We worked hake nets all the year round. They had a 4⅝ inch mesh. We worked a false footrope under the nets to keep them up, so that the hake wouldn't be down on the ground and infested with lice. We worked six tiers of 10 nets when I started and we were five crew. In the 1980s the smaller boats like the small *Boy Anthony PZ 518*, the *Loyal Partner PZ 30* and the *Boy Gary PZ 576* worked out of Scilly and came home to Newlyn to land. We worked out here in the Channel [Bristol Channel] about 50 to 70 miles off. Years ago, that would have been the lining grounds. We have worked on wrecks but it was mostly haking. As time went on, we had to work further off, down on the Labadie and places like that. We did two or three trips off the Isle of Man. We had 120 kits of hake there one time and landed in Douarnenez, as Traz was in their Breton Producer Organisation. We had another good shot of black jacks [coley] and landed them in France as there was a better price there than in Newlyn.

In the early 1990s Cornish netters began to join the tuna fishery in the Bay of Biscay, using tuna drift nets. This fishery was even further from home, so only boats with cooling equipment in their fish rooms were able to join in. In 2002 Europe banned tuna drift netting, after concerns about the number of dolphins entangled in tuna nets. By this time, there were strict limits on the numbers of nets worked. To the fury of Cornish fishermen, the *Charisma BA 45* of Padstow was arrested by the Royal Navy and taken into port to check the length of her fleet. It may be that alternative methods of catching tuna, e.g. pair trawling, will kill not only some dolphins, but also the healthy tuna stock, an unintended consequence of an environmental law. In October 1999 the yellow-painted *Charisma* broke down with gearbox problems 30 miles off Trevose, and was towed in by the Padstow and St Ives lifeboats in worsening weather.

Spain has a large fleet of pole and line tuna boats and is anxious to preserve this fleet. Three Cornish boats, the *Ben Loyal WK 3*, *Charisma BA 45* and *Nova Spero CN 187*, have tried fishing this way, towing lures from the stern and two long poles, but the market price for tuna in the UK may not support this ecological but labour-intensive way of fishing.

In May 2002 Skipper Nick Chapman of Wadebridge took over the steel 15-metre netter *Berlewen PW1* from her builders, Parkol Marine of Whitby. *Fishing News* reported that

*Berlewen
PW 1.*

the *Berlewen* would carry 12 tonnes of nets, 3 tonnes of anchors, 12 tonnes of fuel and 3 tonnes of ballast. She went to sea with 700 turbot nets and 100 whitefish nets (i.e. 38 miles and 7 miles of nets).[27] January 2013 saw the *Berlewen* landing her catch at Bloscon, Roscoff, one of many Cornish netters to seek better prices for their catches in France. In October 2002 Skipper Anthony Hosking took delivery of the 60-foot steel *Silver Dawn PZ 1196*, built by Riverside Fabrications of Falmouth. She replaced the 19-metre ex-French *Boy Anthony PZ 498*.[28] With the arrival of these steel boats, it is unlikely that anymore wooden fishing boats will be built for Cornwall, where the choice is now GRP or steel.

More recently, in view of the high cost of new boats, the trend has been to give second-hand vessels very extensive refits. In March 2010, the 22-metre wooden *Govenek of Ladram PZ 51* started fishing from Newlyn under Skipper Phil Mitchell and his four young crew. Owned by Rowan and Robin Carter of Waterdance, she replaced the steel *Carol H*. Formerly the Scots twin rig trawler *Regent Bird III*, she had been completely refitted by Macduff shipyard, Scotland. The biggest netter in the port, she was expected to make trips of seven–eight days, up to 200 miles from home. *Govenek* is Cornish for 'hope'. In April 2011 Skipper Simon Porter of Padstow and his crew landed their first shot at Newlyn from the 17-metre steel former longliner *Sparkling Line PW 3*. Like the *Govenek*, she had been completely refitted as a netter for Waterdance by Macduff shipyard.[29]

The netter *Girl Patricia* sprang a leak and sank 28 miles north-west of Land's End on 29 May 2008. Her four crew were rescued by a helicopter from Culdrose.[30] She had a long and successful record after being built by Porthleven shipyard as the liner/trawler *Girl Pat PZ 87* for Skipper Tommy Thomas in 1974.

On 11 March 2011, the veteran Newlyn netter *Ben my Chree PZ 645* was lost after springing a leak in her way to the fishing grounds. Skipper Stephen Hicks decided to abandon the vessel and her crew were rescued by helicopter and the St Mary's lifeboat. The *Ben my Chree* was built in France in 1965 as the tunnyman *Gloria Maris Gv 317521*. She came to Newlyn in 1979 and had a successful thirty-year career as a trawler and netter.[31]

Govenek of
Ladram PZ 51.
(F. McWilliams)

Breaking up
decommissioned
fishing boats
at Newlyn old
slipway, 1994.
(Glyn Richards)

(An earlier *Ben my Chree* was a top-earning Mousehole herring drifter that often worked at the Isle of Man and was later sold to Ireland.)

Inshore netters work from all of the Cornish fishing harbours. Newlyn is one of the most important netting ports in Britain, though its fleet has been much reduced in recent years.

In December 2012 Skipper Hosking of Newlyn bought the steel French netter *Stelissa III* from Lorient, surely a vote of confidence in the Cornish fishing industry. She was joined in June 2013 by another sleek ex-French netter, the *Joy of Ladram E 22* for Waterdance to replace the veteran *CKS*. Later in the year, the hefty *Ocean Pride FH 24* arrived for Pete Laity and Jonathan Hamilton to replace the *Ocean Spray*, which was sold to Scarborough, and *Britannia V*, which continues to work from Newlyn. A former Scots boat, the *Ocean Pride* was built by Jones of Buckie as the *Diamond LK 128* in 1987. She was converted for netting by Parkol Marine of Whitby. Many netters and other vessels land at Newlyn for immediate transhipment to Plymouth, Brixham or other markets.

From the late twentieth century, EEC rules brought in decommissioning, aimed at drastically reducing European fishing, in an effort to take the pressure off fish stocks. This scheme saw dozens of Cornish boats, many of them netters, broken up. Many of these vessels were fine seaworthy craft that could have been put to other uses, and it was sad to see them smashed up by diggers at Newlyn old slipway.

CHAPTER 13

Scalloping

Scallops have been fished in Britain for over a century but not on the large scale now seen. In the late nineteenth and early twentieth centuries, large Essex smacks went scalloping in the English Channel off the French coast from Boulogne.[1] Between the world wars, the remaining large smacks were fitted with engines. They were joined by several steam drifters, which were very suitable for deep-water scalloping.

Skipper Alfred Pengelly of Looe recalled his experience in the mid-1930s, after the herring fishery at Brixham ended, when the *Our Daddy FY 7* filled in with scallop dredging:

> We had however, brought with us an escallop dredge that my father had made some years before at Brixham and we now tried this out in company with other boats from Exmouth and Brixham. Our dredge was a large one of nine feet across the mouth which enabled us to keep up with the top boats catchwise, although the first time we tried it, we shot it over the side upside down and drew a blank! After a short season with the dredge we left for home.[2]

However, in the West Country, large-scale scalloping, like beam trawling and netting, is another relatively new fishery, which got going in the 1970s when local boats began to

The 65-foot Essex scalloper *Hilda CK 297* from Brightlingsea, photographed in Mount's Bay in the early twentieth century. Built in 1886 she was fitted with an engine in 1927 and fished until 1935.

fish the extensive scallop grounds east of the Lizard. Many of the larger boats were from Brixham and Plymouth, which had about 60 per cent of the British scallop fleet in the late 1970s. In 1976, small boats from St Mawes and Falmouth fished Veryan and Gerrans bays. When catches eased up, they reverted to trawling. In 1978, £2 million worth of scallops were landed nationally. There are several scallop beds east of the Lizard, stretching from Falmouth Bay to Start Point.[3] Scalloping has been part of the Mevagissey fishing calendar since the 1970s. Off West Cornwall there is an important ground south of the Wolf Rock and another at the Isles of Scilly. In June 2002 the Isles of Scilly fisheries officer visited seventeen scallopers, mainly from the Falmouth area, which were fishing east of the islands. The local Sea Fisheries Committee wanted enforcement of bye-laws banning vessel of over 10 tons and 11-metre length from fishing inside the 6-mile limit, limiting the number of dredges to four a side.[4]

Nigel Stevens recalls scalloping from Newlyn in the 1970s:

> During the very hot Summer of 1976 I was working aboard the *Sea Eagle LT 369*, Skipper George Lawry. The *Sea Eagle* was built as a ring-netter in 1933 in Scotland, and was 53' overall. Legend had it that the grounds we were working had been discovered some years earlier by an Isle of Man beamer who, when he left Castletown, would steam around the top of Ireland on his way to go fishing South of the Isles of Scilly so as to keep his discovery secret. In those days the main electronic aid to navigation was Decca Navigator, derived from the Wartime Oboe aircraft navigation system. The sea-bed in that area is very flat, with the main danger to fouling the dredges coming from the many 2nd World War wrecks.
>
> The dredges we towed were two Baird Sledge Dredges, each two metres wide, and having a 'tooth bar' of steel teeth, set four inches apart and approximately eight inches long, which would dig the scallops out of the sea-bed and thence back into the 'belly' of the dredge. So as to keep the dredges a little distance apart, they were towed from two small derricks that were fixed to the tabernacle that the mizzen mast was footed into.
>
> We would tow the dredges for two hours at a time before hauling them up to empty them. A good tow would produce about fifty dozen scallops, whereas the much bigger, more powerful, beamers would catch ten times that amount, so a good forty eight hour trip for us was up to a thousand dozen, but the Castletown boats were catching up to twelve thousand dozen for the same length of time.

The scallops found off South Cornwall are usually smaller and slower growing than those found off Newhaven in the Channel, off Fishguard and in Morecambe Bay. Modern scallopers are usually specially designed or adapted vessels. They can and do migrate to fish all around Britain, e.g. in 1980, many West Country scallopers worked from Fishguard in Wales. Similarly, large scallopers from the Solway Firth and other west of Scotland ports are often seen at Newlyn during the summer.

Scallops spawn from about April to September, and mature at about three years. Their age can be seen from growth rings on the shell. Those fished are usually about three–four years old, with a minimum shell length of about 90 mm. The scallop digs itself a shallow depression in the seabed and filter-feeds from the surrounding sea. So a suitable piece of kit is needed to prise it from its base. This is often the Newhaven dredge.[5]

The scallop dredge is a bag towed from a triangular steel frame. The bottom of the bag is made of metal rings, and the top of strong nylon netting. At the bottom of the entrance is a spring-loaded toothed bar which scoops the scallops into the dredge as it is towed along. The spring allows it to spring over stones. A set of scallop dredges is fastened to a steel beam with rubber wheels on each end. Scallopers tow two beams, one on either side, in the same way as twin beam trawlers. In smaller scallopers, when the dredges come aboard, a gilson is used to tip them. Large modern scallopers are usually fitted with self-tipping systems along the side to empty the dredges, conveyors to handle the catch and fish room chilling to keep it at top quality.

Thirty years ago, a 35-foot-long boat with a 120-hp engine would tow three dredges a side. A 50-footer would tow up to six a side. Modern large scallopers tow massive arrays of dredges; the *Jacoba PZ 307* of Newlyn has seventeen a side. A modern 12-metre scalloper tows six dredges a side.[6]

Scallop dredging has aroused concerns among environmentalists, who feel that sensitive areas of seabed such as coral can be damaged by dredging. Areas of Lyme Bay and Cardigan Bay have been closed to scalloping.

It may be that something can be learned from North Brittany, where the fishermen themselves very tightly control the scallop fishery, the number of dredges worked, the size of the boats and the hours of fishing. Fishermen who break the rules are condemned to remain in harbour and lose fishing time. Ports like Erquy enjoy a thriving scallop industry. The Breton scallop fishermen feel that their future is secure.

Other areas, such as Guernsey and the Isle of Man, successfully control their own local fishing industries. The Scallop Fishing (England) Order 2012 restricts the number of dredges worked between the 6- and 12-mile limits to eight a side. This was challenged by the owners of large vessels, but supported by inshore fishermen, including Cadgwith and Helford and District Fishermen's Society, whose chairman David Muirhead wrote to

The little *Charlotta PW 362* of Mevagissey tows three dredges off her stern and works single-handed.

The new Falmouth scalloper *Golden Promise FH 401*, February 2010. She tows seven dredges each side.

Fishing News, 'Areas of previously rich ground broken in and worked by large scallop vessels has never recovered.'[7]

In October 2012 there were clashes between British and Normandy fishermen in the Seine Bay. The French scallopers observed a voluntary closed season on these grounds and took a dim view of British boats reaping the fruits of their abstinence. In reply the British asserted that they were legally entitled to work there.[8] It was reported that the British vessels had very high earnings from this fishery.

The scallop fishery from the Cornish and other West Country ports has expanded with the development of markets in Europe and North America. Much of the catch is exported to France and Spain. Scalloping has certainly made a valuable contribution to the regional economy. At present, quotas are not applied to scallop fishing, and several large beam trawlers have been bought in Holland for conversion to scallopers in the UK since there are seen to be profitable opportunities. There is a feeling among some fishermen that further regulation may be needed to safeguard the future of the industry.

Acknowledgements

I have been fortunate to receive very generous help from many friends in compiling this book. Tony Pawlyn of National Maritime Museum Cornwall has been hugely generous in sharing his research and photographs. I am particularly grateful for material on early boat losses in the Irish fishery, the drift net fisheries in St Ives and Mount's Bay in the seventeenth century, the Lowestoft smacks and other vessels recorded in the 1911 Census and many other leads. Michael Pellowe has again allowed me to use his beautiful watercolours, and Glyn Richards has given me access his collection of excellent local 'at sea' photographs, taken during his work as Cornwall Sea Fisheries Officer.

For the use of photographs I am most grateful to the Royal Cornwall Museum Truro, Belinda Ratnayake, Brian and Margaret Stevens of St Ives Museum, Paul Martin, Jan Pentreath, Janet Axten and Mike Murphy of St Ives Archive, Newquay Old Cornwall Society, Margaret Perry, Sarah Parsons of the National Maritime Museum Cornwall, Jenni Pozzi of Penzance Morrab Library, Lisa Coombes of Plymouth City Council Archives, Katie Herbert of Penlee House Museum Penzance, the Rose, Shore Shelter and Shamrock lodges St Ives, Francis McWilliams, Gibsons of Scilly, National Maritime Museum Greenwich, Tim and Rita Lait, Ken Brown, William Thomas, Matthew Ferrell, Jack Daussy of Fecamp, Steve Johnson, Mike Smylie, Bill Ball, Ulster Museums, Mrs E. Murrish, Leon Pezzack, Robert and Susie Jones, John Hornsey, David Berriman, John Lambourn, Carole Catteral, Andy Smith, Stanley Earl of the Port of Lowestoft Research Society, Collection Treizour Douarnenez: Christian Signor, Steve Martin, Andrew Besley, Brenda Bennett of J. Salmon Ltd, Steve Bassett and Johnnie Payter.

For sharing their recollections, thanks to Raymond Peake, Nigel Stevens, Raymond Stevens, Barney Thomas, Gordon Stevens, James 'Maffis' Perkin, Donald Perkin, Paul Stevens, Chris 'Bish' Care, Robert George and many Cornish fishermen.

For advice with research, information and other help, thanks to Kim Cooper and the Cornwall Centre Redruth, Cornwall Records Office, Plymouth Library, Bartlett Library: National Maritime Museum Cornwall, Margaret Stratton and John M. McWilliams.

Every effort has been made to trace and acknowledge the photograph copyright holders. The photographs which are not acknowledged are from my collection and a very few where I have not been able to find the origin.

Notes

1 THE GREAT CORNISH PILCHARD SEINES

1. The *Survey of Cornwall*, Richard Carew; Tamar Books 1602.
2. *St Ives Weekly Summary* 2 September 1893.
3. *St Ives Weekly Summary* 14 October 1893.
4. *Cornish Seines & Seiners*, Cyril Noall; Bradford Barton 1972.
5. *Cornish Seines & Seiners*, Cyril Noall; Bradford Barton 1972.
6. Union Seine Company's ledger of 1843.
7. *The Chatham Directory of Inshore Craft*, pp 159–62; Chatham 1997.
8. *Cornish Seines & Seiners*, pp 98–9, Cyril Noall; Bradford Barton 1972.
9. *St Ives Weekly Summary*, 1911.
10. *Evening Tidings*, 2 December 1893.
11. *Cornish Seines & Seiners*, Cyril Noall; Bradford Barton 1972.
12. *St Ives Weekly Summary*, 2 February 1893.
13. Article by Tony Pawlyn in *Cornwall & the Coast, Mousehole & Newlyn*, Joanna Mattingly; Phillimore 2009.
14. Information from Tony Pawlyn, October 2012.
15. *St Ives Weekly Summary*, 1911.
16. *St Ives & the Burning Mountain*, Cyril Noall in *Cornish Magazine*, August 1963.
17. *Ships Annual 1958*, Ian Allan. *The Black Sea Tramp*, Captain H. Daniel OBE.
18. *Prisoner of War in France 1804–14*, ed. Sir Edward Hain; Duckworth 1914.
19. Knill Trust Deed, 12 May 1797.
20. *West Briton*, 31 July 1818.
21. *The Present Position of the Cornish Pilchard Industry*, Cuthbert Lloyd Fox, 1943.
22. *West Briton*, 8 January 1891.
23. *Cornishman*, 7 October 1897.
24. *St Ives Weekly Summary*, 30 December 1905.
25. *The Motor Boat*, 13 October 1910.
26. *Western Echo*, 21 October 1922.

2 PILCHARD DRIVING

1 A *Survey of Cornwall*, Richard Carew, 1602.
2 RCI St Aubyn estate documents (Henderson).
3 *West Briton*, 30 April 1819.
4 *Royal Cornwall Gazette*, Friday morning, 14 December 1877.
5 *West Briton*, 7 March 1828.
6 *Prisoners of War in France 1804–1814*, ed. Sir Edward Hain; Duckworth 1914.
7 *Evening Star*, Ken Shearwood; Bradford Barton.
8 *Cornishman*, 15 September 1910.
9 *St Ives Weekly Summary*, 1911.
10 *Western Morning News*, 13 August 1921.

11 Gordon Stevens.

12 *Western Morning News*, 13 August 1921.

13 *Cornishman*, 8 September 1920.

14 *Cornishman*, 5 May 1949.

15 *The Present Position of the Cornish Pilchard Industry*, Cuthbert Lloyd Fox; Royal Cornwall Polytechnic Society 1943.

16 *Cornishman*, 16 April 1924.

17 *Cornishman*, 29 September 1926.

18 *Cornishman*, Wednesday 11 June 1930.

19 *Western Echo*, 13 August 1932.

20 *Western Echo*, 10 September 1932.

21 Gordon Stevens.

22 *Western Echo*, 9 September 1933.

23 *Cornishman*, 31 August 1938.

24 Gordon Stevens.

25 *Cornishman*, 21 January 1946.

26 *Western Echo*, 3 July 1948.

27 *St Ives Times & Echo*, 27 September 1957.

28 *Cornishman*, 2 October 1947.

29 *Cornishman*, 30 November 1950.

30 *Cornishman*, 9 November 1950.

31 *Cornishman*, 4 February 1960.

32 *Cornishman*, 28 January 1960.

33 *Scottish Fishing Craft*, Gloria Wilson.

34 *A Boatbuilder's Story*, Percy Mitchell; Kingston, Mevagissey 1968.

35 *Cornishman*, 30 November 1950.

36 *Cornishman*, 20 September 2007.

37 *Fishing News*, 28 January 1972.

38 *Fishing News*, 23 March 2001

39 *Fishing News*, 12 November 2010.

40 *Western Morning News*, 22 December 2011.

3 CORNISH MACKEREL SEASON

1 *The Book of St Ives*, Cyril Noall; Barracuda 1977.

2 'West Cornwall Fishing Luggers Before 1850', R. Morton Nance, in *Mariner's Mirror Volume 30*.

3 *Merchant Shipping Register*, St Ives.

4 *Cornishman*, 2 October 1947.

5 *Prisoners of War in France 1804–1814*, Sir Edward Hain, 1914.

6 *West Briton*, 1 June 1827.

7 *West Briton*, 21 October 1836.

8 *Prisoners of War in France 1804–1814*, Sir Edward Hain, 1914.

9 *Prisoners of War in France 1804–1814*, Sir Edward Hain, 1914.

10 *West Briton*, 14 May 1871.

11 *West Briton*, 4 May 1882.

12 *Cornishman*, Thursday 17 May 1883.

13 *West Briton*, 17 May 1886.

14 *Newlyn, a View from Street an Nowan*, John Jenkin, info: Tony Pawlyn.

15 *St Ives Weekly* Summary, 26 May 1894.

16 *Western Morning News*, 10 October 1980, Tony Pawlyn.

17 Record of the *Jane SS 563*, M. Stevens. Courtesy of Mrs M. Stratton.

18 St Ives Harbour records, Cornwall County Records.

19 *West Briton*, 21 May 1896.

20 *Western Echo*, 6 April 1901.

21 *Sailing Drifters*, E. J. March; P. Marshall 1952.
22 *West Briton*, 5 June 1899.
23 *Western Echo*, 18 May 1901.
24 *The Numerical Fleet of Yarmouth*, L. W. Hawkins, 1982.
25 *Cornishman*, 9 April 1903.
26 *Cornishman*, 30 May 1903.
27 *La Pêche Boulonnaise du Temps des Chalutiers à Vapeur*, F. Guennoc.
28 *Western Echo*, 16 April 1904.
29 *St Ives Weekly Summary*, 18 February 1905.
30 *St Ives Weekly Summary*, 25 May 1907.
31 *St Ives Weekly Summary*, 15 March 1912.
32 *Cornishman*, 25 April 1912.
33 *Western Echo*, 27 March 1920.
34 Parliamentary Report into the Application of Devon & Cornwall Sea Fisheries Committees for Grants from the Development Fund, 1913.
35 Letter M. McWilliams to Sup't of Customs, Tower Hill, January 1912.
36 Cornish Fishing Vessels Insurance Society documents, Box 1.
37 *Western Echo*, 26 April 1919.
38 *Western Echo*, 13 March 1920.
39 *Western Echo*, 21 June 1924.
40 *Western Echo*, 4 April 1925.
41 *Western Echo*, 23 May 1925.
42 *Cornishman*, 6 April 1927.
43 *Western Echo*, 9 March 1929.
44 *Cornishman*, 18 May 1938
45 *Growing up with Boats*, Billy Stevenson, ed. Margaret Perry, 2001.
46 Edwin Stevens, 2011.
47 *Cornishman*, 23 February 1950.
48 Information courtesy of K. Brown, Newlyn.
49 R. Stevens, St Ives, 2012.
50 Lilli Colin, Douarnenez, 2012.
51 Website: Listes de Bâteaux Douarnenistes.

4 CORNISH HERRING: THE NORTH COAST

1. RCI St Aubyn Estate documents (Henderson) HA/8/14 (223b).
2. *Prisoners of War in France 1804–1814*, Sir Edward Hain; Duckworth 1914.
3. *St Ives Weekly Summary*, 11 March 1893.
4. *St Ives Weekly Summary*, 24 February 1894.
5. *St Ives Weekly Summary*, 18 February 1894.
6. *St Ives Times & Echo*, Cyril Noall, 14 January 1983.
7. 'Herrings & Other Fish', Keith Ross, in *St Ives Times & Echo*, 3 February 1995.
8. *Western Echo*, 20 December 1902.
9. *St Ives Times & Echo*, 5 January 1979.
10. *St Ives Weekly Summary*, 12 November 1910.
11. *The Motor Boat*, 9 December 1909.
12. *The Motor Boat*, 12 January 1911.
13. *A Word in Your Ear*, Tom Richards, 2006.
14. *Western Echo*, 12 December 1903.
15. *Western Echo*, 27 September 1919.
16. *Western Echo*, 22 November 1919.
17. *Western Echo*, 4 December 1920.
18. *Cornishman*, 26 December 1923, and E. Murt's St Ives FV records.
19. *Western Echo*, 17 January 1925.
20. *St Ives Times*, 2 December 1927.

21. *Cornish Guardian*, 30 November 1928.
22. *Western Echo*, 16 November 1929.
23. *La Pêche Boulonnaise du Temps des Chalutiers à Vapeur*, F. Guennoc; Punch Editions.
24. *Western Echo*, 19 June 1926.
25. *Western Echo*, 27 November 1937.
26. Cyril Stevens, St Ives, 2011.

5 PLYMOUTH HERRING

1. *Cornishman*, Thursday 10 October 1907.
2. *Sailing Drifters*, E. J. March; Percival Marshall 1952.
3. *Cornishman*, Thursday 16 January 1908.
4. *Cornishman*, Thursday 24 December 1908.
5. *Cornishman*, Thursday 7 January 1909.
6. *The Motor Boat*, 12 January 1911.
7. *Looking back to Yesterday*, Bert Cowls, Porthleven.
8. *Once Aboard a Cornish Lugger*, Paul Greenwood; Polperro Heritage Press 2007.
9. *Cornishman*, 9 January 1924.
10. *Western Echo*, 21 March 1925.
11. Herring Investigations at Plymouth III. The Plymouth Winter Fishery 1924–25, 1925–26 & 1925–27. E. Ford ARCS.
12. *The Driftermen*, David Butcher; Tops'l Books 1979.
13. Herring Investigations at Plymouth III. The Plymouth Winter Fishery 1924–25, 1925–26 & 1925–27. E. Ford ARCS.
14. *La Pêche Boulonnaise du Temps des Chalutiers à Vapeur*, F. Guennoc; Punch Eds 2000.
15. *Western Echo*, February 1930.
16. *A Mousehole Man's Story*, John J. Pender, 1982.
17. Herring Investigations at Plymouth III. The Plymouth Winter Fishery 1924–25, 1925–26 & 1925–27. E. Ford ARCS.
18. *Western Morning News*, 13 January 1931.
19. *Western Echo*, 5 September 1931.
20. *Western Echo*, 9 January 1932.
21. *Western Echo*, 19 March 1932.
22. *Western Echo*, 16 December 1933.
23. *Cornishman*, 18 March 1935.
24. *Western Echo*, 8 January 1938.

6 IRISH HERRING

1. *Cornishman*, 13 July 1938, Herbert Richards.
2. *West Briton*, 10 August 1827.
3. *West Briton*, 29 August 1828.
4. *Royal Cornwall Gazette*, 17 May 1839.
5. *Prisoners of War in France*, ed. Sir Edward Hain; Duckworth 1914.
6. *The Deep Sea & Coast Fisheries of Ireland*, W. Brabazon, 1848.
7. *Prisoners of War in France*, ed. Sir Edward Hain; Duckworth 1914.
8. *Sailing Drifters*, E. J. March; P. Marshall 1952.
9. Information referring to the Castletown, Peel & Newry boats, Mike Craine, IOM, 2004.
10. *St Ives Weekly Summary*, 20 May 1893.
11. Summary St Ives Fishing Boat Registers, St Ives Archive.
12. *The Motor Boat*, 9 December 1909.
13. *The Motor Boat*, 9 December 1909.
14. *Western Echo*, 20 September 1919.
15. *The Motor Boat*, 2 February 1923.
16. *Cornishman*, 30 December 1954.

17. D. Perkin, St Ives, 2011.
18. *Pair Trawling & Pair Seining*, David Thomson; *Fishing News* Books 1978.
19. *World Fishing*, April 1962.

7 THE NORTH SEA VOYAGE

1. *Prisoners of War in France 1804–1814*, Sir Edward Hain; Duckworth 1914.
2. *Sailing Drifters*, E. J. March; P. Marshall 1952.
3. *St Ives Times & Echo*, 26 June 2005, Brian Stevens.
4. *Western Morning News*, Review of the Year 1892.
5. *St Ives Weekly Summary*, 7 July 1894.
6. *St Ives Weekly Summary*, 1 September 1894.
7. *St Ives Weekly Summary*, 13 July 1895.
8. Record of the *Jane SS 536*, M. Stevens, courtesy Mrs M. Stratton.
9. *Western Morning News*, 9 September 1896.
10. *Cornishman*, Thursday 8 October 1896.
11. *Western Echo*, 28 March 1903.
12. *Western Echo*, 26 July 1902.
13. E. Murt, Record of St Ives fishing vessels, *SS 623 Jane Lander*.
14. *Cornishman*, Thursday 23 July 1903.
15. *Cornishman*, Thursday 20 August 1903.
16. *Cornishman*, Thursday 3 September 1903.
17. *Cornishman*, Thursday 24 September 1903.
18. *Cornishman*, Thursday 22 September 1904.
19. *A Fisherman's Diary*, Nicholas Polmeor 1881–1963; David Berriman 2010.
20. *Cornishman*, Thursday 8 August 1907.
21. *Yachting Monthly*, Volume 7, 1909.
22. *Western Echo*, 11 September 1920, and E. Murt, Record of St Ives fishing vessels.
23. *Cornishman*, 5 November 1938.
24. *The Prunier Herring Trophy*, L. W. Hawkins, 1982.

8 LONGLINING

1. B. Thomas, St Ives, 1981.
2. *The Motor Boat*, 9 December 1909, 30 June 1910.
3. *La Pêche Maritime*, J. Kerzoncuf, 1917.
4. Cornwall Fishing Vessel Insurance documents, Box 1.
5. *The Motor Boat*, 4 August 1922.
6. *The Motor Boat*, 7 August 1925.
7. *Western Echo*, 10 March 1934.
8. *Western Echo*, 11 August 1934.
9. *Western Echo*, 9 July 1938.
10. D. Perkin, St Ives, 2011.
11. *Western Echo*, 3 April 1915.
12. *Western Echo*, 29 March 1919.
13. *Cornishman*, 9 January 1924.
14. *Western Echo*, 17 May 1924.
15. St Ives fishing vessel records, E. Murt.
16. *Western Echo*, 23 May 1925.
17. *Western Echo*, 28 June 1928.
18. *Western Echo*, 26 September 1931.
19. *Cornishman*, 16 March 1927
20. *Cornishman*, 12 October 1978.
21. *Cornishman*, 18 July 1963.
22. *Western Echo*, 26 September 1931.

23. *Western Echo*, 26 September 1936.
24. *Western Echo*, 6 May 1933.
25. *Western Morning News*, 21 May 1935.
26. *The Motor Boat*, 27 July 1934.
27. *Cornishman*, 27 March 1935.
28. *Western Echo*, 24 April 1937.
29. *Western Echo*, 15 May 1937.
30. *Fishing News*, 11 July 1975, J. Madron.
31. Website: Les Dundees d'Audierne, Alain Gourret.
32. *Western Echo*, 25 May 1945.
33. *Cornishman*, 6 January 1949.
34. *Cornishman*, 22 September 1949.
35. *Cornishman*, 5 October 1950.
36. *Cornishman*, 6 April 1950.
37. *Cornishman*, 16 August 1962.
38. *Cornishman*, 27 September 1962.
39. *Cornishman*, 4 July 1963.
40. *Cornishman*, 23 April 1964.
41. *Cornishman*, 22 February 1968
42. *Fishing News*, 6 March 1970.
43. *Fishing News*, 24 October 1969.
44. *Fishing News*, 1 September 1978.
45. *Sputniks and Spinningdales*, S. Henderson and P. Drummond; The History Press 2011.
46. *Cornishman*, 29 June 1978.
47. *Fishing News*, 18 October 1996.

9 CRABBING: FISHING FOR LOBSTERS, CRABS AND CRAWFISH

1. Parliamentary Report on the Crab & Lobster Fisheries, 1877.
2. *An Account of the Fishing Gear of England & Wales*, F. M. Davis; HMSO.
3. Chasse Marée No. 42, E. McKee.
4. *The Cruise of the Kate*, E. Middleton, 1870.
5. *Mast & Sail in Europe & Asia*, H. Warington Smyth.
6. Ar Vag 2.
7. Quoted by *Western Echo*, 18 April 1903.
8. *St Ives Weekly Summary*, 31 August 1907.
9. *St Ives Weekly Summary*, 18 June 1910.
10. *The Sea Fishing Industry of England & Wales*, F. G. Aflalo; Stanford 1904.
11. Parliamentary Report into the Application of Devon & Cornwall Sea Fisheries Committees for Grants from the Development Fund, 1913.
12. *Cornishman*, 15 April 1905.
13. *Western Echo*, 8 March 1919.
14. *Western Echo*, 21 June 1924.
15. E. Murt's records of St Ives fishing boats.
16. *Western Echo*, 30 May 1925.
17. M. Peters, St Ives.
18. Cornishwillowcraft.com
19. *The Fishermen of Port Isaac*, Geoff Provis, 2009.
20. *World Fishing*, August 1962.
21. *Cornishman*, 30 August 1962.
22. *Le Télégramme*, 4 November 1965.
23. J. Richards, 2007.
24. *World Fishing*, December 1961.
25. *Land's End Radio Book III Casualties*, W. R. Hocking and M. Pellowe.
26. Website: Les Dundees d'Audierne, Alain Gourret.

27. *Land's End Radio Book III Casualties*, W. R. Hocking and M. Pellowe.
28. *Fishing News*, 13 April 2012.
29. *Fishing News*, 1985.
30. *Fishing News*, 18 April 1975.

10 TRAWLING

1. *Sailing Trawlers*, E. J. March; P. Marshall.
2. *The Trawlermen*, D. Butcher; Tops'l Books 1980.
3. *Padstow Lifeboats*, N. Leach; The History Press 2012.
4. *Lowestoft East Coast Port*, R. Malster; T. Dalton 1982.
5. Website Brixham Sailing Trawler Archive.
6. *Cornishman*, February 1911.
7. 1911 Census, Research by Tony Pawlyn.
8. *Coastwise Craft*, T. C. Lethbridge; Methuen 1952.
9. *Cornishman*, 20 April 1911.
10. *Shipwrecks on the Isles of Scilly*, F. E. Gibson, 1967.
11. *Western Echo*, 16 April 1904.
12. Information, Tony Pawlyn.
13. *Cornishman*, 1 January 1920.
14. W Bennetts, St Ives.
15. *The Trawlermen*, D. Butcher; Tops'l Books 1980.
16. *Westcountry Shipwrecks*, J. Behenna; David and Charles 1974.
17. *Cornishman*, 3 March 1937.
18. Raymond Peake, Newlyn, 2012.
19. E. Murt's records of St Ives fishing vessels.
20. *St Ives Times*, 28 May and 4 June 1920.
21. *Western Echo*, 17 July 1920.
22. *Western Morning News*, 18 May 1931.
23. *Western Morning News*, quoted in *Western Echo*, 10 May 1930.
24. *Western Echo*, 26 September 1931.
25. *Cornishman*, 6 April 1927.
26. *Western Morning News*, 14 January 1931.
27. *Western Echo*, 12 May 1934.
28. *Western Morning News*, 20 and 21 May 1935.
29. Kustvolk in de Vuurlign, Deel 3, Jean Marie Pylyser.
30. *Growing up with Boats*, Billy Stevenson, 2001.
31. *Olsen's Fisherman's Nautical Almanack 1937*.
32. *Cornishman*, 6 January 1949.
33. *Cornishman*, 9 October 1947.
34. *Cornishman*, 6 April 1950.
35. *Cornishman*, 9 November 1950.
36. *Cornishman*, 9 March 1961.
37. *Sputniks & Spinningdales*, S. Henderson and P. Drummond; History Press 2011.
38. *Fishing News*, 16 August 1968, 24 October 1969 and 6 March 1970.
39. *Fishing News*, 22 January 1971.
40. *Land's End Radio Book III Casualties*, W. R. Hocking and M. Pellowe.
41. *Sputniks & Spinningdales*, S. Henderson and P. Drummond; History Press 2011.
42. *Fishing News*, 26 June and 1 September 1978.
43. *Growing up with Boats*, Billy Stevenson, 2001.
44. *Cornishman*, 13 January 2011.
45. 'Through the Gaps' Newlyn blog, Laurence Hartwell.
46. *Fishing News*, February 8 1980.
47. 'Through the Gaps' Newlyn blog, Laurence Hartwell..
48. *Fishing News*, 12 November 2010.

11 MACKEREL HAND LINES AND THE INDUSTRIAL FISHERY OF THE 1970S

1. *Inshore Fishing*, S. Judd, 1971.
2. *A Boatbuilder's Story*, Percy Mitchell, 1968.
3. *Cornishman*, 24 March 1949.
4. *Cornishman*, 29 October 1964.
5. *Cornishman*, 11 June 1969.
6. *Fishing News*, 3 October and 21 November 1975, 20 February and 7 May 1976.
7. *Fishing News*, 12 April 1974.
8. *Fishing News*, 28 June and 8 December 1974, 20 April 1975 and 9 April 1976.
9. *Western Morning News*, 7 February 1976.
10. Glyn Richards 2012.
11. *Cornishman*, 16 October 1975.
12. *Sputniks & Spinningdales*, S. Henderson and P. Drummond; History Press 2011.
13. *Fishing News*, 13 August 1976.
14. *Commercial Fishing*, 1977, Vol. 8, No. 4.
15. *Cornishman*, 7 October 1976.
16. *Fishing News*, 23/30 December 1977.
17. *Land's End Radio Book III Casualties*, W. R. Hocking and M. Pellowe.
18. *Land's End Radio Book 1 History, The Great Mackerel Fishery 1977–81*, W. R. Hocking.
19. *Land's End Radio Book 1 History, The Great Mackerel Fishery 1977–81*, W. R. Hocking.
20. *Cornishman*, 29 December 1979.
21. *Fishing News*, 11 January 1980.
22. *Cornishman*, 21 February 1980.
23. *Fishing News*, 9 November 1979.
24. *Land's End Radio Book 1 History, The Great Mackerel Fishery 1977–81*, W. R. Hocking.
25. *Fishing News*, 1 February 1980.
26. Glyn Richards, 2012.

12 CORNISH NETTERS

1. Ar Vag Tome 2.
2. *Cornishman*, 25 March 1903.
3. *Cornishman*, 8 December 1910.
4. *The Motor Boat*, 12 January 1911.
5. *Western Echo*, 10 August 1912.
6. M. Peters, St Ives.
7. Parliamentary Report on the Crab & Lobster Fisheries 1877.
8. Steve Bassett, St Ives, 2012.
9. *Fishing News*, 1 December 1978, 25 May 1979, 15 January 1982 and 25 March 1983.
10. *Fishing News*, 13 September 1985, 1 November 1985, 28 March 1986, 2 May 1986, 27 June 1986 and 19 February 1988.
11. *Cornishman*, 6 June 1974.
12. *Land's End Radio Book III Casualties*, W. R. Hocking and M. Pellowe.
13. *Fishing News*, 8 May 1987.
14. *Fishing News*, 8 May 1987.
15. *Fishing News*, 11 March 1988.
16. 'Through the Gaps' Newlyn blog, Laurence Hartwell.
17. *Fishing News*, 15 April 1988.
18. *Land's End Radio Book III Casualties*, W. R. Hocking and M. Pellowe.
19. *Fishing News*, 15 May 1987.
20. *Built by Nobles of Girvan*, S. Henderson and P. Drummond; History Press 2010.
21. *Fishing News*, 27 April 1990.
22. *Fishing News*, 13 July 1990.
23. *Land's End Radio Book III Casualties*, W. R. Hocking and M. Pellowe.

24. *Western Morning News*, 12 March 1997.
25. *Western Morning News*, 28 October 1997.
26. *Western Morning News*, 26 June 1992.
27. *Fishing News*, May 2002.
28. *Fishing News*, 18 October 2002.
29. *Fishing News*, 12 March 2010 and 11 March 2011.
30. *Western Morning News*, 30 May 2008.
31. *Fishing News*, 18 March 2011.

13 SCALLOPING

1. *Pioneer, Last of the Skillingers*; Jardine Press 2002.
2. *Oh for a Fisherman's Life*, Alfred John Pengelly; Glasney Press 1979.
3. *Fishing News*, 24 October 1980.
4. *Western Morning News*, 27 June 2002.
5. *The Scallop & Its Fishery in England & Wales*, A. Franklin, G. D. Pickett and P. M. Connor; MAFF Lowestoft 1980.
6. *Fishing News*, 18 November 2011.
7. *Fishing News*, 30 November 2012.
8. 'Through the Gaps' Newlyn blog, Laurence Hartwell, October 2012.